Studies in Abhidharma Literature
and the Origins of Buddhist Philosophical Systems

SUNY Series in Indian Thought: Texts and Studies
Wilhelm Halbfass, Editor

STUDIES IN ABHIDHARMA LITERATURE AND THE ORIGINS OF BUDDHIST PHILOSOPHICAL SYSTEMS

Translated from the German
by Sophie Francis Kidd

under the supervision of
Ernst Steinkellner

Erich Frauwallner

State University of New York Press

Published by
State University of New York Press, Albany

Printed in the United States of America

For information, address State University of New York Press,
State University Plaza, Albany, N.Y., 12246

Production by Diane Ganeles
Marketing by Bernadette LaManna

Library of Congress Cataloging in Publication Data

Frauwallner, Erich, 1898–1974
Studies in Abhidharma literature and the origins of Buddhist philosophical systems / Erich Frauwallner : translated from the German by Sophie Francis Kidd under the supervision of Ernst Steinkellner.
p. cm. — (SUNY series in Indian thought)
ISBN 0–7914–2699–8 (alk. paper). — ISBN 0–7914–2700–5 (pbk. : alk. paper)
I. Kidd, Sophie Francis. II. Steinkellner, Ernst. III. Series.
BQ4195.F73 1995
294.3'824—dc20 95–36
CIP

To the memory of
Ortrun Zangenberg, née Frauwallner

Contents

Foreword

"The Buddhist systems are among the major achievements of the classical period of Indian philosophy. Nevertheless our knowledge of them, especially as regards their origin and development, is still fragmentary." These words of the late Professor Erich Frauwallner with which he introduced a lecture in 1971 at the academy in Göttingen (cf. p. 119) indicate both the reasons for and the goal of his last major scholarly interest.

The quest for the origins of the philosophical systems properly speaking implied an attempt at drawing a picture of the doctrinal development which led to their eventual establishment from their historical background, the works of the Abhidharmapiṭaka, the more recent layers of the Buddhist canon. To survey and analyze this literature, to explain the methods and structures of its individual texts, to uncover traces and lines of its development in order to find clues towards establishing the nature and tendencies of presystematic canonical doctrines, and finally to determine the origins of systematic philosophical thought was the main objective of a last connected series of articles written by Frauwallner.

Towards the end of his activity as professor of Indian and Iranian Antiquity at the University of Vienna, Frauwallner resumed work on his great life project of a comprehensive history of Indian philosophy.[1] He turned to a third volume, on the Buddhist systems,[2] and began his work by clarifying the beginnings and earliest developments in Buddhist systematical thought.[3] With hardly any previous studies of a historical kind available even then—history of philosophy to Frauwallner was the history of philosophical problems—he again undertook this task according to his usual approach. This meant working from the texts themselves, scrutinizing the motifs and solutions, connecting parts of texts and ideas, thus elaborating from the available masses of textual material distorted by the vicissitudes of transmission clear conceptual complexes, theorems, doctrinal tendencies, first approaches towards, and finally the first complex and consistent systematic edifices of Buddhist thought.

The article "Pañcaskandhaka und Pañcavastuka" (cf. chapter VI) appeared in 1963 and determined two important steps towards the development of systematic Abhidharma thought. Then, instead of following this development, he found it "necessary to cast our net further and examine the early period of Abhidharma" (p. 147) and turned to an investigation of the canonical Abhidharma literature. He developed the next article "Abhidharmastudien II. Die kanonischen Abhidharma-Werke", published in 1964, into an explanation of the characteristic features and methods of the canonical Abhidharma (cf. chapter I) and an analytical survey of the Abhidharma works of the Sarvāstivādin (cf. chapter II).

A subsequent break in these interests, from 1962–1967, was taken up with studies in the Navyanyāya tradition and early Mīmāṃsā epistemology, the results of which appeared from 1965 to 1970. He then resumed the Abhidharma studies, following the development in the Sarvāstivāda school up to its first systematic creation, the *abhisamayavāda* of Dharmaśrī. The article "Abhidharmastudien III. Der Abhisamayavādaḥ" appeared in 1971 (cf. chapter VII). However, he also continued the survey of the canonical Abhidharma with the works of the Pāli school and the Śāriputrābhidharma. The resulting articles "Abhidharmastudien IV. Der Abhidharma der anderen Schulen" appeared in 1971 and 1972 (cf. chapters III and IV).

By this time, Frauwallner had gained a clear picture of the presystematic development in the canonical Abhidharma literature, as well as of the beginnings of systematic Buddhist philosophy. His lecture in Göttingen "Die Entstehung der buddhistischen Systeme", published in 1971, presents the results in form of a historical summary (cf. chapter V).

With the last article, "Abhidharmastudien V. Der Sarvāstivādaḥ. Eine entwicklungsgeschichtliche Studie", published in 1973, Frauwallner started his investigation of the development of the major philosophical problems which occurred within the historical framework provided by the previous studies, starting with the problem of time (cf. chapter VIII). He continued this line of approach with the major systematical themes, for example, theories of causality, of the path of meditation, until his death (July 5, 1974). The remaining short sketches reveal that he was already fighting time:[4] he no longer intended to continue this series of separate studies, but was already starting to write the third volume of his history, which by then had assumed a concrete conceptual shape in his mind. The loss to scholarship could hardly have been greater.

The plan to produce an English translation of these articles was conceived above all because of the striking neglect of these important contributions by that part of the academic world which does not read German. With a very few exceptions, studies on the canonical Abhidharma and early Buddhist philosophical thought continue to be written as if these studies had never been published. Ms. Sophie Kidd, lecturer in the English department of the University of Vienna, expressed an interest in translating these articles and work began in 1990. A fluent English text was produced which attempted to remain faithful to the meaning and style of the original. The main purpose of the revision, which was my task, was to preserve this closeness of meaning. I am very grateful indeed to Ms. Kidd for her painstaking efforts and untiring willingness to discuss often the most subtle terminological problems and alternatives of expression over the years.

Notwithstanding our joint efforts to produce a translation of a high standard that was also faithful to the meaning of Frauwallner's words, for all purposes of research and criticism, the original German versions of the articles collected here should be referred to. Easier access to these original papers and further dissemination of Frauwallner's insights and findings are the main purpose of the present translation.

With a view to systematic coherence, I have chosen to present this series of articles in the form of a systematically arranged book rather than in its temporal sequence of origination. However, this is the only liberty I have taken. I have not changed anything within the body of the individual articles. Since Frauwallner did not compose a balanced book but proceeded step by step in presenting his observations, he repeatedly referred to previous steps either by short references or even by brief summarizing paragraphs. These, then, will account in the present book for some redundancies which, in view of their residual usefulness, I have retained, only changing the references to conform to the format of the present book. Except for these changes, all other changes, additional texts, or editorial supplementations are given in square brackets.

In the case of Sanskrit and Pāli names, I have used the stem forms, whereas Frauwallner always preferred the nominative forms. However, in the case of all other terms and phrases the original style has been retained. In order to facilitate an overview of his discussions, Frauwallner made deliberate and abundant use of figures. I have therefore not edited such cases, even when he chose to write "4 Noble Truths" while elsewhere using "Four Noble Truths".

The style of quotations in the notes, however, has been standardized to a moderate extent. Pāli texts are abbreviated in accordance with the system in the *Epilegomena to Vol. I* of *A Critical Pāli Dictionary*, except where Frauwallner preferred to give a more or less full name. The titles of certain frequently cited works have also been abbreviated.

The new arrangement of the different texts under two main headings—literature and philosophical development—puts the first article of this series, "Pañcaskandhaka und Pañcavastuka", in a somewhat odd place. The academic reader interested in the progress of Frauwallner's research as a gradual revelation of the structures and developments of a vast mass of early Buddhist literature is better advised to read this article first before attempting the survey of the literary heritage of canonical Abhidharma.

No attempt has been made to "update" these contributions by supplementing information on research in the areas touched upon or on new editions of texts that have appeared since the writing of the last article in 1972. However, indices have been added together with a list of abbreviations.

The translation was made possible with a grant from the Austrian Academy of Sciences from its Holzhausen Bequest in 1989 for which I would like to express my sincere gratitude.

Many colleagues and friends have given their support and help in producing this volume. To all of them I extend my warmest thanks. Professor David Seyfort Ruegg read and commented upon an initial trial translation. Professor Richard Gombrich and Professor Alexis Sanderson aided the enterprise with their moral support and good counsel. Professor Wilhelm Halbfass accepted this volume for the series "Indian Thought, Texts and Studies", of which he is editor. The manuscript was prepared and corrected by Dr. Michael Torsten Much, and finally checked by Monika Pemwieser M.A. and Dr. Helmut Krasser, both of whom also helped with the proofreading. Also Horst Lasic M.A. assisted in reading the proofs. Last but not least I would like to thank William D. Eastman, the director of State University of New York Press, for his interest, concern, and understanding.

ERNST STEINKELLNER

Translator's Note

The challenge of translating a work of this kind is both stimulating and daunting at the same time. A translator is always expected to become an "instant" expert in numerous fields of human knowledge as required. However, in the case of the present work, with its closely argued exposition of a highly specialized area written in an idiosyncratic German, this approach would have inevitably proved inadequate. The aim of this translation was not only to give an accurate rendering of the contents of the original but also to preserve its author's characteristic style, and without the painstaking supervision of Professor Steinkellner, the project would have been doomed to failure. His scholarly rigour was an invaluable support as well as a source of inspiration. I would like to thank Monika Pemwieser M.A. for checking the manuscript so meticulously, Dr. Helmut Krasser for starting me off on the road to a modicum of computer competency, and Dr. Michael Torsten Much for his friendly encouragement and the sheer hard work involved in preparing the manuscript for publication. Last and most, my thanks are due to Professor Ernst Steinkellner, not least for his near-saintly (and, I fear, all too frequently tried) qualities of patience.

SOPHIE KIDD

Concordance

I. The Earliest Abhidharma—"Abhidharma-Studien", *WZKSO* 8, 1964, pp. 59–99: II. Die kanonischen Abhidharma-Werke. 1. Der älteste Abhidharma, pp. 59–69.

II. The Canonical [Abhidharma] Works [of the Sārvastivāda School]—"Abhidharma-Studien", *WZKSO* 8, 1964, pp. 59–99: 2. Die kanonischen Werke, pp. 70–99.

III. The Abhidharma of the Pāli School, 1. Vibhaṅga, 2. Dhātukathā, 3. Puggalapaññatti, 4. Paṭṭhāna, 5. Yamaka, 6. Dhammasaṅgaṇi—"Abhidharma-Studien", *WZKSO* 15, 1971, pp. 103–121: IV. Der Abhidharma der anderen Schulen. Der Abhidharma der Pāli-Schule und der Śāriputrābhidharma. A. Der Abhidharma der Pāli-Schule.
a. Cittakaṇḍa, α. The Path of Meditation, β. The Psychology in the Cittakaṇḍa, b. Rūpakaṇḍa, c. The Commentaries, 7. Kathāvatthu, 8. Paṭisambhidāmagga, 9. Vimuttimagga and Visuddhimagga—"Abhidharma-Studien", *WZKSO* 16, 1972, pp. 95–152: IV. Der Abhidharma der anderen Schulen (Fortsetzung), pp. 95–132.

IV. The Śāriputrābhidharma—"Abhidharma-Studien", *WZKSO* 16, 1972, pp. 95–152: IV. Der Abhidharma der anderen Schulen (Fortsetzung). B. Der Śāriputrābhidharmaḥ, pp. 133–152.

V. The Origin of the Buddhist Systems—*Die Entstehung der buddhistischen Systeme*. Nachrichten der Akademie der Wissenschaften in Göttingen, I. Philosophisch-historische Klasse Jg. 1971, Nr. 6, Göttingen 1971, pp. 115–127.

VI. Pañcaskandhaka and Pañcavastuka—"Abhidharma-Studien", *WZKSO* 7, 1963, pp. 20–36: I. Pañcaskandhaka and Pañcavastuka.

VII. The Abhisamayavāda—"Abhidharma-Studien", *WZKSO* 15, 1971, pp. 69–102: III. Der Abhisamayavādaḥ.

VIII. The Sarvāstivāda—"Abhidharma-Studien", *WZKSO* 17, 1973, pp. 97–121: V. Der Sarvāstivādaḥ. Eine entwicklungsgeschichtliche Studie.

Abbreviations or Frequently Cited Works

Bareau, *Dhammasaṅgaṇi*	André Bareau, *Dhammasaṅgaṇi*, traduction annotée, Paris 1951.
BB	Bibliotheca Buddhica
Earliest Vinaya	E. Frauwallner, *The earliest Vinaya and the beginnings of Buddhist literature,* Roma 1956 (Serie Orientale Roma 8).
Lamotte, *Histoire*	Etienne Lamotte, *Histoire du Bouddhisme Indien, des origines à l'ère Śaka,* Louvain 1958 (Bibliothèque du Muséon 43).
MCB	Mélanges chinois et bouddhiques
T	Taishō Issaikyō, Tōkyō 1924ff.
VP	Louis de la Vallée Poussin, *L'Abhidharmakośa de Vasubandhu,* traduit et annotée, vol. I-VI, Louvain 1923–31.
WZKSO	Wiener Zeitschrift für die Kunde Süd- und Ostasiens.

Part 1

The Canonical Abhidharma Literature—
Its Development and Methodology

I

The Earliest Abhidharma

The question as to how the system of the Sarvāstivāda originated, the last authoritative summary of which is represented by Vasubandhu's Abhidharmakośa and Saṃghabhadra's Nyāyānusāra, can be answered—at least as far as the earliest period is concerned—with reference to a wealth of material in the canonical Abhidharma works of this school. Thus, it is with these works that research must begin, and the following essay is an attempt to characterize these works, assign them a place in the overall development, and demonstrate the contribution of each particular work to this development. However, consideration should be given to the following factor: the philosophical development as such began at a later period, and was then only gradual. The period prior to this was confined to collecting and working through the doctrinal material contained in the Buddha's sermons. Since this period represents the soil that nurtured the later development, however, and since the approach and method which were developed at that time continued to influence even the last canonical works of the Abhidharma, this period must first be briefly described.

The oldest Buddhist tradition has no Abhidharmapiṭaka but only *mātṛkāḥ*.[1] What this means is that besides the small number of fundamental doctrinal statements, the Buddha's sermons also contain a quantity of doctrinal concepts. The most suitable form for collecting and preserving these concepts would have been comprehensive lists. Lists of this kind were called *mātṛkā*, and it was from these lists that the Abhidharma later developed.

This must have happened in more or less the following fashion: first the attempt was made to collate all the more important doctrinal concepts scattered among the sermons without distinction and as comprehensively as possible. An early list of this kind has come down to us in the Saṃgītisūtra of the Dhīrghāgama.[2] In this list, completely heterogeneous concepts are combined indiscriminately and arranged numerically in a purely superficial way.[3] However, this purely superficial arrangement of a variety of concepts was hardly a suitable vehicle for the propounding and explanation of the doctrine. For this reason, from an early date onwards, we also encounter shorter lists which group related doctrinal concepts together. One of these lists, which comprises several groups of elements of import for entanglement in the cycle of existence and which is modelled on the Oghavagga of Saṃyuttanikāya,[4] can be found, for example, in the Jñānaprasthāna,[5] and recurs in a variety of other texts.[6] A further list of doctrinal concepts which are of importance for the path of liberation, forms the basis of the first section of the Dharmaskandha[7] and also appears in the seventh chapter of the Prakaraṇa. Shorter lists of this kind can also be found throughout the early works of the Abhidharma.

Especial importance must be assigned to those lists containing fundamental concepts under which it was attempted to subsume all the various elements. Concepts of this type in the sermons which offered themselves were in particular the 5 *skandhāḥ*, the 12 *āyatanāni,* and the 18 *dhātavāḥ*, and these therefore repeatedly occur as a group. Occasionally the 5 *upādānaskandhāḥ* appear side by side with the 5 *skandhāḥ*, and the 6 *dhātavaḥ* beside the 18 *dhātavaḥ*. These are frequently also associated with the 22 *indriyāṇi*.[8] Lists of this kind constitute the first attempt at systemization and formed the basis for the Pañcaskandhaka.[9]

These lists were all intended to serve as a basis for communicating the doctrine, and were accompanied as a matter of course by explanations. Originally delivered orally, they were later preserved in written form. Examples of these will be dealt with in the discussion of the individual works of the Abhidharma. The works invariably start with the list and the individual elements are then discussed in the same order as they appear in this list. The first explanations are little more than involved circumstantial paraphrases.[10] Progress towards clear terminology and definitions was made only gradually. This descriptive method was retained even after new doctrines began to be developed. Thus, we encounter it both in the first section of the Dhātukāya, the first independent attempt at a systematic psychology, and later in the Pañcavastuka. It offered an alternative to the sūtras of the Brahmanic philosophical systems and made the creation of similar sūtras for the Buddhists superfluous.

Parallel to this simple method of explaining the lists of elements, we find quite early on a further, somewhat curious method. It consists of composing a list of attributes and discussing the nature of the relevant elements with the aid of this list. I have dubbed these lists "attribute-*mātṛkāḥ*". They originally consist of dyads, of which the question is asked whether an attribute can be assigned to these items or not, whether they possess a particular attribute or its opposite, whether, for example, they are conditioned or not, whether they are internal or external. Sometimes they consist of triads, where three possibilities are considered: for example, whether something is past, future, or present. Some of these groups regularly appear together and recur frequently. They must originally have been associated with particular problems, for example the following five dyads:

rūpi	*arūpi*
sanidarśanam	*anidarśanam*
sapratigham	*apratigham*
sāsravam	*anāsravam*
saṃskṛtam	*asaṃskṛtam*

From their meaning we can see that they represent fundamental divisions between the elements in general. With the first three groups, an attempt is made to distinguish between material and non-material entities, a matter which was not at all easy at this early period. I therefore believe that these groups were originally intended to define more precisely the general fundamental concepts of *skandhāḥ, āyatanāni,* and *dhātavaḥ*, and to facilitate categorization. In any case, they are still closely linked with the Pañcaskandhaka even at a relatively late date.[11]

A similarly close link is evident in five triads which also recur from the earliest times onwards. These are as follows:

atītam	*anāgatam*	*pratyutpannam*
kuśalam	*akuśalam*	*avyākṛtam*
kāma-	*rūpa-*	*ārūpya-pratisaṃyuktam*
śaikṣam	*aśaikṣam*	*naivaśaikṣanāśaikṣam*
darśana-	*bhāvanā-*	*a-prahātavyam*

They seem originally to have been connected with the doctrine of entanglement in and liberation from the cycle of existence, which I refer to as the Abhisamayavāda.[12] Attribute-*mātṛkāḥ* of this kind could of course easily be extended and applied to any of the groups of elements. And by and large this is what happened.

Nonetheless, the explanation dealt not only with the nature of the elements collected in the lists, but also with their relationship to one another. The question of which of the various elements were included *(saṃgrahaḥ)* in the *skandhāḥ*, *āyatanāni*, and *dhātavaḥ* arose quite early on. What this meant was that when the need was felt to collect all the elements in groups and a serviceable principle of classification was being sought in the Buddha's sermons, only the series of the 5 *skandhāḥ*, the 12 *āyatanāni*, and the 18 *dhātavaḥ* were found to be suitable for the purpose. Thus, in order to classify any element systematically, the only possibility was to determine the *skandhāḥ*, *āyatanāni*, or *dhātavaḥ* to which they belong. This method was then adopted extensively, and works such as the Dhātukathā of the Pāli Abhidharma are to all intents little more than a subsumption of the various elements under *skandhāḥ*, *āyatanāni*, and *dhātavaḥ*. Eventually, in the Pañcaskandhaka, the *āyatanāni*, *dhātavaḥ*, and particularly the *skandhāḥ* also served as the framework for a first, consistent attempt at systematization. The inconvenient factor here was that there were three different principles of classification. However, it was impossible for any one of them to be omitted if the Buddha's word was to be adhered to. Therefore an attempt had to be made to harmonize them and to establish their relationships to one another. This led to the question of which of the *skandhāḥ* included the various *āyatanāni* and *dhātavaḥ* and vice versa. The discussion of this question occurs regularly at the end of the various versions of the Pañcaskandhaka.

A further question concerning the relationship of the elements to each other is the question of their association with each other *(saṃprayogaḥ)*. It had been observed that certain elements only occur together, not alone, and thus it seemed only logical to attempt to establish which elements this applied to. This also occupies a major part of works such as the Dhātukathā. Later it was also observed that in groups of elements of this kind, one of them could represent the center, or support of the others, and the question arose as to which elements this was accompanied by *(samanvāgamaḥ)*.

It was often observed that the spheres of two elements overlapped. This prompted the question of whether the first was completely or only partially included in the second and vice versa. Discussions of this kind occur frequently in the Jñānaprasthāna and long stretches of the Yamaka of the Pāli Abhidharma are constructed on the formulation of such questions.

Finally, mention should be made here of a factor which is characteristic of the early Abhidharma, that of the form of the catechesis. Subjects are generally not described and explained; it is rather that questions are asked which demand an answer. Unfortunately the answers confine themselves all too often to nothing more than a superficial statement of the facts, often merely in the form of an enumeration. One searches in vain for explanation or substantiation.

We have now examined the most important ways in which the old Abhidharma treats the transmitted doctrinal material. The occurrence of other, unusual forms is rare. One case of this, however, is to be found in the Dharmaskandha, where the list of elements to be treated is not simply enumerated and explained as such; the individual elements from the list are attested by passages from the sūtras which are then explained.[13] A strangely artificial use of an attribute-*mātr̥kāḥ* occurs in the Daśottarasūtra, which was early enough to have been incorporated into the Sūtrapiṭaka.[14] Here the question treated is that of which things are efficacious *(bahukaraḥ)*, which of them have to be practised *(bhāvayitavyaḥ)*, which of them must be cognized *(parijñeyaḥ)* and so forth. However, the discussion of whether these attributes can be assigned to them or not does not follow a list of elements; rather, those things are enumerated that occur singly, in pairs, in threes etc., and which possess these attributes.

However, these are exceptions, and have no lasting influence. In general, it is the approaches already discussed which predominate, and which were developed into a proper method that could be used for the various subjects. The term "scholasticism" springs to mind as a characterization of this method.[15] However, it is scholasticism of a special kind. I have described scholasticism in Indian philosophy elsewhere[16] as a form of philosophizing that does not start out from a direct perception of things but is based instead on given concepts, which it develops into a system. However, in terms of content, nothing new is created. It remains the same, merely being considered from continually new aspects and presented in ever new forms. Thus, it is perhaps more accurate to speak of "formal" or "formalistic" scholasticism.

To a certain degree, however, the use of this method was justified. For in the early period it was not deemed necessary to create something entirely new. The sole aim was to preserve safely what the Buddha had taught and to illuminate it from a variety of different angles. Even if this was done in a fairly superficial manner, the aim had nevertheless been achieved to a large extent. However, the method that had been developed for this bore the seeds of degeneration within itself. The constant endeavor to say something new while presenting the same content and each time giving the material a new form naturally led to exaggeration and excess.

On examining these phenomena individually, the first impression gained is that of a tedious prolixity. At certain levels of Buddhist literature, such long-winded treatment has occasionally been explained by the fact that it was a matter of religious merit to produce as many of these texts as possible. Here in the early Abhidharma the impression of bombastic pomposity preponderates. Typically, when a short, clear basic exposition would have sufficed, each individual case is treated in minute detail according to a stereotype, frequently with very little variation. A typical example of this is the first chapter of the Dhammasaṅgaṇi, which treats the question of which mental elements are good, evil, or indeterminate. Here one author has managed to spin out to 130 pages what Vasubandhu says in under two pages in the Abhidharmakośa,[17] by enumerating all the elements that could conceivably be considered in each possible case.

This excessive breadth of treatment is combined with an abuse of the method by applying it in the wrong place. It is, for example, entirely appropriate for a list presenting a series of elements to be followed by explanations of these elements. However, the repetition of the same explanations whenever these elements are mentioned in any context whatsoever becomes nonsensical. The same is true of the subsumption under the general fundamental concepts *(saṃgrahaḥ)*. When elements are introduced and explained for the first time, it is quite appropriate to establish how they should be assigned to *skandhāḥ*, *āyatanāni*, or *dhātavaḥ* etc., but not each time that these same elements occur in any context whatsoever. The above-mentioned chapter in the Dhammasaṅgaṇi offers a wealth of examples of both kinds.[18]

In other cases, the method degenerates into artificiality and senseless exaggeration. A particularly blatant example of this is the development of the attribute-*mātṛkāḥ*. As we have seen, these originally appear to have been short lists intended for a particular purpose. They were then also used for other subjects, their original purpose having been forgotten, and were then extended in a variety of different ways. The questions posited included, for example, whether the elements concerned were internal or external, high or low, large or small, limited or unlimited, mundane or supramundane and so forth. Methods were soon found for extending these lists in such a way without effort or imagination. Dyads were easily formed by the negation of a concept. Thus, old triads could be transformed into three dyads, for example, by distinguishing between *kāmāvacarā—na kāmāvacarā, rūpāvacarā—na rūpāvacarā* and *arūpāvacarā—na arūpāvacarā dhammā* instead of *kāmāvacarā, rūpāvacarā* and *arūpāvacarā dhammā* (Dhammasaṅgaṇi, pp. 13,25–14,4). Triads were easily formed by either combining or negating both concepts of a dyad. Thus, *ajjhattabahiddhā dhammā* was placed beside *ajjhattā* and *bahiddhā dhammā,* for example (Dhammasaṅgaṇi, p. 5,17–19. cf. p. 11,19f.). Pairs of concepts proved an especially rich vein for the formation of tetrads. One only needed to distinguish the four possibilities: whether either one or the other, both, or neither of the two concepts occur. It was asked for instance which elements were *kuśalā na kuśalahetukāḥ, kuśalahetukā na kuśalāḥ, kuśalahetukāś ca kuśalā ca* and *naiva kuśalā na kuśalahetukāḥ* (numerous examples in the Prakaraṇa, T 1541, p. 633b13ff. = T 1542, p. 733b29ff.). Furthermore, newly occurring concepts could be used to form new groups. In connection with the development of the doctrine of causality, the question that was often asked was which elements represented the bases *(ālambanapratyayaḥ)* of particular mental processes. Accordingly, the question was now not simply one of which elements were *parīttā* etc., *atītā* etc., and *ajjhattā* etc., but also which of them were *parīttārammaṇā* etc., *atītārammaṇā* etc.

and *ajjhattārammaṇā* etc. (Dhammasaṅgaṇi, pp.4,18–23; 5,11–16; 5,17–22).

Wholesale extensions of attribute-*mātṛkāḥ* were made possible in the following manner: *mātṛkāḥ* of this type were not only suitable for use with a particular given group of elements; but the questions concerned could also be asked in regard to the elements in general; not, for example, by asking which *skandhāḥ* were conditioned or non-conditioned etc., but to which elements these attributes should be assigned in the first place. Now, the form of the catechesis determined that regardless of what elements were discussed, this discussion had to be clothed in the form of questions and answers. It was not, for example, stated that "There are a fixed number of fetters *(saṃyojanāni).*" Instead the question was asked: "Which elements are fetters?" Questions of this type, however, corresponded in form to the questions of a generally applicable attribute-*mātṛkāḥ* and could therefore be added to the latter without further ado. Thus, "mixed" *mātṛkāḥ* came into being in which both types were combined promiscuously. In this type of *mātṛkāḥ*, unlimited groups of elements could be added as desired to a wide variety of attributes. We thus come across *mātṛkāḥ* of this type consisting of well over one hundred questions (e.g. Prakaraṇa T 1541, p. 644b6ff. = T 1542 p. 711b7ff.).

In addition, the development of Buddhist doctrine facilitated the continued creation of new groups. In the area of psychology, for example, a distinction had come to be made between *cittam* and *caitasikā dharmāḥ*, which were then augmented by the concepts of *cittasaṃprayuktā dharmāḥ, cittasahabhuvo dharmāḥ, cittānuparivartino dharmāḥ* etc., all of them being subsumed in a "bundle" *(gucchakam)*. Each member of this bundle, together with its negation, provided a dyad for the *mātṛkāḥ* (Prakaraṇa T 1541, p. 644b10-15 =T 1542, p. 711b12-18; Dhammasaṅgaṇi, p. 10,21–11,18). Bundles and dyads were also formed by starting out from the concepts of *karma* and *bhāvaḥ* (Prakaraṇa T 1541, p. 644b15ff. = T 1542, p. 711b18ff.). Similarly, *sahetukā dharmaḥ, hetusaṃprayuktā dharmāḥ* were placed beside the concept of the *hetavaḥ*, and dyads were again formed from each of these three concepts and its negation (Prakaraṇa T 1541, p. 644 c 4ff. = T 1542, p. 711c7f.). On the same model, the Dhammasaṅgaṇi reorganized all the members of the old Oghavagga[19] into bundles and dyads (p. 7,7-10,18). This process could, of course, be continued indefinitely if desired.

A similarly blatant process of degeneration occurred with the discussion of the relation of the elements to each other. The question of the degree to which elements are included in other elements *(saṃgrahaḥ)* or are connected with each other *(saṃprayogaḥ)* in itself offered unlimited possibilities to the imagination. New combinations were thought up; for example, the question of what the included and non-included elements were included in, what the connected and non-connected elements are connected with and so forth.[20] This opened the floodgates as it were; volume after volume could be filled using this method if one so wished.[21]

These are the essential features that characterize the scholasticism of the early Abhidharma. The process of the development and degeneration of the method naturally took a different course within each of the various schools. Thus, for example, the short attribute-*mātṛkāḥ* in the early works of the Yogācāra school[22]—which were of course taken over from Hīnayāna schools—demonstrate that the exaggerated inflation of these *mātṛkāḥ* was not taken up everywhere. This degeneration was probably at its worst in the Pāli school, which confined itself exclusively to the transmitted doctrinal material and never really developed any original thought of its own. The compulsion always to say the same things while expressing them in a different form helped to promote these methodological excessess and aberrations. Ultimately, this "method" was also applied to other areas, running riot in the Yamaka and Paṭṭhāna. The Sarvāstivāda school did not go so far as this, yet even there, although there are signs of exaggeration and degeneration in the early period, they keep within certain bounds and eventually disappear completely. The reason for this was that a new, dynamic development had begun and new ideas and problems had arisen which attracted increasing interest, with the result that the old scholasticism faded away, appearing in the later texts of the school merely as the fossilized remains of an ancient heritage.[23]

II

The Canonical [Abhidharma] Works [of the Sarvāstivāda School]

Following this general outline of the type and methods of the early Abhidharma, I would now like to direct my attention to the individual Abhidharma texts of the Sarvāstivāda school. These works are enumerated by Yaśomitra in his commentary to the Abhidharmakośa as follows:

1. the Jñānaprasthāna by Kātyāyanīputra,
2. the Prakaraṇapāda by Vasumitra,
3. the Vijñānakāya by Devaśarman,
4. the Dharmaskandha by Śāriputra,
5. the Prajñaptiśāstra by Maudgalyāyana,
6. the Dhātukāya by Pūrṇa,
7. the Saṃgītiparyāya by Mahākauṣṭhila.[1]

Other transmissions give a different order and in some cases different authors.[2] However, more important than this is the following: P'ou-kouang, a disciple of Hiuan-tsang, at the beginning of his commentary to the Abhidharmakośa,[3] lists the seven works mentioned above, gives their length and adds that Śāriputra's Saṃgītiparyāyapādaśāstra, Mahāmaudgalyāyana's Dharmaskandhapādaśāstra, and Mahākātyāyana's Prajñaptipādaśāstra were composed during the Buddha's lifetime, that Devakṣema's Vijñānakāyapādaśāstra was written during the 100 years after the nirvana, Vasumitra's Prakaraṇapādaśāstra and Dhātukāyapādaśāstra at the beginning of the fourth century after the nirvana and Kātyāyanīputra's Jñānaprasthānaśāstra at the end of the fourth century after the nirvana. We do not know where he derived his information from nor consequently how much weight to accord it. However, examination of the works themselves shows that—with one exception—the relative chronology which it provides is correct. The Saṃgītiparyāya, Dharmaskandha and Prajñaptiśāstra constitute the oldest layer. The Vijñānakāya and—as we shall see—the Dhātukāya derive from the middle period. The Prakaraṇa and Jñānaprasthāna are the most recent of the works named. I therefore concur with this relative chronology and shall proceed to discuss the works in the order it prescribes.[4]

1. Saṃgītiparyāya (T 1536)

The Saṃgītiparyāya is a commentary on the Saṃgītisūtra of the Dīrghāgama.[5] The Saṃgītisūtra itself contains a comprehensive enumeration of the most important doctrinal concepts. At first glance, it seems an arid and unrewarding work. However, if one considers the purpose and intentions of this work, one begins to appreciate it as a remarkable achievement. The sūtra is contained within a framing narrative, which relates how disputes and schisms arose in the Jaina community after the Jina's death due to differing interpretations of the doctrine, and how Śāriputra, in order to prevent similar disputes within the Buddhist community, recited a systematic collection of the Buddhist doctrinal concepts and how the Buddha approved of and endorsed Śāriputra's recital.[5] Regardless of whether this report actually has a basis in historical fact, it well expresses the aim and import of the sūtra. The Buddha had not preached a doctrinal system as such; he had demonstrated the path to enlightenment and had supplied the necessary theoretical justification for it. This represented the core of his message. Throughout the long years of his teaching, as he preached this message to an increasing body of followers, constantly adapting it to the capacities of his audience, certain concepts were also touched upon which formed a valuable complement to his basic message. However, since these concepts were dispersed throughout his sermons, they could thus be easily overlooked and gradually forgotten. Therefore it is these concepts in particular which were collected in the Saṃgītisūtra, in order to ensure their preservation. It was perhaps inevitable that they should be collected in a purely superficial form by simple enumeration. For these doctrinal concepts were scattered amongst the numerous sermons and did not in themselves form a system. Nor was there either intention or desire to create a system from these doctrinal concepts; the aim was merely to record the words of the Buddha. In this respect the Saṃgītisūtra represents an important achievement which contributed greatly to the subsequent development of Buddhist doctrine, and in particular to that of the Abhidharma.

It is only natural that a recitation of the doctrine, such as that kind contained in the Saṃgītisūtra, could not simply be confined to an enumeration of the doctrinal concepts collected in the sūtra. Some form of explanation was indispensable; this would originally have been given in the form of an oral commentary. This is a phenomenon which we encounter again and again in India in very different fields: doctrinal texts were memorized, retained in concise form and accompanied by varying explanations. The explanations of the Saṃgītisūtra were eventually recorded in written form by the Sarvāstivādin, and thus came to form the Saṃgītiparyāya.

This explains the essence and import of the text. It demonstrates the development of the Abhidharma of the Sarvāstivādin from its canonical beginnings, and it also shows how this tradition was continually adhered to. However, the text can only be used with caution as evidence for the development of the individual doctrines of the Abhidharma. The kind of explanations contained in the Saṃgītiparyāya were continually being renewed, especially while they were still being delivered orally. It was natural that explanations which no longer corresponded to the current state of doctrinal development were not employed. Thus any utilization of the text must always take this into account.

2. Dharmaskandha (T 1537)

While the Saṃgītiparyāya is very much within the tradition of the early Abhidharma, the Dharmaskandha is a highly idiosyncratic and interesting work. It has been characterized as being simply a collection of sūtras.[7] This is, however, misleading, for it merely describes the form and not the subject matter. Closer examination reveals that it divides into three parts.

The first part, which constitutes roughly two thirds of the work (p. 453b24–494b29), deals with the following doctrinal concepts:

1. 5 *śikṣāpadāni*	(p. 453c6)
2. 4 *srotaāpattyaṅgāni*	(p. 458b22)
3. 4 *avetyaprasādāḥ*	(p. 460b17)
4. 4 *śrāmaṇyaphalāni*	(p. 464a16)
5. 4 *pratipadaḥ*	(p. 465a22)
6. 4 *āryavaṃśāḥ*	(p. 466b15)
7. 4 *samyakpradhānāni*	(p. 467c23)
8. 4 *ṛddhipādāḥ*	(p. 471c12)
9. 4 *smṛtyupasthānāni*	(p. 475c24)
10. 4 *āryasatyāni*	(p. 479b24)
11. 4 *dhyānāni*	(p. 482a26)
12. 4 *apramāṇāni*	(p. 485a26)
13. 4 *ārūpyāṇi*	(p. 488b18)
14. 4 *samādhibhāvanāḥ*	(p. 489a29)
15. 7 *bodhyaṅgāni*	(p. 491b8)

One glance is enough to tell us that this is a *mātṛkā*, a list containing a collection of concepts which concern the path to liberation. It is quite clear that this list was regarded as a *mātṛkā*, since the same list was taken over into the Prakaraṇa[8] with only one minor divergence,[9] and since in both cases it is preceded by a verse which summarizes it.[10] The treatment of the doctrinal concepts contained in the list consists first of a short sūtra text containing the relevant doctrinal concepts, followed by a detailed commentary on both the text and the doctrinal concepts it contains.

The second part, which follows on from this, is far shorter (p. 494c1–498b7). It consists merely of a short sūtra text enumerating a long sequence of elements, which were later held to be the *kleśāḥ* and *upakleśāḥ*. Following this text, these elements are discussed and explained individually. This part is called the "Kṣudravastuka" (Tsa che) and is also referred to by this name in later texts.[11]

The third part (p. 498b12–513c10) again can be seen as the treatment of a *mātṛkā*. In this case, it is a list of fundamental general concepts concluding with a discussion of the tenet of dependent co-arising, that is.

1. 22 *indriyāṇi*	(p. 498b12)[12]

2. 12 *āyatanāni* (p. 499c25)[13]
3. 5 *skandhāḥ* (p. 500c26)
4. 62 *dhātavaḥ*, i.e.18,6,6,6,4 etc. (p. 501b24)
5. *pratītyasamutpādaḥ* (p. 505a9)

The same treatment as before is also followed here, that is a sūtra containing the relevant doctrinal concepts is quoted and the latter are then subsequently discussed.

Even this brief description demonstrates the idiosyncratic nature of this work in contrast to the Saṃgītiparyāya. We are here no longer dealing with an indiscriminate enumeration of very different doctrinal concepts; rather, individual groups of particular interest are singled out: the basic concepts used in the earliest attempts at the creation of a system, the doctrinal concepts that were of especial importance for the practice of liberation, together with a group of mental elements considered especially significant with regard to entanglement in the cycle of existence. In addition, there is the quite unusual method of first of all quoting instances from the sūtras and then continuing with their discussion, a procedure that is completely unprecedented in the Abhidharma of the Sarvāstivādin. Finally, one should also mention the detailed elaboration of the doctrinal concepts enumerated, which goes far beyond the uniform paraphrases of the early Abhidharma method.

All of this supports the view that the text is of special value. However, in order to evaluate its significance correctly, we must also consider the period to which it belongs. According to the tradition in P'ou-kouang, it belongs to the earliest layer of Abhidharma texts. We must therefore examine the question of whether this can be justified.

Aid is fortunately at hand in the form of the Pāli Abhidharma, which contains a text, namely the Vibhaṅga, which displays remarkable similarities to the Dharmaskandha.[14] If we survey the structure of this work in general, we will see that it consists of the following 18 sections:

1. 5 *khandhā* (p. 3)
2. 12 *āyatanāni* (p. 83)
3. 18 *dhātuyo* (p. 102)
4. 4 *ariyasaccāni* (p. 126)
5. 22 *indriyāni* (p. 156)

6. *paṭiccasamuppādo* (p. 173)
7. 4 *satipaṭṭhānā* (p. 238)
8. 4 *sammappadhānā* (p. 255)
9. 4 *iddhipādā* (p. 264)
10. 7 *bojjhaṅgā* (p. 276)
11. *aṭṭhaṅgiko maggo* (p. 285)
12. 4 *jhānāni* (p. 294)
13. 4 *appamaññāyo* (p. 327)
14. 5 *sikkhāpadāni* (p. 342)
15. 4 *paṭisambhidā* (p. 350)
16. *ñāṇavibhaṅgo* (p. 366)
17. *khuddakavatthuvibhaṅgo* (p. 409)
18. *dhammahadayavibhaṅgo* (p. 480)

It is already evident from this that—apart from a few additions—the Vibhaṅga is constructed from the same material as the Dharmaskandha, the only difference being that the third part of the Dharmaskandha has here been placed at the beginning of the work.

On examining this part (Nos. 1–6), we find that *indriyāṇi*, *āyatanāni*, *skandhāḥ*, *dhātavaḥ*, and *pratītyasamutpādaḥ* are discussed in both texts. While it is true that *indriyāṇi*, *āyatanāni*, *skandhāḥ*, *dhātavaḥ* frequently constitute a group, the addition of the *pratītyasamutpādaḥ* is unusual. Moreover, whenever the *dhātavaḥ* are subsumed in a group as primary concepts together with the *skandhāḥ* and *āyatanāni*, it is generally only the 18 *dhātavaḥ* which are treated. Drawing on the Bahudhātukasūtra (and in connection with this the discussion of numerous groups of *dhātavaḥ* in the Dharmaskandha) is exceptional. Although the Vibhaṅga gives broad treatment only to the 18 *dhātavaḥ*, it also lists at least three of the hexads from the Dharmaskandha (p. 102–108), including groups which are rarely mentioned elsewhere, i.e. *sukha-*, *dukkha-*, *somanassa-*, *domanassa-*, *upekkhā-*, and *avijjādhātu* and *kāma-*, *vyāpāda-*, *vihiṃsā-*, *nekkhamma-*, *avyāpāda-* and *avihiṃsādhātu*. The connection is thus unmistakable. The *ariyasaccāni* added on after the *dhātuyo* are taken from the first part of the Dharmaskandha (No. 10). However, in the Pāli Abhidharma they frequently appear with the fundamental concepts.[15]

The first part of the Dharmaskandha, which here follows in second place (Nos. 7–16), only displays partial correspondence, since it is obvious that the group of doctrinal concepts that it contains were here no longer regarded as a *mātṛkāḥ*.[16] This is connected with the generally negligent treatment of the contents in the Pāli Abhidharma, in which formalistic scholasticism flourishes at the expense of intellectual content. However, 9 out of 15 topics are also present here: Dharmaskandha I (=Vibhaṅga 14), 7 (=8), 8 (=9), 9 (=7), 10 (=4), 11 and 13 (=12),[17] 12 (=13), and 15 (=10). Only three topics have been added here: Vibhaṅga 11, 15 and 16.

The second part of the Dharmaskandha, the Kṣudravastuka, follows in third place (No. 17). It is in itself a very singular text and its appearance in both works is a strong indication of their relatedness.[18] Finally, the last section of the Vibhaṅga, the Dhammahadayavibhaṅga (No. 18), is a complete work in its own right, containing its own list of elements *(khandhā, āyatanāni, dhātuyo, saccāni, indriyāni, hetū, āhārā, phassā, vedanā, saññā, cetanā,* and *cittāni,*[19] which are treated in the usual fashion of the early Abhidharma. It was obviously added to the Vibhaṅga proper at a later date.

However, the Dharmaskandha and the Vibhaṅga display virtual correspondence not only in terms of content, since the general form of the material is also very similar. I have already pointed out that the presentation of the material is both characteristic of the Dharmaskandha and unique within the Abhidharma of the Sarvāstivādin, in that a sūtra text containing the relevant doctrinal concepts is first presented and then subsequently explained. The Vibhaṅga uses the same method. Here, parts of various sūtra are presented and then explained. To a certain extent they are even the same passages as those in the Dharmaskandha,[20] except that the typical setting of the sūtra, the Nidāna, has been omitted. This method of treatment is, however, also unusual and rare in the Pāli Abhidharma and thus signifies a further, important feature of correspondence between the two texts.

However, in individual details of form, the two works differ considerably from one another. In the Dharmaskandha we find detailed explanations of the subject matter; in the Vibhaṅga, the material is treated in accordance with the formalistic methods of the Abhidharma that proliferated within the Pāli school.

The question now arises of how to account for the correspondence and differences between these works. The differences can readily be explained as arising from a long period of separate transmission, since examples of the different courses of development taken by similar works can repeatedly be seen in the Buddhist canon.[21] However, it is inconceivable that in two different works the same three groups of material were united by mere accident and treated in the same, unusual way merely by chance. A connection must therefore be assumed. There are only two posibilities: either one was based on the other, or they both derive from the same source. It should also be noted that the great differences of detail between the two works presuppose a long period of separate development before the text assumed its ultimate form. At all events, we must therefore presume that they originated at a very early date. In these circumstances it seems to me very probable indeed that they derived from a common source, as does the majority of the canonical literature collected in the Sūtrapiṭaka and Vinayapiṭaka. We are thus dealing with a work from the period before the Pāli and the Sarvāstivāda schools separated, a work which was then taken over and transmitted by both schools. Thus, the Dharmaskandha proves to be a very early work from the time before Aśoka's missions and can therefore also be regarded as the Sarvāstivadin's earliest Abhidharma work after the Saṃgītiparyāya.

This also provides us with a criterion for the accurate evaluation of this work. In singling out particular groups of doctrinal concepts and treating them in a completely new way, the Dharmaskandha takes the first step beyond the old Abhidharma, beyond the latter's superficial compilation of lists and its impersonal and worn-out methods of interpretation. It constitutes the first individual work of the Sarvāstivāda school. We can thus also see why Tsing-mai in his epilogue to the Chinese translation (p. 513c, 14ff.) characterizes it as the basic text of the Abhidharma and the primary source for the school of the Sarvāstivādin.

In conclusion, the fact that the Dharmaskandha and the Vibhaṅga can be established as two versions of the same work is also of importance for the evaluation of the transmission and provides a measure of the extent to which such texts may be regarded as representative of the original work. It is evident that it is only the actual core of the work, the basic ideas that constitute its essential content, which has been to any extent reliably transmitted. However, even here we must reckon with corruptions. This is clearly illustrated by the distortion of the first part of the Dharmaskandha in the Vibhaṅga. Extensive alterations in the individual details of the explanations are to be expected where the two versions differ most from one another. In this respect, the Dharmaskanda would seem to offer the more reliable transmission; however, it is suspicious that the explanations it carries often presuppose a highly developed stage of the Sarvāstivāda doctrine. Thus, the the same holds true here as for the Saṃgītiparyāya: that the explanations were adapted as a matter of course to the progressive development of the doctrine and that this must always be borne in mind when working on these texts.

3. Dhātukāya
(T 1540)

I would next like to discuss the Dhātukāya, which in my opinion belongs to the middle group of the early works of the Abhidharma. It is divided into two parts; a short, fundamental section (p. 614b7–616a28), and a broad treatment of the doctrinal concepts contained in the first section, after the fashion of the early Abhidharma (p. 616a29–625c2).

The first of these parts is of particular importance and must therefore be examined in more detail. It enumerates a series of elements divided into groups, which are then explained one after the other. It is therefore a work of the *mātṛkā* type accompanied by an explanatory text. The *mātṛkā* is composed of the following groups:[22]

1. 10 *mahābhūmikā dharmāḥ* (1. *vedanā*, 2. *saṃjñā*, 3. *cetanā*, 4. *sparśaḥ*, 5. *manaskāraḥ*, 6. *chandaḥ*, 7. *adhimuktiḥ*, 8. *smṛtiḥ*, 9. *samādhiḥ*, 10. *prajñā)*.

2. 10 *kleśamahābhūmikā dharmāḥ* (1. *āśraddhyam*, 2. *kausīdyam*, 3. *muṣitasmṛtitā*, 4. *vikṣepaḥ*, 5. *avidyā*, 6. *asamprajanyam*, 7. *ayoniśomanaskāraḥ*, 8. *mithyādhimokṣaḥ*, 9. *auddhatyam*, 10. *pramādaḥ)*.

3. 10 *parīttakleśabhūmikā dharmāḥ* (1. *krodhaḥ* 2. *upanāhaḥ* 3. *mrakṣaḥ,* 4. *pradāśaḥ,* 5. *īrṣyā,* 6. *mātsaryam,* 7. *māyā,* 8. *śāṭhyam,* 9. *madaḥ,* 10. *vihiṃsā).*

4. 5 *kleśāḥ* (1. *kāmarāgaḥ,* 2. *rūparāgaḥ* 3. *ārūpyarāgaḥ,* 4. *pratighaḥ,* 5. *vicikitsā).*

5. 5 *dṛṣṭayaḥ* (1. *satkāyadṛṣṭiḥ,* 2. *antagrāhadṛṣṭiḥ,* 3. *mithyādṛṣṭiḥ,* 4. *dṛṣṭiparāmarśah,* 5. *śilavrataparāmarśaḥ).*

6. 5 *saṃsparśāḥ* (1. *pratigha-,* 2. *adhivacana-,* 3. *vidyā-,* 4. *avidyā-,* 5. *naivavidyānāvidyāsaṃsparśaḥ).*

7. 5 *indriyāṇi* (1. *sukhendriyam,* 2. *duḥkhendriyam,* 3. *saumanasyendriyam,* 4. *daurmanasyendriyam,* 5. *upekṣendriyam).*

8. 5 *dharmāḥ* (1. *vitarkaḥ,* 2. *vicāraḥ,* 3. *vijñānam,* 4. *āhrīkyam,* 5. *anapatrāpyam).*

These are joined by 6 hexads which correspond to the six inner and outer spheres *(āyatanāni)*, that is,

1. 6 *vijñānakāyāḥ,*
2. 6 *sparśakāyāḥ,*
3. 6 *vedanākāyāḥ,*
4. 6 *saṃjñākāyāḥ,*
5. 6 *saṃcetanākāyāḥ,*
6. 6 *tṛṣṇākāyāḥ.*

A cursory glance at this list reveals that it consists exclusively of mental elements. Thus it constitutes an attempt to create a system of psychology through the systematic collation of all the mental factors. This represents something new and therefore important, for it goes much further than the rudimentary efforts to be found in the sūtras and also beyond the scattered collections of individual groups of psychic elements in the earliest Abhidharma. However, if we examine the way in which this has been carried out, various aspects stand out.

First of all, one notices certain discrepancies. The list begins with a number of large, fundamental groups, leading one to expect a large-scale, clear structure. However, it loses itself in the enumeration of minor groups, the systematic integration of which into the whole remains unclear. The last of these groups are in fact merely a repetition of themes that have already been dealt with, but in a different form. The explanation for this is not hard to find. The first groups display a new, independent arrangement. However, the author obviously felt obliged to also include older groups which had already been present, and their incorporation inevitably led to discrepancies. This is particularly evident in the 6 hexads right at the end of the list. They are already to be found in the Saṃgītisūtra, in all its versions[23], and have here been incorporated in total and in the same order.

Another characteristic feature is the author's endeavor to create numerically equal groups. The three decads are followed by five pentads. Some of these have obviously been devised solely to form groups of the required number. With the *dr̥ṣṭayaḥ* and the *indriyāṇi* the number five was given in any case. However, the five *kleśāḥ* have obviously been spun out of the three *akuśalamūlāni.*[24] The combination of *pratigha-* and *adhivacanasaṃsparśaḥ*[25] with the other three *saṃsparśāḥ* also seems artificial, as does the arbitrary integration of the five *dharmāḥ* into one group.

There is also a striking absence of a group of good mental elements as a counterpart to the *kleśamahābhūmikāḥ* and *parīttakleśabhūmikā dharmāḥ*. This was also felt to be lacking in later times, and as early as the Prakaraṇa[26] we find 10 *kuśalamahābhūmikā dharmāḥ* inserted between the *mahābhūmikāḥ* and the *kleśamahābhūmikā dharmāḥ*, and they continued to maintain their position afterwards. Their absence in the Dhātukāya can perhaps only be explained by the fact that the interest of the early period was mainly concentrated on those elements that determined entanglement in the cycle of existence.[27]

On the whole, however, despite its shortcomings, the achievement which this text represents should not be underestimated. Up to this point, the Abhidharma had dealt exclusively with traditional concepts. The Dharmaskandha had, it is true, made innovations in the organization of the material and in its approach, but in terms of content nothing new had been achieved. Here, in the Dhātukāya, especially in the first groups, psychology is for the first time considered separately and from a new viewpoint. This represents a major step forward for the subsequent development of the Abhidharma. Although this achievement may seem slight at a first glance, it is important to remember what breaking with old ties in an age bound to tradition signified. This is reflected in the great influence which the work exerted in subsequent times. This section was not only incorporated into the Prakaraṇa; from the system of psychology later developed by the Sarvāstivāda school to the last systematic summary of the same school's dogmatics in Vasubandhu's Abhidharmakośa, the Dhātukāya had a lasting effect on the classification of the mental elements.

Of interest less in terms of content than for other reasons is the second part of the work (p. 616a29–625c2). It deals with the list of mental elements from the beginning of the first part in the style of the early Abhidharma, under the aspects of connectedness *(saṃprayogaḥ)* and includedness *(saṃgrahaḥ)*. The first question which is asked and answered (p. 616b5–617b7) is that of how many of the elements of the list are connected or not connected with the 5 *vedanendriyāṇi*, the 6 *vijñānakāyāḥ* and the two elements *āhrikyam* and *anapatrāpyam*, that is, the connection of the elements of the *mātṛkā* with the elements of individual groups of the same *mātṛkā* is discussed.[28] The next question posed (p. 617b13–625c2) is that of how many of the *dhātavaḥ*, *āyatanāni*, and *skandhāḥ* contain the elements of the list. This is done in the following, rather unusual fashion: each of the elements of the list are considered in turn and in each case the question is that of how many *dhātavaḥ* etc. contain the elements which are connected to that particular element and which are not connected to one of the following elements. The whole presentation corresponds to a type which is common in the early Abhidharma but which here appears in a peculiar modification. However, before we ask what purpose this method of presentation serves and where it originated from, we must deal with yet another question.

The afterword to the Chinese translation (p. 625c6ff.) indicates that there were three versions of this work; a longer one of 6,000 lines, a medium-length one of 900 lines and a shorter version of 500 lines. The translation is of the medium-length version. It might therefore be presumed to give an incomplete picture of the work and to omit important features. However, it is stated in the text itself (p. 616b1–4 and 625c1–2) that although the total number of approaches *(nayāḥ)* amounts to 88, only 16 of them are presented. This would seem to indicate that the longer version was probably nothing more than a broad presentation of all 88 cases. The version that has been preserved thus merely avoids going into unnecessary detail, but in all other respects gives a complete account of the work.

Let us now return to the question of the origin and significance of the second part. L. de La Vallée Poussin, in the introduction to his translation of the Abhidharmakośa (p. XLIf.), was the first to point out the close relationship between the Dhātukāya and the Dhātukāya of the Pāli Abhidharma. This relationship is unmistakable. The two works display the same structure. Both begin with a *mātṛkā* which is treated under the aspects of *saṃprayogaḥ* and *saṃgrahaḥ*. The *samanvāgamaḥ* is conspicuously absent in both works. A particularly striking feature is the complicated method by which the Dhātukāya deals with the *saṃgrahaḥ*, that is, by asking which connected and non-connected elements are contained in the *dhātavaḥ* etc., a method which has its counterpart in the Dhātukathā. Added to this are similarities in turns of phrase. There are, however, also marked differences. The *mātṛkā* which constitutes the basis for the exposition is different in each case. Concerning the *saṃprayogaḥ*, the Dhātukāya asks which of the other elements of the *mātṛkā* are connected to the elements of this same *mātṛkā*. The Dhātukathā asks only whether they are related to the *dhātavaḥ*, *āyatanāni*, and *skandhāḥ*. Furthermore, the Dhātukāya merely poses the question of connectedness and non-connectedness. The other complex questions in the Dhātukathā are absent here. On the other hand, in the case of the *saṃgrahaḥ*, it employs only one of these complex questions. The simple question of includedness and non-includedness is absent, as are the other variants. Thus, the assessment of the relationship between the two works remains at first uncertain.

Fortunately, however, we have the aid of another text, which demonstrates with particular clarity at the same time not only the sort of fluctuations that were possible in the transmission of texts in the earlier period, but also that one should not be misled by these fluctuations. The Prakaraṇa, which is largely a reworking of earlier texts,[29] contains in its 4th chapter a reworking of the Dhātukāya as well (T 154 1, p. 634a10–636c28 = T 1542, p. 698b27–702a6). In this version, the second section now displays the following form: first the question is asked of which *dhātavaḥ*, *āyatana*, and *skandhāḥ* include the elements of the list. This involves seven ways of questioning: how many include the elements themselves, how many include those elements included in themselves, how many include those elements not included in themselves and so forth (T 1541, p. 636a13ff. = T 1542, p. 701b1ff.). Then follows the question of how many *dhātavaḥ* etc. are connected or not connected to the elements of the *mātṛkā* (T 1541 p. 636b20ff. = T 1542, p. 701c6ff.). Given the great similarity between the texts and above all the fact that the Prakaraṇa is in other ways too a reworking of older texts, it cannot be doubted that this section is in actual fact a reworking of the Dhātukāya. Nonetheless, this version displays several important differences. *Saṃprayogaḥ* and *saṃgrahaḥ* are discussed in the reverse order. The discussion of the *saṃgrahaḥ* is conducted using not only the one, complex form found in the Dhātukāya but, according to a variety of ways of questioning. Finally, in the case of the *saṃprayogaḥ*, the question asked is not that of whether the elements of the *mātṛkā* are connected to the other elements but rather to which of the *dhātavaḥ*, *āyatanāni*, and *skandhāḥ* they are connected. However, in all these points the version in the Prakaraṇa corresponds to that in the Dhātukathā. Thus, the fact that the Dhātukāya displays marked differences to the latter is merely due to the transmission and does not preclude their being closely related.

The relationship between Dhātukathā, Dhātukāya and the 4th chapter of the Prakaraṇa is thus as follows. Compared to the Dhātukāya, the Prakaraṇa further developed the doctrine contained in its first section, as we shall see.[30] The second part was left largely unchanged. By contrast, the second section was reworked in the Dhātukāya, namely, after the work had been incorporated into the Prakaraṇa. That it was reworked at a very late date is also clear from the fact that the discussion of whether the individual elements are included in *dhātavaḥ*, *āyatanāni* and *skandhāḥ* is still conducted using the categories of the Pañcavastuka. Finally, Dhātukathā seems to have changed very little in general. What is quite clearly secondary in this work is the supplementary incorporation of the Dhammasaṅgaṇi's *mātṛkā* (p. 19ff. and 55ff.). Otherwise, apart from those differences that are quite common in the transmission of works from the early period, the three works are so similar in structure and realization that one would be inclined to trace them back to one and the same original. There is, however, one major disparity: the *mātṛkā* of the Dhātukathā is completely different to the *mātṛkā* of the Dhātukāya. Thus, the similarity of the works could also be explained as deriving merely from the fact that they were both written according to the same method.

Nonetheless, in view of the correspondence in structure and realization and particularly in view of the fact that on both sides, in the Abhidharma of the Sarvāstivādin and that of the Pāli school, only one work of this type exists, it seems more likely that both derive from a common ancestor. Furthermore, the Dhātukathā is based on the *mātṛkā* of the Vibhaṅga (=Dharmaskandha).[31] This can be traced back to the early period and clearly must be the original. By contrast, the basis of the Dhātukāya is not a *mātṛkā* of the early type. The list given here, together with the explanations is, rather, an independent work in its own right, as is, for example, the later Pañcavastuka. However, there would have been no occasion to have revised this text according to the fashion of the Dhātukathā, had not an already extant model of this type suggested it. This model, however, is in all probability the same work that lived on in the form of the Dhātukathā[32] in the Abhidharma of the Pāli school. In order to circumvent this assumption, we would have to presume that the original model was another work of the same type which later disappeared without trace. The reworking of the original which resulted in the Dhātukāya was effected by replacing the old *mātṛkā* with a new list of mental elements together with their explanations and reworking the second part accordingly.

It merely remains to discuss the date of the text. P'ou-kouang places it together with the Prakaraṇa at the beginning of the fourth century after the nirvana. This is clearly because P'ou-kouang attributes it to the same author as the Prakaraṇa, that is, Vasumitra. However, this attribution is fairly doubtful. Yaśomitra names Pūrṇa rather than Vasumitra as the author. In view of the general tendency to attribute the works of lesser-known authors to famous personalities, the less well-known name is always the likelier option in such cases. To attempt a dating of the work myself, I should say that its connection with a work also held in common with the Pāli school would seem to indicate an early date. A further indication is the old-fashioned way in which, in the first part, the enumerated elements are explained by paraphrases in the style of the earliest Abhidharma.[33] L. de La Vallée Poussin thus writes appositely of the "Sarvāstivāda archaïque."[34] On the other hand, a very early dating is precluded by the fact that the Pāli school did not participate in the innovations made in it in the field of psychology. The separation of the two schools had therefore already taken place by this time. It would thus seem best to place the work between the Dharmaskandha and the Prakaraṇa.

4. Vijñānakāya (T 1539)

The next work, Devaśarman's Vijñānakāya, constitutes an important step forward in the development of the early Abhidharma of the Sarvāstivādin. It divides into two parts, one polemic (p. 531a21–547b21) and the other systematic (p. 547b22–614b1).

The polemic consists of two sections. The first combats the doctrine of Mou-lien (Maudgalyāyana), which asserted that it is only the present that exists, not the past and the future (p. 531a21–537a26). The second section directs itself against the Pudgalavāda of the Vātsīputrīya (p. 537a27–547a2). The work concludes with a discussion of the Pratītyasamutpāda (p. 547a3–b21).

L. de La Vallée Poussin indicated both the significance of this part for the history of the Buddhist sects as well as its close relationship to the Kathāvatthu of the Pāli canon.[35] Since closer examination demands a broader-based approach, we shall thus have to return to this later. In any case, we can see here the origins of the fundamental differences in dogmatics which later led to the two most important schools separating. At the same time, this confirms the dating given by P'ou-kouang, which assigns the work to the middle layer of the canonical literature of the Abhidharma.

Of far more importance for the development of the Abhidharma of the Sarvāstivādin itself, however, is the second part, which deals mainly with the problems of cognition and which gives the work its name. It is divided into the following four sections:

1. *hetupratyayaskandhakam*	(p. 547b22–559a20)
2. *ālambanaskandhakam*	(p. 559a25–582b13)
3. *saṃkīrṇaskandhakam*	(p. 582b18–593a24)
4. *samanvāgamaskandhakam*	(p. 593b4–614b1)

The first section treats the causality of cognition in general. First of all, the four kinds of causes, *hetupratyayaḥ, samantara-*

pratyayaḥ, ālambanapratyayaḥ, and *adhipatipratyayaḥ,* are enumerated, and this is followed by an explanation of what these four causes consist of in the case of a cognition, that is, what *hetupratyayaḥ* etc. is in the case of a cognition, and for what this itself is *hetupratyayaḥ* etc. (p. 547b22–c4). Then further determinants are adduced. The question is asked of whether a past, present, or future cognition has past, future, or present causes (p. 547c12–548a28), whether a good, evil, or indeterminate cognition has good, evil, or indeterminate causes (p. 548a29–c3), whether eliminated or non-eliminated *(prahīnaḥ)* mental moments *(cittam)* have eliminated or non-eliminated causes (p. 551a8–553b5 and 553b11–555c5). Includedness in the various spheres is also considered here. The *anuśayāḥ* play a special role: the question is asked of which *anuśayāḥ* adhere to good, evil, or indeterminate cognition (p. 5c4–21), which are the reason and cause of good, evil, or indeterminate cognition (p. 548c22–549c10), and so forth. The various additional determinants are also taken into account here.

The second section deals with the cause that is of particular importance for cognition, the *ālambanapratyayaḥ,* that is, the object. The discussion is conducted along similar lines to the previous section. The question is asked whether the object of past, future, or present cognition is the past, future, or present, either singly or together (p. 559b2–14), whether the object of good, evil, or indeterminate cognition is good, evil or indeterminate, either singly or together (p. 559b14–26), whether a mental moment belonging to a particular sphere cognizes elements belonging to this or other spheres, either singly or together (p. 559c29–562a25) etc. Here, too, there is a detailed discussion of the workings of the *anuśayāḥ*. Of particular importance is the paragraph which explains the different modes of cognition in sense cognition and mental cognition (p. 559b27–c28). It contains the sentence *cakṣurvijñānasamaṅgī nīlam vijānāti no tu nīlam iti*[36] which is so frequently quoted in later texts.

The third section contains, as the name tells us, a miscellany. This consists in part of questions which are contingent on the doctrine of cognition, such as the first question, as to which type of cognition is capable of producing or eliminating a defilement (p. 582b21–c8), or by how many types of cognition the elements are cognized, which are *rūpi* or *arūpi* and so forth. (p. 582c9–19).[37]

Some of these are questions which occur randomly and out of context, such as the question of how color *(varṇaḥ)* and shape *(ākāraḥ)* are apportioned to matter *(rūpam)* (p. 583a14-19), or the question of what is meant by *adhipatipratyayaḥ* (p. 586a14–26).

The fourth and last section deals with the accompaniedness *(samanvāgamaḥ)*[38] by the various types of cognition, that is, first of all, 12 types of mental moments *(cittam)* are enumerated, followed by an examination of the various combinations of mental moments which can accompany an individual. The twelve types are: good, evil, defiled-indeterminate and undefiled-indeterminate mental moments in the sphere of desire *(kāmadhātuḥ)*, good, defiled-indeterminate, and undefiled-indeterminate in both the sphere of forms *(rūpadhātuḥ)* as well as the sphere of formlessness *(ārūpyadhātuḥ)*; and finally, mental moments of the one who is to be trained *(śaikṣaḥ)* and the adept *(aśaikṣaḥ)*. The questions now asked are of whether an individual who is accompanied by a good mental moment belonging to the sphere of desire can also be accompanied by an evil mental moment etc. in all possible combinations (p. 593b10ff.); whether in the case of an individual who has relinquished the accompaniedness of a good spiritual moment belonging to the sphere of desire and achieved non-accompaniedness, the same applies to the evil mental moment etc. (p. 606a8ff.); whether somebody who has not yet relinquished a good mental moment belonging to the sphere of desire is accompanied by that mental moment etc. (p. 611b14ff.) and so on in the same vein. This concludes the work.

Taken as a whole, this seems at first glance to differ very little from what we have encountered in the other works of the Abhidharma. However, the external form is deceptive. What we have here in fact represents a fundamental change. Up to this time, these works had consisted solely of the explanation and description of the transmitted doctrinal concepts. Even the Dhātukāya had only contributed something new to the degree that it had extended the circle of these concepts. Here, by contrast, we encounter new problems and a new approach. The most important feature in this is the doctrine of causality. Although the doctrine of the four causes is derived from sūtras,[39] the way in which it is presented here is entirely new. Causal events here take a different course to the causal linkage in the Pratītyasamutpāda. Mind and the mental elements are thereby given a different position and thus new significance. The operation of the *anuśayāḥ* is also viewed in a new light. However, the most important aspect in all this is that, from this point on, the thought takes a new, independent course. Up to this point, everything had been held in the thrall of tradition; here the spell has been broken.

Nevertheless, the forms of thought used are still largely the same. The aspects under which the mental elements are viewed in their causal relationship, the temporal arrangement, moral quality and inclusion in the various spheres, have been taken from an old attribute-*mātṛkā*.[40] The old form of the catechesis was still influential. The new perceptions are not presented with reasons; the results are rather stated in the form of answers to questions. The influence of the traditional forms is particularly marked in the treatment of the *samanvāgamaḥ*, in the circuitous discussion of the various possible combinations.

A further characteristic feature of the Vijñānakāya's presentation is the absence of a larger, systematic framework. Although a large and complex problem has been singled out and discussed, it is nevertheless treated in isolation. This is also true of the smaller, individual problems touched on in the Saṃkīrṇaskandhaka.

All this results in a picture which is both singular and characteristic, but one which is not confined to the Vijñānakāya alone. We find the same features in a much later work, in the Jñānaprasthāna, the last canonical work of the Abhidharma of the Sarvāstivādin. I thus feel justified in regarding this singular and characteristic method of treating the material as a separate stage of development, one which superseded with the Sarvāstivādin the old, purely formalistic scholasticism and remained paramount for a considerable length of time. It was in turn eventually supplanted by a new movement, the characteristic expression of which is, in my opinion, the Pañcavastuka. However, we will return to this later. First there is another work from the literature of the early Abhidharma to be examined: the Prakaraṇa.

5. Prakaraṇa (T 1541 and 1542)

Vasumitra's Prakaraṇa is again a work of a completely different character. It could perhaps best be described as a compendium. Earlier, the Saṃgītisūtra had gathered together a wealth of doctrinal concepts, albeit without any intrinsic coherence and presented in a form that verges on the chaotic. The attempts to combine groups of related doctrinal concepts as in the Dharmaskandha had created order in minor areas, yet these areas were isolated and lacked coherence. Similarly, the attempts to treat individual subjects systematically, signs of which begin to appear in the Vijñānakāya, had not done anything to change this fragmentary state of affairs. It became, rather, ever more noticeable, the more of these isolated attempts at systemization were juxtaposed. This development made compilation all the more necessary, and this is exactly what the Prakaraṇa attempts to do.

However, this compilation is not systematic. Rather, Vasumitra makes a purely outward attempt to unite in one work all the most important achievements that had been made up to his time. His work therefore consists of a number of sections, all virtually independent of each other and complete in themselves. Some of these sections reproduce the essential content of earlier works, while others deal with a single subject of greater significance. A short survey of the individual chapters will soon reveal the character of this work.

The first chapter (T 1541, p. 627a6–628c27 = T 1542, p. 692b19–694b2) is nothing other than a rendering of the Pañcavastuka. In both works the 5 categories are first enumerated and then explained, with both the enumeration and the explanation corresponding in all essentials. The individual details of phrasing cannot be discerned through the refraction of the Chinese translation.

The second chapter (T 1541, p. 628c28–631b23 = T 1542,p. 694b3–696b13) contains a discussion of the 10 kinds of knowledge *(jñānāni)*. They are the same as the 10 enumerated in the Pañcavastuka (T 1541, p. 628b7ff. and T 1542, p. 693c 22ff. = T 1556, p. 997b14ff.), and which Vasubandhu still discusses in the 7th chapter of his Abhidharmakośa. The discussion itself follows that in the Vijñānakāya. The questions asked are which objects *(ālambanam)* are possessed by each type of knowledge and why it has this particular object; to what degree each type of knowledge is included in the other kinds and why this should be the case; which type of knowledge is defiled *(sāsravam)* and which is undefiled *(anāsravam)*; which has a defiled and which an undefiled object; and finally, which type is conditioned *(saṃskṛtam)* and which is not conditioned *(asaṃskṛtam)*, and which has a conditioned and which a non-conditioned object.

The third chapter (T 1541, p. 631c5–634a9 = T 1542, p.696b14–698b26) forms a counterpart to the Pañcaskandhaka. In the latter, the 5 *skandhāḥ* are first enumerated, then discussed according to an attribute-*mātṛkā*. Finally, their relationship to the *āyatanāni* and the *dhātavaḥ* is discussed. Here the 12 *āyatanāni* serve as a starting point. The attribute-*mātṛkā* according to which they are discussed displays extensive similarities to the *mātṛkāḥ* that appear in the various versions of the Pañcaskandhaka. In the concluding discussion of the relationship between *skandhāḥ*, *āyatanāni*, and *dhātavaḥ*, the 22 *indriyāṇi* and the 98 *anuśayāḥ* are also included. Despite these differences, however, the chapter clearly displays the same structure as that of the Pañcaskandhaka.

The fourth chapter (T 1541 p. 634a10–636c28 = T 1542, p. 698b27–702a6) represents a reworking of the Dhātukāya. The first part (T 1547, p. 634a11–636a12 = T 1541, p. 698b28–701a29) corresponds in essence almost exactly to the first part of the Dhātukāya. The same groups of elements are enumerated and explained in the same way, the numerical order being identical to that in the Dhātukāya.[41] Divergences in the explanations are minimal.[42] There is only one important difference: inserted between the 10 *mahābhūmikāḥ* and the 10 *kleśamahābhūmikā dharmāḥ* is a group of 10 *kuśalamahābhūmikā dharmāḥ* (1. *śraddhā*, 2. *vīryam*, 3. *hrīḥ*, 4. *apatrapā*, 5. *alobhaḥ*, 6. *adveṣaḥ*, 7. *praśrabdhiḥ*, 8. *upekṣā*, 9. *apramādaḥ*, 10. *avihiṃsā)*. This remedies a critical deficiency in the system of the Dhātukāya.

Vasumitra made a number of additions to this basic core. He prefaced the groups of elements taken from the Dhātukāya with an enumeration of the general basic concepts, mentioning 18 *dhātavaḥ*, 12 *āyatanāni*, 5 *skandhāḥ*, 5 *upādānaskandhāḥ,* and 6 *dhātavaḥ* (T 1541, p. 634a11;15–24 = T 1542, p. 698b28; c2–10).

He also explains these fundamental concepts at the relevant point in the text (T 1541, p. 634b12–635a3 = T 1542, p. 699a3–c7).[43] The relationship of the second part of the chapter to the second part of the Dhātukāya has already been demonstrated in the discussion of the latter work.

The fifth chapter (T 1541, p. 637a5–644a23 = T 1542, p. 702a 7–711b5) is, like the second chapter, devoted to a detailed discussion of one single topic, the doctrine of the *anuśayāḥ*, a theme repeatedly touched upon in the earlier works. However, since we will have to examine this subject more closely in another context, we shall avoid going into details here.

The last three chapters employ *mātṛkāḥ* after the fashion of the early Abhidharma and are thus again presumably based on older works. The sixth chapter (T 1541, p. 644b5–662c26 = T 1542. p. 711 b6–733a16) discusses the elements *(dharmāḥ)* in general, using a long, miscellaneous *mātṛkā* (T 1541, p. 644b6-646b23 = T 1542, p. 711b7-713c19). This is the same procedure as in the 3rd and 4th chapters of the Dhammasaṅgaṇi. Concerning the composition of the *mātṛkā*: since the Sarvāstivādin *mātṛkāḥ*—in contrast to those of the Dhammasaṅgaṇi—generally begin with the numerically inferior groups, random groups of elements (in addition to the triad) were added in numerical order, while the Dhammasaṅgaṇi had to confine itself to taking over the dyads from the Saṃgītisūtra. The basic core is provided by the attribute *mātṛkā* contained in the dyads and triads. Both groups begin wholly or at least partly with the five old pairs of *rūpi—arūpi* etc. and the five triads of *kuśalam—akuśalam—avyākṛtam* and so forth. Only in the dyad are a number of concepts premised.[44] The subsequent elaboration of the two groups displays a number of striking correspondences with the Dhammasaṅgaṇi, for example in the groups of *cittam* etc. (p. 644b10ff. and 711b12ff., cf. Dhammasaṅgaṇi, p. 10,21ff.), or *vipākā dharmāḥ, vipākadharmadharmāḥ,* and *naivavipākanavipākadharmadharmāḥ* (p. 712 a,1f. = Dhammasaṅgaṇi, p. 3,7ff.). It thus appears that this section of the Prakaraṇa evolved from the same beginnings as the 3rd and 4th chapter of the Dhammasaṅgaṇi. The explanations are unfortunately unsuitable for purposes of comparison since they were naturally subject to the forces of change and modernization; thus also the two chapters from the Dhammasaṅgaṇi give two different series of explanations.

In the Prakaraṇa there follows yet another section (T 1541, p. 654b6ff. = T 1542, p. 723c3ff.), which discusses how many of the *dhātavaḥ, āyatanāni,* and *skandhāḥ* include the concepts of the *mātṛkā,* how many kinds of knowledge they are known by, how many kinds of cognition they are cognized by and how many *anuśayāḥ* adhere to them. This would seem to be a later addition, since it is unusual to find a discussion of this kind following an attribute-*mātṛkā*.

The seventh chapter (T 1541, p. 663a5–688c10 = T 1542, p. 733a17–765c25) is based on the *mātṛkā* of the Dharmaskandha. The only omissions are the *srotaāpattyaṅgāni* from the 15 doctrinal concepts of the first part, the Pratītyasamutpāda, which represents a heterogeneous constituent in itself, from the basic general concepts of the third part, and finally the Kṣudravastuka. Even the sequence is the same. The discussion is not conducted in the same way as in the Dhātukathā, i.e. under the aspects of includedness *(saṃgrahaḥ)* or connectedness *(saṃprayogaḥ),* but according to 50 questions by means of a long attribute-*mātṛkā*. This *mātṛkā* (T 1541, p. 663a10–c15 = T 1542, p. 733a28–734a4) consists essentially of attributes which are arranged in dyads, triads and tetrads. The dyads and triads are again headed by the five old groups of *rūpi* etc. and *atītam* and so forth. The great length of the list is due to the large number of tetrads, in which four possibilities are postulated for each of the two concepts treated: that one, both or neither are present, for example, *karma na karmavipākaḥ, karmavipāko na karma, karma ca karmavipākaś ca, naiva karma na karmavipākaḥ.*

The eighth and last chapter (T 1541, p. 688c11–692a23 = T 1542, p. 766a4–770a19) is closely connected to the previous chapters and displays nothing new in terms of either form or content. It starts out from the attribute *mātṛkā* of the 3rd chapter which it incorporates unchanged,[45] making only a few additions, namely the *skandhāḥ, āyatanāni, dhātavaḥ,* and *indriyāṇi,* i.e. the basic general concepts. Also added are the *anuśayāḥ,* arranged according to the spheres they belong to and to whether they can be eliminated by the seeing of suffering and so forth. Like the *mātṛkā,* the mode of treatment is also taken from the earlier chapters. As at the end of the 6th chapter, the question is posed of which *dhātavaḥ, āyatanāni,* and *skandhāḥ* the elements are included in, which possess the attributes of the *mātṛkā*, how many kinds of knowledge they are known by, how many kinds of cognition they are cognized by and how many *anuśayāḥ* adhere to them.

This concludes the work. The achievement it represents can only be judged with reference to its character. As I said at the outset, and as our examination of the work has clearly shown, we are here dealing with a compendium which is largely based on older material. Thus, the real achievement lies above all in the attempt to collect the existing material systematically. Innovations of content can only be expected to a limited degree, and are even then more likely to be found in the way the material was reformed and augmented. However, this can only be properly gauged where the source is still extant, as, for example, in the case of the 4th chapter, which is based on the Dhātukāya. We can probably ascribe the addition of the basic general concepts and the insertion of the 10 *kuśalamahābhūmikā dharmāḥ* into the list of the Dhātukāya to the author of the Prakaraṇa. However, there is a further element of uncertainty involved in deliberations of this kind. Kumārajīva reports in the Mahāprajñāpāramitopadeśa (T 1509, p. 70a16f.) that only four chapters of the work are by Vasumitra, while the other four were written by the Arhats of Kaśmir. The accuracy of this report is upheld by the proximity of heterogeneous parts, such as chapter 1 (=Pañcavastuka) and chapter 4 (=Dhātukāya), the psychology of which contradict each other. If we believe this account, however, we are confronted by the difficult question of which chapters are old and which are later additions. I feel that the beginning, chapters 1–3, are likely to be a later addition, as well as chapter 8, on account of its close relationship to the *mātṛkā* in chapter 3. This means that chapters 4–7 would represent the earlier part. This is, however, only a conjecture. It will perhaps become clearer when more research has been done on the literature of the early Abhidharma.

This concludes my brief survey of the canonical works of the Abhidharma of the Sarvāstivādin. The last work, which has not been discussed, the Jñānaprasthāna by Kātyāyanīputra, occupies a special position,[46] and it would thus be advisable to discuss it separately. In the meantime, I should like to summarize briefly the conclusions we have arrived at so far.

The general picture that has emerged is as follows. The canonical works of the Abhidharma of the Sarvāstivādin contain largely a transmitted heritage of material from earlier times. Much of this was held in common with the Pāli school. Innovations occurred only gradually. The Saṃgītiparyāya is still based entirely on the early Abhidharma, and even the Dharmaskandha contains only formal innovations. Innovation in terms of content first occurs in the psychology of the Dhātukāya. However, it is not until the Vijñānakāya that truly new paths are trodden. What is new in the Prakaraṇa, which is essentially a compilation of transmitted material, is above all what came from the Pañcavastuka. This, however, already belongs to a new era, an era which saw the end of the old Abhidharma.

Thus, in terms of content, there is little that can be regarded as an independent achievement in these works. Nevertheless, the broad lines of a process of development can be distinguished in them. Furthermore, there is a certain amount concealed below the surface of these works which must first be brought to light, since it is obscured by the unfortunate way it is usually presented. Its significance, however, is no less for all that. This is particularly true of the fundamental reworking of the doctrine of liberation, which I would like to call the "Abhisamayavāda." This will be the subject of my next essay.[47]

III

The Abhidharma of the Pāli School

Very few of the canonical works of the Abhidharma of the Hīnayāna schools have survived. Apart from the Abhidharma of the Sarvāstivādin, we possess only the Abhidharma of the Pāli school and the Śāriputrābhidharma, which A. Bareau attributes to the school of the Dharmaguptaka.[1] There is also a variety of additional material, for example Harivarman's Tattvasiddhi. This is, it is true, a late work; Harivarman is credibly attested as being a pupil of Kumāralāta, which would mean he was an approximate contemporary of the elder Vasubandhu.[2] However, the work is based on old tradition. Some material is provided by Asaṅga's Abhidharmasamuccaya, which represents a Mahāyānistic reworking of a Hīnayāna Abhidharma. However, the only works that have survived without adulteration are those mentioned above and thus it is to these that we will turn our attention first. I shall begin with the Abhidharma of the Pāli school.

In the second part of these studies [cf. p. 13ff.] I have shown that certain works of the Sarvāstivāda Abhidharma display marked similarities to corresponding works of the Pāli Abhidharma, from which I have drawn the conclusion that they share a common heritage and are derived from one and the same original work. However, since objections have been raised against this view, with reference to the fact that they display not only correspondences but also marked discrepancies, I would like to make some additional remarks on the subject.

We will never arrive at a satisfactory conclusion if we emphasize only the correspondences on the one hand or the discrepancies on the other. Any attempt at a solution which is based on either the former or the latter must also attempt to explain the other. Assuming the texts are completely different makes the similarities I have demonstrated very difficult to explain. It seems to me, for example, to be extremely unlikely to be mere coincidence that the *mātṛkāḥ* of the Dharmaskandha and the Vibhaṅga are based on the same three constituent parts, especially as they contain such an idiosyncratic text as the Kṣudravastuka. Conversely, assuming that the texts have a common source, it seems to me that the differences can be easily explained. As I have pointed out elsewhere [p. 4f.], the Buddhist *mātṛkāḥ* together with their commentaries correspond most closely to the Brahmanical sūtras. They both consist of a brief text which was committed to memory and which was supplemented by (originally oral) explanations, which were adapted to the gradual development of the doctrine before eventually being replaced by written commentaries. On the Brahmanical side, too, the sūtras, many of them orginating from ancient times, have come down to us only in late versions with written commentaries. However, we can still clearly see the constituent parts of which they are composed, as, for example, in the case of the Nyāyasūtras or the Yogasūtras. The Vaiśeṣikasūtras in particular display as it were the annual rings of development. We must imagine a similar state of affairs within the Buddhist Abhidharma. The Buddhist *mātṛkāḥ*, as mere enumerations, were even more subject to change, whether by addition or omission. The commentaries also have only been transmitted in the late versions in which they were ultimately preserved. However, this happened long after the schools had separated and these works had frequently assumed a quite different appearance after a long period of individual development. I should therefore like to adhere to my view that the correspondences between the Abhidharma works of the Sarvāstivādin and those of the Pāli school derive from a common heritage and I believe that the differences between them can be easily explained in the manner indicated above.

Evidence of a common source thus establishes the oldest stratum in the Pāli Abhidharma, from which the later development continued. At the same time, this also provides a basis for dating this oldest stratum. Both the Sarvāstivāda school in the remote northwest and the Pāli school in Ceylon are mission schools owing their origin to Aśoka's missions. The common source must therefore derive from the period before they separated, i.e. before these missions. If we also bear in mind that the first missionaries are unlikely to have brought the whole of the canon as it then existed with them, a date of before 200 B.C. would seem probable for the origin of the oldest layer. All the Abhidharma works that were written later come after this point.

Turning now to this later stage of development, the following question still has to be clarified first. Were these Abhidharma works written in the missionary areas or were they written in the area the missions had started out from and taken to the missionary areas later? The possibility cannot be dismissed if there was constant traffic between the two areas. Nonetheless, since both the extant Abhidharma collections—that of the Sarvāstivādin and of the Pāli school—are quite different from each other (apart from their old, common heritage), at least one of them must have been written in the missionary area and only one can perhaps have originated in the mother country.

I am firmly convinced that the Sarvāstivāda Abhidharma originated in the missionary area. It displays such obvious signs of a keen, markedly individual development, (even within the bounds of the Abhidharma tradition), which continued uninterruptedly into more brightly illuminated historical times that it seems justified to assume that this entire development occurred in one and the same area.

The situation is different in the case of the Pāli Abhidharma. Here it is in particular the linguistic conditions which are remarkable. While the northwest, the home of the Sarvāstivādin, seems to all appearances to have used a northwestern form of Prakrit before the adoption of Sanskrit, we have in this case an alien language which was not the language of the original canon. In Ceylon itself, commentaries on the canonical works were written in Singhalese. Pāli did not become the ecclesiastical language until much later, from approximately the 3rd century A.D. onwards.[3] It is therefore unlikely that here comprehensive works were written in Pāli at this early period and incorporated into the canon. This leads to the conclusion that the works of the Pāli Abhidharma originated in the mother country and were taken from there to Ceylon.

However, this assumption implies further conclusions. To begin with, it follows that Pāli was the language of the area the mission came from. For it is unlikely that a foreign language would have been used for works that were written there. The mission appears to have originated in Vidiśā.[4] Pāli would therefore be the language of this region. Nothing stands in the way of this argument. Linguistic data, in particular the relationship to the Girnār version of the Aśoka inscriptions, clearly points to the west and the location of Pāli in this region has therefore been repeatedly advocated.

Our assumption also presupposes that there was lively traffic between Ceylon and the mother country long after Aśoka's missions, so that works were taken from there to Ceylon long afterwards. S. Lévi has demonstrated that traffic of this kind did in fact exist right into the 2nd century A.D.[5] and I myself have already dealt with this topic elsewhere.[6] I am therefore of the opinion that the works of the Pāli Abhidharma—apart from the oldest core of texts—were written in the period between 200 B.C. and A.D. 200 in the mother country and were brought to Ceylon from there.

Turning to the works themselves, we find ourselves dealing in the first place with the 7 works of the Abhidhammapiṭaka. These are in the usual order: 1. Dhammasaṅgaṇi, 2. Vibhaṅga, 3. Dhātukathā, 4. Puggalapaññatti, 5. Kathāvatthu, 6. Yamaka and 7. Paṭṭhāna. In addition there is the Paṭisambhidāmagga, which is usually counted as part of the Khuddakanikāya. That this is clearly a work of the Abhidharma has always been recognized. The reason why it was included in the Khuddakanikāya and not in the Abhidhammapiṭaka is easily explained. It is the latest of the Abhidharma works and was written at a time when the formation of the canon had been essentially completed. At that time, it was only the Khuddakanikāya in which late works such as the Niddesa were included. However, any examination of the Abhidharma must take the Paṭisambhidāmagga as well as the canonical works of the Abhidharma into account.

I shall now go on to discuss the individual works. I shall begin with those which I believe represent the earliest tradition and then proceed to treat those in which the later development is evident. Initially I shall consider only the ancient core of texts. The commentaries will be treated where they belong according to when they assumed their final form. I shall limit myself to briefly characterizing the works and emphasizing what was important for the development of the doctrine and for the philosophical development in general. I shall not deal with any other aspects.[7]

1. Vibhaṅga

The core of the Vibhaṅga consists of three *mātṛkāḥ*. These are the same ones which form the Dharmaskandha of the Sarvāstivādin.[8] They thus represent a common ancient heritage. The *mātṛkāḥ* are accompanied by two shorter texts, the Ñāṇavibhaṅga (p. 366–408) and the Dhammahadayavibhaṅga (p. 480–521). Such a combination of essentially unrelated texts is unremarkable; the Abhidharma texts were after all not composed according to a program; the canon was compiled from all the relevant extant texts, whereby shorter texts which were not comprehensive enough to form an Abhidharma work on their own were combined with longer texts.

The first of the three *mātṛkāḥ* is constituted as follows:

1. 5 *khandhā*	(p. 3)
2. 12 *āyatanāni*	(p. 83)
3. (a) 6 *dhātuyo (pathavīdhātu* etc.)	(p. 102)
(b) 6 *dhātuyo (sukhadhātu* etc.)	(p. 106)
(c) 6 *dhātuyo (kāmadhātu* etc.)	(p. 107)
(d) 18 *dhātuyo*	(p. 108)
4. 4 *ariyasaccāni*	(p. 126)
5. 22 *indriyāni*	(p. 156)
6. *paṭiccasamuppādo*	(p. 173–237)

It contains a list of basic general concepts and is identical to the third *mātṛkā* of the Dharmaskandha, except that in the latter the 4 *āryasatyāni* are in a different place. However, as we shall see, it is the Vibhaṅga that has preserved the original structure.

The second *mātṛkā* consists of the following items:

1. 4 *satipaṭṭhānā*	(p. 238)
2. 4 *sammappadhānā*	(p. 255)
3. 4 *iddhipādā*	(p. 264)
4. 7 *bojjhaṅgā*	(p. 276)
5. *aṭṭhaṅgiko maggo*	(p. 285)
6. 4 *jhānāni*	(p. 294)
7. 4 *appamaññāyo*	(p. 327)

8. 5 *sikkhāpadāni* (p. 342)
9. 4 *paṭisambhidā* (p. 350-365)

It contains a list of concepts concerning the path of liberation and corresponds to the first *mātṛkā* of the Dharmaskandha. However, there are numerous individual differences between the two. The question of what is original can be answered with the help of another text. The 1st and 2nd *mātṛkā* of the Vibhaṅga namely occur again in the Dhātukathā, and the second *mātṛkā* appears in the following form:

1. 4 *satipaṭṭhānā*
2. 4 *sammappadhānā*
3. 4 *iddhipādā*
4. 4 *jhānāni*
5. 4 *appamaññāyo*
6. 5 *indriyāni*
7. 5 *balāni*
8. 7 *bojjhaṅgā*
9. *aṭṭhaṅgiko maggo*

This list corresponds to another list which is already present in the old canon[9] and which later survived in the 37 *bodhipakṣikā dharmāḥ.*[10] Only the 4 *jhānāni* and the 4 *appamaññāyo* have been added. We may therefore regard this list in the Dhātukathā as the oldest version of the second *mātṛkā,* which was subsequently altered and extended in the Vibhaṅga and the Dharmaskandha.

The third *mātṛkā* (p. 409–479) is based on the Kṣudravastuka, which takes the second place in the Dharmaskandha. Here, however, it has been expanded to an excessive degree. The first part has preserved its original character and exhibits the concepts that are characteristic for this work. It has been extended by adding 27 variants of *mado* and 12 variants of *māno*. However, after the much-favored numbered scheme of dyads, triads, and tetrads etc., these are followed by a long series of concepts which only partly belong here. In most cases the connection is purely superficial.[11]

To recapitulate: the three *mātṛkāḥ* that form the core of the Vibhaṅga constitute in all essentials an ancient heritage, albeit occasionally distorted and expanded. There is no further development or any new thought.

And now a brief word about the commentary. This is divided into three parts: the Suttantabhājanīya, the Abhidhammabhājanīya and the Pañhāpucchaka. As the name tells us, the Suttantabhājanīya is linked to sūtra texts, while the Abhidhammabhājanīya and the Pañhāpucchaka supply explanations in the manner of the Abhidharma.[12] This otherwise unusual manner of dividing the commentary can probably be explained as follows. As we have seen in the discussion of the Dharmaskandha,[13] the explanation of the individual concepts of the *mātṛkāḥ* after sūtra texts is characteristic of this work. And the Suttantabhājanīya, which has the same type of explanation, is thus based on an ancient heritage. However, this does not seem to have satisfied the rampant scholasticism of the Pāli Abhidharma, and thus further explanations along the lines of this Abhidharma were added. That these are later additions is evident not only from the fact that the Pañhāpucchaka uses the *mātṛkā* of the Dhammasaṅgaṇi, but also in its formulations and concepts, which also appear in the Dhammasaṅgaṇi and are characteristic of it and which thus belong to a considerably later period than the old core of the Vibhaṅga.[14]

Let us turn now to the two texts which, as we established above, were originally independent works and were only combined with the old core of the Vibhaṅga at a later date. There is little to say about the Ñāṇavibhaṅga; it is one of those texts that occur frequently in the Abhidharma, where an unending series of miscellaneous varieties of some object or other are enumerated.[15] The core consists of a number of old, well-established divisions, such as the 4 cognitions which form the basis for the process of liberation: *dukkhe, dukkhasamudaye, dukkhanirodhe* and *dukkhanirodhagāminiyā paṭipadāya ñāṇaṃ*, or the 4 cognitions which we have already encountered in the discussion of the Abhisamayavāda [cf. below p. 168]: *dhamme, anvaye, pariye,* and *sammutiñāṇaṃ*. In addition there are other topics, such as the 10 *tathāgatabalāni*. However, these are combined in dull and meaningless fashion with a variety of other distinctions: first varieties of the 5 *viññāṇā*, then varieties of the *paññā*, arranged according to dyads and triads with the aid of attribute-*mātṛkāḥ*, and so forth. In this way, long lists of variations for all possible objects could be easily compiled. If these were comprehensive enough, they could even appear as works in their own right. We will meet an example of this in the

Puggalapaññatti. A shorter list, such as the one we are dealing with here, would be incorporated into a larger work, in this case the Vibhaṅga. It is impossible to date these lists with any accuracy, since they were constantly being augmented. However, in their vapidity they are of little importance for the development of the doctrine.

The second text, the Dhammahadayavibhaṅga, is of far greater importance. It is divided into three sections. The first section (p. 480–502) starts with a short *mātṛkā*, which is then explained (p. 480–482). Then follows a discussion of how the elements in the list are distributed among the various spheres (p. 482–491), and which of them are assigned to the various beings if they arise in these spheres (p. 492–502). The second section has no connection with the initial *mātṛkā* (p. 502–509). It deals with the following questions: which elements occur in the various spheres (p. 502–503), what acts will cause one to be reborn among the beings of this sphere (p. 503–504), and how long the life span of these beings is (p. 504–509). The third and last section takes up the original *mātṛkā* once again and discusses it with the aid of a short attribute-*mātṛkā*.

What is striking about this text is its interest in the spheres the world is composed of and in the beings that inhabit them. However, it is the initial *mātṛkā* which is of far greater importance both in terms of thought and for the general development of the doctrine. It consists of the following items:

1. 5 *khandhā*
2. 12 *āyatanāni*
3. 18 *dhātuyo*
4. 4 *saccāni*
5. 22 *indriyāni*
6. 9 *hetū*
7. 4 *āhārā*
8. 7 *phassā*
9. 7 *vedanā*
10. 7 *saññā*
11. 7 *cetanā*
12. 7 *cittāni*

It starts with the list of basic general concepts familiar to us from the basic text of the Vibhaṅga. It omits only the *paṭiccasam-*

uppādo, which would be out of place here. Instead a number of new concepts have been added which are explained as follows.

The 9 *hetū* are the 3 *kusalahetū*, *alobho*, *adoso*, and *amoho*, the 3 *akusalahetū*, *lobho*, *doso*, and *moho* and the 3 *avyākatahetū*, *alobho*, *adoso*, and *amoho*, which are *avyākatā* inasmuch as they arise from the maturation of good elements or inasmuch as they are, with respect to the acts, indeterminate elements *(kusalānaṃ vā dhammānaṃ vipākato kiriyāvyākatesu vā dhammesu)*. This is both new and important, since it brings into the description the doctrine of good and evil acts and their retribution. This may be connected with the interest of the text in rebirth in the various spheres.

The 4 *āhārā* are explained as *kabalīkārāhāro*, *phassāhāro*, *manosañcetanāhāro* and *viññāṇāhāro*. They already appear in the old canon in this form and it is from there that they have been taken.[16]

Phasso, *vedanā*, *saññā*, and *cetanā* are more closely connected. They have also been taken from the old canon, where they already formed a group and served to explain *nāmaṃ* in *nāmarūpaṃ*.[17] The connection between them is evident in the uniformity of the explanation. For, after the 7 *phassā* have been explained as *cakkhu-*, *sota-*, *ghāna-*, *jivhā-*, *kāya-*, *manodhātu-*, and *manoviññāṇadhātusamphasso*, the 7 *vedanā*, *saññā*, and *cetanā* are explained in corresponding fashion as *cakkhusamphassajā vedanā*, *saññā*, and *cetanā* and so forth.

Finally, the 7 *cittāni* are determined as *cakkhuviññāṇaṃ*, *sotaviññāṇaṃ*, *ghānaviññāṇaṃ*, *jivhāviññāṇaṃ*, *kāyaviññāṇaṃ*, *manodhātu*, and *manoviññāṇadhātu*.

The addition of these concepts to the old list of basic general concepts shows the concern to give a position of fundamental importance to the mental elements and processes which these had lacked among the old general and indeterminate basic concepts. The fact that this was achieved with the aid of concepts and expressions taken unaltered from the old canon instead of creating something new is characteristic of the Pāli school. Nonetheless, a step forward had been taken. I see in this an endeavor to create a new system. This is also indicated in the name of the work, Dhammahadaya,[18] which says that it is the essence, the core of the doctrine which is to be described. If the discussion of the concepts treated using an attribute-*mātṛkā* at the end of the work belonged to the text from the start, it is possible that it might represent a distant parallel to the Pañcaskandhaka, which in other schools formed the starting point for a more developed system.

That the text possessed a certain standing and was not unimportant for the development of the Pāli Abhidharma is evident from the fact that the group of mental elements included in its *mātṛkā* was also added to the old *mātṛkā* in the Dhātukathā. The list of mental elements in the Dhammasaṅgaṇi begins with this group, and the Dhammasaṅgaṇi also works with the concepts it included elsewhere.[19] There is also a remarkable account in the Aṭṭhasālinī that in the dispute over the authenticity of the Kathāvatthu one of the suggestions made was to include the Mahādhammahadaya among the seven works of the Abhidharma in its stead.

Finally, as far as the age of the text is concerned, its inclusion in the Vibhaṅga does not, of course, prove that it was older than the latter. It merely indicates that it was available to the redactors of the Pāli Abhidharma who inserted it. I should therefore not like to date it any earlier.

2. Dhātukathā

The Dhātukathā, like the Vibhaṅga, also derives from an ancient heritage. Its core corresponds to the Dhātukāya of the Sarvāstivādin. It is constituted as follows:

Its point of departure is a *mātṛkā* which corresponds essentially to the 1st and 2nd *mātṛkāḥ* of the Vibhaṅga. There follows a discussion of which *khandhā*, *āyatanāni*, and *dhatuyo* include the members of this *mātṛkā* and with which they are connected. This is conducted according to various aspects: namely, whether they are included, not included, not included in what is included, included in what is not included and so forth. Their connectedness is also discussed according to the same method. Finally, both includedness and connectedness are linked to one another.

The following points are particularly important. In the Dhātukāya, the *mātṛkā* has been replaced by a comprehensive list of mental elements. In contrast to this, the Dhātukathā, with its *mātṛkā* which corresponds to that in the Vibhaṅga, has obviously preserved the original features. The innovations it contains are insignificant and superficial. Apart from occasional changes in the formulation of the questions concerning includedness and connectedness, the following aspect should be mentioned. The following members have been added to the *mātṛkā*:

1. *phasso*
2. *vedanā*
3. *saññā*
4. *cetanā*
5. *cittaṃ*
6. *adhimokkho*
7. *manasikāro*

The first five of these have been taken from the Dhammahadayavibhaṅga. The only extra additions are *adhimokkho* and *manasikāro*.[20] Furthermore, in the discussion of includedness and connectedness, the *mātṛkā* of the Dhammasaṅgaṇi is also discussed immediately after the *mātṛkā* belonging to the text and according to the same method.

We can thus say that the essence of this work also consists of an ancient core, the additions made to it being purely superficial. There is no independent development or original thought.

3. Puggalapaññatti

We may pass over this work quickly. It belongs to the type already described in the discussion of the Ñāṇavibhaṅga. A long series of variants of a concept, here that of the *puggalo*, is listed in numerical order, as is usual in the Pāli Abhidharma.

In the Buddha's sermons different types of human beings are often mentioned for the purposes of instruction or comparison. Here these are collected and enumerated and the relevant sūtra texts given in the explanations. Thus, in one of his sermons the Buddha differentiates between three types of human beings: *nirāso, āsaṃso,* and *vigatāso*, i.e. those who have no wish to achieve liberation, those who have this wish and those who have already fulfilled this wish. He describes their behavior on their hearing of a monk who has achieved liberation.[21] In another sermon, he compares various human beings and their behavior with three types of sick person,[22] and so forth. We also find here the various distinctions made according to the way in which the disciple strives for liberation or according to the level he has attained, which we discussed in our treatment of the Abhisamayavāda. [Cf. below p. 162ff.] However, it is characteristic of the dull manner in which the text was compiled that *ubhatobhāgavimutto, paññāvimutto* etc. are first cited and explained, after which they appear collectively as a septad and finally, with the addition of *sammāsambuddho* and *paccekasambuddho*, form a new group together with the same explanations.[23]

All in all, it can be said that this text represents a mere compilation of material without independent value.

4. Paṭṭhāna

We now come to texts which go beyond the inherited material and introduce innovations, albeit initially of a purely formal nature. For this did not mean the introduction of new subjects or thought; rather, questions were asked about the occurrence of the subjects discussed and about the application of the given concepts. Here the Pāli Abhidharma is inexhaustible in inventing new cases and exceptions. And when something has already been discussed in the greatest possible detail, some variant or other is introduced and the whole thing is repeated again in the same fashion from the beginning.

The Paṭṭhāna deals with the doctrine of causality. First of all, 24 kinds of causes are enumerated and briefly explained. The discussion is then conducted in the following manner. The point of departure is the formulation of a question which, in its basic form, runs as follows: *siyā (kusalaṃ) dhammaṃ paṭicca (kusalo) dhammo upajjeyya (hetu-) paccayā*, that is, whether a particular object of a certain property arises through another object of a certain property due to a certain causal relationship. Then 4 cases are distinguished according to which the description is by and large divided. Either the relevant property is present in the case of both objects (vol. I p. 20–vol. V p. 520), or it is absent in both (vol. VI p. 3–134), or it is present in the first object and absent in the second (vol. VI p. 135–307), or it is absent in the first object and present in the second (vol. VI p. 309–444). The properties of the objects are taken from the *mātṛkā* of the Dhammasaṅgaṇi and are discussed in the order given there, i.e. first the triads (vol. I p. 20–vol. II p. 517), then the dyads (vol. III p. 3–vol. IV p. 458), and then both in various combinations (vol. V p. 3–520). Then the various causal relationships of these properties are treated one after the other. Here even more variations arise from a change in the original formulation with the word *paṭicca* being replaced by *sahajāto* (vol. I p. 64–66), *paccayā* (p. 67–100), *nissāya* (p. 100–104), *saṃsaṭṭho* (p. 104–120) or *sampayutto* (p. 121–123). Finally the following variant appears: *(kusalo) dhammo (kusalassa) dhammassa (hetu-)paccayena paccayo* (p. 123–270).

This is not the place to discuss other distinctions and variants. What has been said will suffice to give an idea of the nature of this work. The doctrinal content is meagre and limited to what is said about the various causes. The rest is mere consideration of the various cases, whereby many distinctions are purely superficial and insignificant in terms of content. Here the "method" has replaced genuine thought.

5. Yamaka

The Yamaka is by and large even more deficient in content. It comprises 10 sections, in each of which one group of doctrinal concepts is discussed:

1. *kusalā, akusalā, avyākatā,* and *nāmā dhammā* (vol.I p.3–22)
2. 5 *khandhā* (vol.I p.23–104)
3. 12 *āyatanāni* (vol.I p.105–295)
4. 18 *dhātuyo* (vol.I p.296–310)
5. 4 *saccāni* (vol.I p.311–400)
6. 3 *saṅkhārā*, namely, *kāya-, vacī-,* and *cittasaṅkhāro* (vol.II p.3–79)
7. 7 *anusayā*, namely, *kāmarāgānusayo, paṭighānusayo, mānānusayo, diṭṭhānusayo, vicikicchānusayo, bhavarāgānusayo,* and *avijjānusayo* (vol.II p.81–393)

8. *cittaṃ* (vol.II p.395–433)
9. *dhammā*, namely, *kusalā, akusalā* and *avyākatā* (vol.III p.3–106)
10. 22 *indriyāni* (vol.III p.107–431)

The discussion usually proceeds in the following manner: two things are contrasted with one another and the question is asked of whether when the one arises and vanishes the other also arises etc., and vanishes and whether when one is cognized the other is also cognized. Every question is followed by its inversion and it is the way in which the questions occur in pairs that gives the work its name. Here, too, of course, a plethora of variants appear. The things are contrasted in an infinite variety of combinations and linkages. And every question is followed by its negation—whether that which one thing is not the other is also not, whether when one thing does not arise the other also does not arise, and so forth.

Only a few sections deviate from this type of presentation. The difference is minimal in section 9 when instead of cognizing *(pariññā)* practising *(bhāvanā)* and fighting against *(pahānaṃ)* the good and evil elements are discussed in third place. However, the divergences in sections 1, 7, and 8 are more significant and it is here that one comes across a number of interesting points in terms of content.[24]

In section 1 the question is asked of whether the *kusalā dhammā* are *kusalamūlā, kusalamūlamūlā, kusalamūlakā,* and *kusalamūlamūlakā*, always with the corresponding variants. The same questions are asked with regard to the *akusalā, avyākatā,* and *nāmā dhammā*. Finally, in true Abhidhamma fashion, *kusalam ūlā* is replaced by *kusalahetū, -nidānā, -sambhavā, -pabhavā, -samuṭṭhānā, -āhārā, -ārammaṇā, -paccayā,* and *-samudayā*.

In section 7, the 7 *anusayā* are first enumerated and explained as to which everyone adheres to (*kattha anuseti*). Then follow the questions. These ask with whom an *anusayo* occurs and what it adheres to (p. 81ff.), who is afflicted with an *anusayo* and why (p. 144ff.), who eliminates an *anusayo* and why (p. 203ff.), who cognizes an *anusayo* and why (p. 260ff.), who has eliminated an *anusayo* and in what respect (p. 320ff.), and finally with whom it arises (p. 379f.). The questions are always presented in pairs in the usual form, for example, whether when the *kāmarāgānusayo* arises in a person the *paṭighānusayo* also arises *(yassa kāmarāgānusayo anuseti tassa paṭighānusayo anusetīti)*, and so forth. The same is always asked of all *anusayā*, and in a variety of combinations. Again, every group of questions is followed by corresponding questions in the negative form. Only in the case of the last group is this procedure incomplete. Finally, a separate section discusses how many *anusayā* arise in someone who passes away from one sphere and is reborn in the same or another sphere (p. 380–393).

In section 8, the arising and vanishing of the mind *(cittaṃ)* and the relationship of both to one another is discussed with reference to all possible cases and in all the different phases of time. The breadth of the presentation arises from the fact that the questions, which are in any case clumsily formulated, are in addition asked from the point of view of the person *(yassa cittaṃ)*, then from the point of view of the mind *(yaṃ cittaṃ)*, and finally with regard to the combination of both *(yassa yaṃ cittaṃ)*. This is a particularly glaring example of how an intrinsically interesting problem can be inflated to the point of inanity using the Abhidhamma "method".

6. Dhammasaṅgaṇi

The Dhammasaṅgaṇi is a work that represents a significant step forward in the development of the doctrine. Here we encounter ideas that are genuinely new, and we must therefore examine it in more detail. However, this work also represents an important stage of development for other reasons. It represents the state of the doctrine that was authoritative for the compilers and redactors of the Abhidhammapiṭaka. It is, of course, obvious that this Piṭaka did not grow gradually on its own but was the result of a conscious effort of compilation. The insertion of the Abhidhammabhājanīya and the Pañhāpucchaka into the Vibhaṅga, for example, the incorporation of originally independent works such as the Ñāṇavibhaṅga and the Dhammahadayavibhaṅga—all this is the work of redactors. The fact that it is the *mātṛkā* of the Dhammasaṅgaṇi which has been worked in here secondarily just as it has been in the Dhātukathā, and that these inserted parts contain the same advanced views and concepts as in the Dhammasaṅgaṇi, shows that it is this work that reflects the form of the doctrine that was prevalent at the time when the Abhidhammapiṭaka was compiled.

The structure of the work is quite clear. It starts with a *mātṛkā*; the *mātṛkā* of the Dhammasaṅgaṇi that has been mentioned so often. However, the commentary belonging to it comes at the end, and in duplicate, too, with two sections known as Cittakaṇḍa and Rūpakaṇḍa inserted between the two versions.

The *mātṛkā* is based on a core of older material, as the correspondences with the 6th section of the Prakaraṇa indicate,[25] but was expanded considerably over the course of time. The last part, taken mostly from the Saṅgītisuttanta, the so-called Suttantamātikā, is a later addition. This is evident from the fact that this part is missing in the Vibhaṅga and the Dhātukathā, where the *mātṛkā* of the Dhammasaṅgaṇi was incorporated. And in the Dhammasaṅgaṇi it is only treated in the Nikkhepakaṇḍa, the first of the two commentaries.

[a. Cittakaṇḍa]

The most comprehensive part of the work is the Cittakaṇḍa, the first of the two inserted sections (p. 18–146). However, its size is merely the result of the "method". Its essence can be summarized relatively briefly.

The question is asked of which elements are *kusalā, akusalā,* and *avyākatā*, i.e. good, evil, and indeterminate. The answer is: when a good, evil, or indeterminate cognition arises, then both this and all its accompanying elements are good, evil, or indeterminate. These elements which accompany the cognition are then enumerated one by one. They are of course different in the case of good, evil, or indeterminate cognitions. However, there are additional circumstances which make for a difference. These include above all the appertaining to a particular sphere. It is true that the evil elements only belong to the *kāmadhātu*. The good elements, on the other hand, can belong to the *rūpa-* and *arūpadhātu* as well as the *kāmadhātu*. Finally, they may also be a *lokuttaraṃ cittaṃ*. In the case of the indeterminate elements, a distinction must be made as to whether they are *vipāko,* i.e. the maturation of previous acts, or *kiriyā*, i.e. acts themselves. As *kiriyā* they belong to all three spheres only if they are the maturation of good acts. The maturation of evil acts belongs exclusively to the *kāmadhātu*. Further distinctions in the higher spheres are contingent on belonging to various levels of meditation, which are discussed in breadth. Finally, a number of further distinctions are treated which I do not propose to discuss here.[26] Since in all of these cases all the elements which accompany a cognition are enumerated and perhaps explained, the whole section has understandably swollen to considerable dimensions.

What purpose, though, does this enumeration of various cognitional complexes serve? This circumstantial method was certainly not chosen to determine which elements are good, evil, or indeterminate. This question can be easily answered, however, if we refer to the works of the Sarvāstivāda for comparison. As we have seen, an attempt was made in the Dhātukāya to collect all the mental elements systematically and arrange them in a list,[27] and as we will see, an attempt was subsequently made to determine how many of these elements are included in each cognitional process.[28] Now the Cittakaṇḍa of the Dhammasaṅgaṇi evidently represents a parallel to this. Thus, the Pāli school had also attempted to cover all the mental elements and to establish how many of them are included in each mental complex. And it is this attempt that has been preserved in the Cittakaṇḍa of the Dhammasaṅgaṇi. The fact that a distinction was made between good, evil, and indeterminate cognitions was obvious for Buddhism and also has a parallel in the Sarvāstivāda school. This has nothing to do with the first *trikaṃ* in the *mātṛkā* of the Dhammasaṅgaṇi. But the correspondence provided a welcome opportunity of including this text in the work, despite the fact that it was otherwise of a completely different character.

This text is naturally premised by a list of all the mental elements, similar to that in the Dhātukāya, and we must assume that there was a list of this kind in the Pāli school as well. The fact that it has not survived is not necessarily significant in itself. Very little apart from the canonical texts has been preserved from the early period. The various shorter texts worked into the canonical works which we have encountered up to this point owe their survival solely to the redactors who inserted them into the canonical works.

Otherwise they, too, would have been lost. This list can in any case easily be reconstructed. The mental elements are always enumerated in the same order with the various cognitions. Thus, in order to complete the list, we merely need to take what has been omitted in one case from the other cases. This would then give the following list:

1. *phasso*, 2. *vedanā*, 3. *saññā*, 4. *cetanā*, 5. *cittaṃ*.

6. *vitakko*, 7. *vicāro*, 8. *pīti*, 9. *sukhaṃ*, 10. *dukkhaṃ*, 11. *upekkhā*, 12. *somanassaṃ*, 13. *domanassaṃ*, 14. *cittassekaggatā*.

15. *saddhindriyaṃ*, 16. *viriyindriyaṃ*, 17. *satindriyaṃ*, 18. *samādhindriyaṃ*, 19. *paññindriyaṃ*, 20. *manindriyaṃ*, 21. *sukhindriyaṃ*, 22. *dukkhindriyaṃ*, 23. *upekkhindriyaṃ*, 24. *somanassindriyaṃ*, 25. *domanassindriyaṃ*, 36. *jīvitindriyaṃ*, 27. *anaññātaññassāmītindriyaṃ*, 28. *aññindriyaṃ*, 29. *aññātāvindriyaṃ*.

30. *sammādiṭṭhi*, 31. *sammāsaṅkappo*, 32. *sammāvācā*, 33. *sammākammanto*, 34. *sammāājīvo*, 35. *sammāvāyāmo*, 36. *sammāsati*, 37. *sammāsamādhi*.

38. *micchādiṭṭhi*, 39. *micchāsaṅkappo*, 40. *micchāvāyāmo*, 41. *micchāsamādhi*.

42. *saddhābalaṃ*, 43. *viriyabalaṃ*, 44. *satibalaṃ*, 45. *samādhibalaṃ*, 46. *paññābalaṃ*, 47. *hirībalaṃ*, 48. *ottappabalaṃ*, 49. *ahirīkabalaṃ*, 50. *anottappabalaṃ*.

51. *alobho*, 52. *adoso*, 53. *amoho*.

54. *lobho*, 55. *doso*, 56. *moho*.

57. *vicikicchā*, 58. *uddhaccaṃ*.

59. *anabhijjhā*, 60. *avyāpādo*, 61. *sammādiṭṭhi*.

62. *abhijjhā*, 63. *vyāpādo*, 64. *micchādiṭṭhi*.

65. *hirī*, 66. *ottappaṃ*.

67. *ahirīkaṃ*, 68. *anottappaṃ*.

69. *kāyapassaddhi*, 70. *cittapassaddhi*, 71. *kāyalahutā*, 72. *cittalahutā*, 73. *kāyamudutā*, 74. *cittamudutā*, 75. *kāyakammaññatā*, 76. *cittakammaññatā*, 77. *kāyapāguññatā*, 78. *cittapāguññatā*. 79. *kāyujukatā*, 80. *cittujukatā*.

81. *sati*, 82. *sampajaññaṃ*.

83. *samatho*, 84. *vipassanā*.

85. *paggāho*, 86. *avikkhepo*.

ye vā pana . . . aññe pi atthi paṭiccasamuppannā arūpino dhammā.[29]

In order to evaluate this list it is instructive to compare it with the list in the Dhātukāya. This begins with the division of the mental elements into *mahābhūmikā dharmāḥ, kleśamahābhūmikā dharmāḥ* and *parīttakleśabhūmikā dharmāḥ*. This is a new systematic idea, and even if it was not successfully applied in general it at least represented an attempt, a path upon which further steps could be taken. There is nothing comparable to this in the Dhammasaṅgaṇi. The list begins with the mental elements from the *mātṛkā* of the Dhammahadayavibhaṅga and is followed by a long series of concepts which are for the most part already in the canon. The only achievement here consists of the collection and arrangement of the elements into groups.

Let us now turn to the actual subject of this section: the arrangement of the mental elements that accompany the individual processes of cognition. At first sight it seems that this proceeds in the monotonously mechanical fashion and in the tedious breadth that is so characteristic of the Pāli Abhidharma. Nonetheless, all of this is based on a system of psychology that has been developed to a certain degree and which gives rise to various interesting problems. However, it is advisable to deal with this separately. The only theme I would like to anticipate here, since it is certainly older and was not newly created in connection with the psychological questions, is the conception of the course of the path of meditation which is presupposed here.

[α. The Path of Meditation]

As I have already said, the presentation of the Cittakaṇḍa does not confine itself to discussing the good, evil, and indeterminate cognitional complexes in ordinary human existence. It also treats the spheres which Buddhism assumes on the basis of meditational experiences and into which the disciple enters during the state of meditation. From this it is possible to establish which views on the course of the path of meditation obtained at the time when the Cittakaṇḍa was written. However, the presentation in this section is extremely circumstantial. Irrelevant material is treated in excessive breadth, resulting in a confused picture. Thus, in order to arrive at any fruitful conclusions we must elaborate the essence of this work, and strip it of the formalism of the Abhidharma which has overgrown and almost smothered it. The method used here is the familiar one which returns again and again. With the things that are being treated a distinction is made between a plethora of variants, all of which are then discussed in tedious detail according to the same formula. All of this is for the most part completely superficial; the essential content is not touched upon. We must therefore first establish which of these variants are present in this section. These we will separate from the core of the text and then examine this core itself. In doing so we will attempt to explain the path of meditation described in the text in all its particularity and then to establish the significance it had within the confines of the general development of the doctrine of the Pāli school.

Looking at the path of meditation in general, it is immediately obvious that besides the series of the 4 *jhānāni* familiar from the old canon, mention is also always made of 5 *jhānāni*. This can be explained as follows: the Buddha's revelation as represented by the old path of liberation posits four *jhānāni* during the decisive process of liberation, the first of which is *savitakkaṃ savicāraṃ* and the second *avitakkaṃ avicāraṃ*. It seemed logical in addition to these two to assume a level of meditation in which only the *vitakko* is missing but where the *vicāro* is present. And in the old canon there is in fact a group of three *samādhī*, the first of which is *savitakko savicāro*, the second *avitakko vicāramatto*, and the third *avitakko avicāro*.[30] In the Sarvāstivāda this led to the assumption of the *dhyānāntaram*, where, in contrast to the regular *dhyānāni*, only the *vicāro* is present and not the *vitarko*.[31] However, this school did not simply add the *dhyānāntaram* to the *dhyānāni* but left it its special standing. In contrast to this, the Pāli school combined this form of meditation with the other stages of meditation, thus creating a series of 5 *jhānāni* which were then treated and discussed beside the 4 *jhānāni* in the same way. The course of the path of meditation itself has not been thereby changed in any way and we will therefore disregard the 5 *jhānāni* in the following examination.

Of the variants distinguished in the individual processes of meditation themselves we find the following kinds.

Particular distinction is made as to whether access to the state of meditation is laborious *(dukkhapaṭipadaṃ)* or easy *(sukhapaṭipadaṃ)* and whether the cognition occurs slowly *(dandhābhiññaṃ)* or quickly *(khippābhiññaṃ)*. If the two are combined the following four variants result: meditation is either *dukkhapaṭipadaṃ dandhābhiññaṃ* or *dukkhapaṭipadaṃ khippābhiññaṃ, sukhapaṭipadaṃ dandhābhiññaṃ* or *sukhapaṭipadaṃ khippābhiññaṃ*. Moreover, this type of distinction is not new but derives from models in the old canon.[32]

A second type of variant is based on the following distinction. A meditation can be limited *(parittaṃ)* or unlimited *(appamāṇaṃ)* and it can have a limited *(parittārammaṇaṃ)* or an unlimited object *(appamāṇārammaṇaṃ)*. If these are combined with one another this again results in four variants: the meditation is either *parittaṃ parittārammaṇaṃ* or *parittaṃ appamāṇārammaṇam, appamāṇaṃ parittārammaṇaṃ,* or *appamāṇaṃ appamāṇārammaṇam*.[33] In addition, both these types of distinction can be combined with one another, resulting in sixteen variants.

A third type of variant distinguishes whether the meditation is weak *(hīnaṃ)*, moderate *(majjhimaṃ)* or excellent *(paṇītaṃ)*. This distinction is also based on similar distinctions in the old canon.[34]

Finally there is a fourth type of variant according to whether the meditation is governed by a wish *(chandhādhipateyyaṃ)*, energy *(viriyādhipateyyaṃ)*, thought *(cittādhipateyyaṃ)* or consideration *(vīmaṃsādhipateyyaṃ)*. Here, too, there is a correspondence with a model in the old canon, since the distinction between the 4 *iddhipādā* is premised by *chando, viriyaṃ, cittaṃ* and *vīmaṃsā*.

I shall now present a survey of the path of meditation according to the Dhammasaṅgaṇi. It is present in its entirety in the discussion of the *kusalā dhammā* and also in the *avyākatā dhammā* as *vipāko,* in part also as *kiriyā*. Moreover, the formulations of the Dhammasaṅgaṇi are frequently used in the Vibhaṅga. I shall list the different forms of meditation in order, state which level of meditation they belong to and give the number of variants presented. The subsequent number in brackets indicates which of the four types of variant discussed it is. It becomes clear that this was too much even for the Ābhidharmika, who otherwise seem so indefatigable in their invention of variants. Frequently variants are not mentioned where they would be expected and there are cases where this has given rise to indistinctness.

kusalā dhammā

I. *rūpāvacarā kusalā dhammā*

1. 8 *kasiṇāni* — with all 4 and 5 *jhānāni*
   including 4 variants (1), 4 variants (2) and 16 variants (1 + 2)[35]
2. 8 *abhibhāyatanāni* — with all 4 and 5 *jhānāni*
   including 4 variants (1), 2 variants (2) and 8 variants (1 + 2)[36]
3. 3 *vimokkhā* — only with the 1st *jhānaṃ*
   no variants
4. 4 *brahmavihārā* — the first three with the first 3 and 4 *jhānāni*; the last only with the 4th *jhānaṃ*
   no variants
5. 10 *asubhajhānāni* — only with the first *jhānaṃ*
   no variants

II. *arūpāvacarā kusalā dhammā*

1. 4 *arūpajhānāni* — only with the 4th *jhānaṃ*
   no variants
   (a)[37] *(paṭhavīkasiṇaṃ)* — with all 4 and 5 *jhānāni*
      3 variants (3), 4 variants (4) and 12 variants (3 + 4)
   (b) 4 *arūpajhānāni* — only with the 4th *jhānaṃ*
      3 variants (3), 4 variants (4) and 12 variants (3 + 4)

III. *lokuttarajhānāni*

1. 1st *bhūmi* — with all 4 and 5 *jhānāni*
   4 variants (1)
   (a) *suññataṃ* — with all 4 and 5 *jhānāni*
      including 4 variants (1)
   {b) *animittaṃ*}[38]
   c) *appaṇihitaṃ* — with all 4 and 5 *jhānāni*
      including 4 variants (1)
      (a) 20 *mahānayā* — only the 1st *jhānaṃ* mentioned
         1 variant *(dukkhapaṭipadaṃ dandhābhiññaṃ)*
      (b) 1st *bhūmi* — with all 4 and 5 *jhānāni*
         4 variants *(dukkhapaṭipadaṃ dandhābhiññaṃ* + 4)

(c) 20 *mahānayā* only the 1st *jhānaṃ* mentioned
4 variants *(dukkhapaṭipadaṃ dandhābhiññaṃ* + 4)
2. 2nd *bhūmi* only the 1st *jhānaṃ* mentioned
1 variant *(dukkhapaṭipadaṃ dandhābhiññaṃ)*
3. 3rd *bhūmi* only the 1st *jhānaṃ* mentioned
1 variant *(dukkhapaṭipadaṃ dandhābhiññaṃ)*
4. 4th *bhūmi* only the 1st *jhānaṃ* mentioned
1 variant *(dukkhapaṭipadaṃ dandhābhiññaṃ)*

avyākatā dhammā

A. *vipākā*
I. *rūpavacarā vipākā*
1. *(paṭhavīkasiṇaṃ)* with all 4 and 5 *jhānāni*
no variants
II. *arūpāvacarā vipākā*
1. 4 *arūpajhānāni* only with the 4th *jhānaṃ*
no variants
III. *lokuttarā vipākā*[33]
1. (1st *bhūmi)*
suññataṃ with all 4 and 5 *jhānāni*
animittaṃ with all 4 and 5 *jhānāni*
appaṇihitaṃ with all 4 and 5 *jhānāni*
4 variants in each case (1)
(a) *(suññataṃ)*
suññataṃ with all 4 and 5 *jhānāni*
animittaṃ with all 4 and 5 *jhānāni*
appaṇihitaṃ with all 4 and 5 *jhānāni*
including 4 variants in each case (1)
(b) *(animittaṃ)*[40]
(c) *(appaṇihitaṃ)*
appaṇihitaṃ with all 4 and 5 *jhānāni*
animittaṃ with all 4 and 5 *jhānāni*
suññataṃ with all 4 and 5 *jhānāni*
including 4 variants in each case (1)
(a) (20 *mahānayā)*
suññataṃ only the 1st *jhānaṃ* mentioned
animittaṃ
appaṇihitaṃ
1 variant *(dukkhapaṭipadaṃ dandhābhiññaṃ)*

(b) (1st *bhūmi)*
suññataṃ with all 4 and 5 *jhānāni*
animittaṃ with all 4 and 5 *jhānāni*
appaṇihitaṃ with all 4 and 5 *jhānāni*
4 variants (1 + *chandādhipateyyaṃ)*
(c) *(suññataṃ)*
suññataṃ with all 4 and 5 *jhānāni*
animittaṃ with all 4 and 5 *jhānāni*
appaṇihitaṃ with all 4 and 5 *jhānāni*
including 4 variants (1 + *chandādhipateyyaṃ)*[41]
(d) *(appaṇihitaṃ)*
appaṇihitaṃ with all 4 and 5 *jhānāni*
animittaṃ with all 4 and 5 *jhānāni*
suññataṃ with all 4 and 5 *jhānāni*
including 4 variants (1 + *chandādhipateyyaṃ)*
(e) (20 *mahānayā)*
suññataṃ only the 1st *jhānaṃ* mentioned
animittaṃ
appaṇihitaṃ
4 variants *(dukkhapaṭipadaṃ dandhābhiññaṃ* + 4)
2. (2nd *bhūmi)*[42]
suññataṃ only the 1st *jhānaṃ* mentioned
1 variant *(dukkhapaṭipadaṃ dandhābhiññaṃ)*
3. (3rd *bhūmi)*
suññataṃ only the 1st *jhānaṃ* mentioned
1 variant *(dukkhapaṭipadaṃ dandhābhiññaṃ)*
4. (4th *bhūmi)*
suññataṃ only the 1st *jhānaṃ* mentioned
1 variant *(dukkhapaṭipadaṃ dandhābhiññaṃ)*

B. *kiriyā*
I. *rūpāvacarā kiriyā*
1. *(paṭhavīkasiṇaṃ)* with all 4 and 5 *jhānāni*
no variants
II. *arūpāvacarā kiriyā*
1. 4 *arūpajhānāni* only with the 4th *jhānaṃ*
no variants

Before we turn to the path of meditation itself, a few brief remarks should be made about the variants. Looking at the path of meditation as a whole, we see that initially only variants 1 and 2 occur. It is not until after all the *rūpāvacarā* and *arūpāvacarā kusalā dhammā* have been discussed that the beginning of the path is returned to and the most important stages of the path are then combined with variants 3 and 4. This gives the impression from the outset of being secondary, an impression strengthened by the fact that variant 3 only occurs here. Variant 4 does occur once more, but again in dubious circumstances. In the case of the *lokuttarajhānāni*, the discussion proper of the first *bhūmi* is followed by the so-called 20 *mahānayā*, a vapid and pointless addition as such. Then the first *bhūmi* is taken up again and combined with variant 4, as are the *mahānayā* subsequently. The secondary nature of this variant could hardly be more clearly revealed. We may thus regard variants 3 and 4 as being in all probability later additions. It is only variant 1 and possibly variant 2 which seem to be closely linked with the path of meditation.

As I have already indicated, however, we shall now disregard all the variants and turn to the path of meditation itself. It will suffice if we confine ourselves at first to the description in the case of the *kusalā dhammā* since it contains all the essential features. Here it is obvious at first glance that while the path of meditation is based on canonical material, as a whole it represents a new creation. We must therefore attempt to establish in which respects it was new and to explain what led to its creation.

As far as canonical models are concerned, the old canon contained two sequences of meditation: the 4 *jhānāni* and the 4 *arūpā*. The 4 *jhānāni* derive from the personal experience of the Buddha. They are the path on which he himself attained enlightenment. He became familiar with the 4 *arūpā* during the time of his striving, while endeavoring to attain enlightenment under the tutelage of Āḷāra Kālāma and Uddaka Rāmaputta. Both sequences appear in the canon, also in combination, such that the meditation progresses via the *jhānāni* to the *arūpā*.[43] This is understandable, since the *arūpā* represent the highest states of consciousness. Nonetheless, this does not mean that the *jhānāni* lose their importance or standing in any way. They are and remain the moments that lead to the liberating cognition. Characteristic for this conception is the account of the end of the Buddha's life. Before the end, he passes through all the levels of meditation up to *nevasaññānāsaññāyatanaṃ*, then returns to the *jhānāni*, ultimately passing into nirvana from the 4th *jhānaṃ*.[44]

By contrast, in the Dhammasaṅgaṇi, we find three sequences of meditation divided among the *rūpāvacarā, arūpāvacarā,* and the *lokuttarā dhammā*. The question thus arises of how the two sequences of meditation from the old canon stand in relation to these. In the case of the 4 *arūpā*, the answer is easy. They correspond to the *arūpajhānāni* of the *arūpāvacarā kusalā dhammā*. But what is the position of the *jhānāni*? According to the canonical model they should be placed before the *arūpā*. But this position is occupied by the *kasiṇāni* and so forth. Neither can they be equated with the *lokuttarajhānāni*, since these are described in a completely different way.

Our survey of the path of meditation of the Dhammasaṅgaṇi has shown that each form of meditation is combined with all or at least some of the 4 and 5 *jhānāni*. That it is the canonical 4 *jhānāni* that are meant here is obvious from the fact that the description of them is identical to that in the canon. However, this means that according to the description in the Dhammasaṅgaṇi the 4 *jhānāni* are not a form of meditation in their own right, separate from other forms, but that they accompany all forms of meditation, constituting their underlying structure. This also implies that they do not determine the character of the individual forms of meditation but that they form the backbone of the path of meditation as a whole.

This signifies a complete change in the position of the *jhānāni* and the question urges itself of how this happened. I believe the following explanation can account for this. Even according to the canonical doctrine there is a fundamental difference between the *jhānāni* and the *arūpā*. It is the content of the meditation—of which one becomes conscious in the meditation itself—which determines the character of the *arūpā*. In contrast to this, the 4 *jhānāni* signify a training of the mind. Through these the *cittaṃ* becomes *parisuddhaṃ pariyodātaṃ anaṅganaṃ vigatūpakkilesaṃ mudubhūtaṃ kammaniyaṃ*, and, when it is directed towards the chosen object, is able to cognize the latter with complete lucidity. However, as soon as this fundamental difference between *jhānāni* and *arūpā* had been realized, they could no longer be put alongside each other as levels of meditation in the same way. It was only the *arūpā* that were and remained levels of meditation. On the other hand, it was only natural to combine the *jhānāni* with all of the levels of meditation as a training for the mind.

However, this fundamental decision necessarily led to further changes. The *arūpā* on their own were not enough as levels of meditation. Thus, the place formerly occupied by the *jhānāni* was filled by the *kasiṇāni* etc. as preparatory levels of meditation so to speak. To form the conclusion of the path the *lokuttarajhānāni* were added. These bring about liberation in the same way as the canonical *jhānāni* and thus seemed especially appropriate as a conclusion. And now let us look at how this happened in detail.

The old canon has a number of forms of meditation which the Buddha himself had probably recommended for practice to his disciples. Here these are strung together and put before the *arūpā*. Various changes were made as necessary under these circumstances.

The sequence starts with the *kasiṇāni*, which consist of 10 members in the canon: 1. *paṭhavī-*, 2. *āpo-*, 3. *tejo-*, 4. *vāyo-*, 5. *nīla-*, 6. *pīta-*, 7. *lohita-*, 8. *odāta-*, 9. *ākāsa-*, and 10. *viññāṇakasiṇaṃ*.[45] The first eight of these were taken over and the last two omitted; the *ākāsakasiṇaṃ* and the *viññāṇakasiṇaṃ* were now redundant, since the *ākāsānañcāyatanaṃ* and the *viññāṇañcāyatanaṃ* follow later under the *arūpā*.

Next come the 8 *abhibhāyatanāni*. These are described in the canon as follows:[46]

1. *ajjhattaṃ rūpasaññī eko bahiddhā rūpāni passati parittāni suvaṇṇadubbaṇṇāni, . . .*
2. *ajjhattaṃ rūpasaññī eko bahiddhā rūpāni passati appamāṇāni suvaṇṇadubbaṇṇāni, . . .*
3. *ajjhattaṃ arūpasaññī eko bahiddhā rūpāni passati parittāni suvaṇṇadubbaṇṇāni, . . .*
4. *ajjhattaṃ arūpasaññī eko bahiddhā rūpāni passati appamāṇāni suvaṇṇadubbaṇṇāni, . . .*
5. *ajjhattaṃ arūpasaññī eko bahiddhā rūpāni passati nīlāni nīlavaṇṇāni nīlanidassanāni nīlanibhāsāni, . . .*
6. *ajjhattaṃ arūpasaññī eko bahiddhā rūpāni passati pītāni pītavaṇṇāni pītānidassanāni pītanibhāsāni, . . .*
7. *ajjhattaṃ arūpasaññī eko bahiddhā rūpāni passati lohitakāni lohitakavaṇṇāni lohitakanidassanāni lohitakanibhāsāni, . . .*

8. *ajjhattaṃ arūpasaññī eko bahiddhā rūpāni passati odātāni odātavaṇṇāni odātanidassanāni odātanibhāsāni,...*

In addition, *tāni abhibhuyya jānāmi passāmīti evaṃsaññī hoti* is appended throughout, which simultaneously explains the name *abhibhāyatananaṃ*. Here, the octonary set is retained in the Dhammasaṅgaṇi. The first two *abhibhāyatanāni* have, it is true, been omitted, but the next two have been taken apart in that they are given first without and then with the addition *suvaṇṇadubbaṇṇāni*, resulting again in the octonary set. In addition, the word *eko* has been omitted in all cases.

The changes in the case of the *vimokkhā*, which follow in third place, are radical. They form a set of eight in the canon and are described as follows:[47]

1. *rūpī rūpāni passati,...*
2. *ajjhattaṃ arūpasaññī bahiddhā rūpāni passati,...*
3. *subhan t' eva adhimutto hoti,...*
4. *sabbaso rūpasaññānaṃ samatikkamā paṭighasaññānaṃ atthaṅgamā nānattasaññānaṃ amanasikārā ananto ākāso ti ākāsānañcāyatanaṃ upasampajja viharati,...*
5. *sabbaso ākāsānañcāyatanaṃ samatikamma anantaṃ viññāṇaṃ ti viññāṇañcāyatanaṃ upasampajja viharati,...*
6. *sabbaso viññāṇañcāyatanaṃ samatikamma natthi kiñcīti ākiñcaññāyatanaṃ upasampajja viharati,...*
7. *sabbaso ākiñcaññāyatanaṃ samatikamma nevasaññānāsaññāyatanaṃ upasampajja viharati,...*
8. *sabbaso nevasaññānāsaññāyatanaṃ samatikamma saññāvedayitanirodhaṃ upasampajja viharati,...*

Of these 8 *vimokkhā* the Dhammasaṅgaṇi has retained only the first three. This is, however, understandable and only appropriate to the consistent structure of the path of meditation. For numbers 4 to 7 only anticipate the 4 *arūpā*, and the *saññāvedayitanirodho* does not, it is true, appear later but it always has a special position with regard to the normal path of meditation. Here, among the preparatory exercises, it was in any case out of place. The fact that the the third member is shortened to *subhan ti* is, I feel, insignificant.

In fourth place appear the 4 *appamaññāyo* or *brahmavihārā*: *mettā, karuṇā, muditā,* and *upekkhā*. These, too, have been taken from the canon, where there are also four of them, but their function has changed. The canon teaches that the mind that is connected with them should radiate in all directions.[48] It appears that this did not fit into the scheme of the other levels of meditation as the Dhammasaṅgaṇi teaches them, where the contemplation of an object is always concerned. Thus, here it is said that on this level the various *jhānāni* are connected with *mettā* etc. *(mettāsahagataṃ)*. It is therefore obviously assumed that the practice of these *jhānāni* constitutes the content of this level of meditation.

In fifth and last place is the contemplation of the offensive, the corpse which gradually decays and decomposes—the *asubhajhānaṃ*. This contemplation, which is intended to effect a turning away from all earthly things is common in the canon. Its most well-known occurrence is perhaps the relevant section in the Mahāsatipaṭṭhānasuttanta.[49] What is missing in the canon is a numerical arrangement of this level of meditation. However, the whole structure of the path of meditation in the Dhammasaṅgaṇi demanded such a division and it is therefore applied here. It survived, incidentally, into later times[50] and we also find similar arrangements in other schools.[51]

Thus the preparatory part of the path of meditation. It is, as we have seen, a conscious innovation. The individual parts, it is true, were taken from the canon, but they have been changed to the extent that it was possible to connect them to one another and form a complete unit.

There is little to say about the *arūpā*, which form the next part of the path of meditation. As we have already said, they were taken as a whole from the old canon and adapted slightly to the new structure. They are connected in particular with the *jhānāni*, and since according to ancient tradition the *arūpā* go beyond the *jhānāni*, they only proceed from the 4th *jhānaṃ*. Therefore, while the old canon has

> *idha bhikkhu sabbaso rūpasaññānaṃ samatikkamā paṭighasaññānaṃ atthaṃgamā nānattasaññānaṃ amanasikārā ananto ākāso ti ākāsānañcāyatanaṃ upasampajja viharati*, etc.

we have here

yasmiṃ samaye arūpūpapattiyā maggaṃ bhāveti, sabbaso rūpasaññānaṃ samatikkamā paṭighasaññānaṃ atthaṃgamā nānattasaññānaṃ amanasikārā ākāsānañcāyatanasaññāsahagataṃ sukhassa ca pahānā dukkhassa ca pahānā pubbe va somanassadomanassānaṃ atthaṃgamā adukkhaṃ asukhaṃ upekkhāsatipārisuddhiṃ catutthaṃ jhānaṃ upasampajja viharati, etc.

The third and final part of the path of meditation, which embraces the *lokuttarajhānāni*, is of especial importance. It contains material which is essentially new and is important for the evaluation of the path of meditation as a whole. Nonetheless, in order to evaluate it correctly we must again eliminate what is inessential. This means above all the usual variants, and also the *mahānayā*, which as we have already said are nothing more than an unimaginative extension. In the first *bhūmi* the distinction between variants by means of the additions of *suññataṃ, animittaṃ,* and *appaṇihitaṃ* is of interest. These are in fact the 3 *samādhī, suññato samādhi, animitto samādhi,* and *appaṇihito samādhi*, familiar from the old canon, which have been incorporated into the text here.[52] The Kathāvatthu[53] shows that the Pāli school was still concerned with these concepts at a much later date. However, here the distinction does not touch on essential concerns and we may therefore disregard it.

Nonetheless, after the shedding of these superficialities little remains that constitutes the actual description of the *lokuttarajhānāni* and what there is is limited to a few parts of sentences. These are:

1. *yasmiṃ samaye lokuttaraṃ jhānaṃ bhāveti niyyānikaṃ apacayagāmiṃ diṭṭhigatānaṃ pahānāya paṭhamāya bhūmiyā pattiyā . . . paṭhamaṃ jhānaṃ upasampajja viharati, . . .*
2. *yasmiṃ samaye lokuttaraṃ jhānaṃ bhāveti niyyānikaṃ apacayagāmiṃ kāmarāgavyāpādānaṃ tanubhāvāya dutiyāya bhūmiyā pattiyā . . . paṭhamaṃ jhānaṃ upasampajja viharati, . . .*
3. *yasmiṃ samaye lokuttaraṃ jhānaṃ bhāveti niyyānikaṃ apacayagāmiṃ kāmarāgavyāpādānaṃ anavasesappahānāya tatiyāya bhūmiyā pattiyā . . . paṭhamaṃ jhānaṃ upasampajja viharati, . . .*
4. *yasmiṃ samaye lokuttaraṃ jhānaṃ bhāveti niyyānikaṃ apacayagāmiṃ rūparāgaarūparāgamānauddhaccaavijjāya ana-*

vasesappahānāya catutthāya bhūmiyā pattiyā . . . paṭhamaṃ jhānaṃ upasampajja viharati, . . .

Little though this is and despite the fact that many details remain unclear, nonetheless the most essential things are said. The *lokuttaraṃ jhānaṃ* is practised on the basis of the first *jhānaṃ*.[54] It is divided into 4 levels *(bhūmi)*. On these the propensities are gradually eliminated. The *diṭṭhigatāni* are eliminated on the first level. On the second, *kāmarāgo* and *vyāpādo* are weakened. On the third level both of these are eliminated completely. On the fourth level, *rūparāgo, arūparāgo, māno, uddhaccaṃ,* and *avijjā* are eliminated completely.

With this, however, liberation is attained. For just as in the canonical descriptions, where the reaching of the fourth *jhānaṃ* brings with it not only the decisive cognition but the elimination of the *āsavā*, through which liberation is gained, so here the propensities are eliminated by the *lokuttarajhānāni*. Thus, the path of meditation in the Dhammasaṅgaṇi is not only a path of meditation but also a path of liberation. It forms a unified whole and proceeds from the initial preparatory exercises to the highest level, which brings liberation.

However, in this way the path of meditation in the Dhammasaṅgaṇi comes close to the Abhisamayavāda. Both are paths of meditation which are developed from the canonical path of liberation, and they provide a good example of how the same doctrine was developed in quite different ways in two different schools of Buddhism.

In the Pāli school, meditation is the decisive element and it eliminates the propensities directly. Here the most essential thing is therefore the expansion of the path of meditation. This was effected, as was usual for the Pāli school, by the collection and organization of transmitted material. However, this was not exclusively the case: the author of the new doctrine was not afraid to alter the preparatory exercises taken from the canon in order to ensure the smooth course of the path of meditation. Pointless repetition, which otherwise occurs frequently,[55] has here been avoided. In addition, the reevaluation of the old *jhānāni* and the introduction of the *lokuttaraṃ jhānaṃ* indicates a certain understanding of the differing natures of the individual processes of meditation. However, this does not represent a thorough and fundamental reworking of the doctrine.

The Abhisamayavāda is quite different. In this work meditation fades into the background. Essentially, it represents the creation of a new doctrine. The canonical material used has either been reworked, or used in a merely superficial fashion in order to preserve the appearance of a connection with the old canon. What has been achieved here is, above all, a compact system of ideas. The causal relation is observed and one thing is consistently derived from another. Here we have the systematic philosophical thought that one seeks in vain in the Pāli school.

[β. The Psychology in the Cittakaṇḍa]

So much for the path of meditation of the Dhammasaṅgaṇi. Now we will return to the psychology of the Cittakaṇḍa, in order to gain an impression of its fundamental psychological concepts. For what we have discussed so far[56] are only the elements that accompany the individual mental processes. We will now examine these processes themselves.

In general, the description of these processes is structured according to the following scheme:

> *yasmiṃ samaye kāmāvacaraṃ (kusalaṃ) cittaṃ uppannaṃ hoti (somanassasahagataṃ ñaṇasampayuttaṃ) rūpārammaṇaṃ vā . . . yaṃ yaṃ vā panārabbha, tasmiṃ samaye phasso hoti . . . avikkhepo hoti ye vā pana tasmiṃ samaye aññe pi atthi paṭiccasamuppannā arūpino dhammā.*

Here the *cittaṃ* is given as the central element and at the same time characterized as good, evil, or indeterminate. The aim of the text as a whole is, after all, to describe the good, evil, and indeterminate mental processes. Then the nature of the respective *cittaṃ* is determined more exactly and its object given. The phrase *tasmiṃ samaye* introduces the enumeration of the elements that accompany it.

In all this, it is obviously the description of the nature of the *cittaṃ* which is of primary importance. However, since this description is different in the case of each mental process, we should make a survey of the various forms it takes before we attempt to explain it.[57]

I. *kusalā dhammā*

1.	*cittaṃ*	*somanassasahagataṃ*	*ñāṇasampayuttaṃ*	
2.	"	"	"	*sasaṅkhārena*
3.	"	"	*ñāṇavippayuttaṃ*	
4.	"	"	"	*sasaṅkhārena*
5.	"	*upekkhāsahagataṃ*	*ñāṇasampayuttaṃ*	
6.	"	"	"	*sasaṅkhārena*
7.	"	"	*ñāṇavippayuttaṃ*	
8.	"	"	"	*sasaṅkhārena*

II. *akusalā dhammā*

1.	*cittaṃ*	*somanassasahagataṃ*	*diṭṭhigatasampayuttaṃ*	
2.	"	"	"	*sasaṅkhārena*
3.	"	"	*diṭṭhigatavippayuttaṃ*	
4.	"	"	"	*sasaṅkhārena*
5.	"	*upekkhāsahagataṃ*	*diṭṭhigatasampayuttaṃ*	
6.	"	"	"	*sasaṅkhārena*
7.	"	"	*diṭṭhigatavippayuttaṃ*	
8.	"	"	"	*sasaṅkhārena*
9.	"	*domanassasahagataṃ*	*paṭighasampayuttaṃ*	
10.	"	"	"	*sasaṅkhārena*
11.	"	*upekkhāsahagataṃ*	*vicikicchāsampayuttaṃ*	
12.	"	"	*uddhaccasampayuttaṃ*	

III. *avyākatā dhammā*

A. *kusalavipākā*

1.-4.	*cakkhuviññāṇaṃ—jivhāviññāṇaṃ*	*upekkhāsahagataṃ*		
5.	*kāyaviññāṇaṃ*	*sukhasahagataṃ*		
6.	*manodhātu*	*upekkhāsahagatā*		
7.	*manoviññāṇadhātu*	*somanassasahagatā*		
8.	"	*upekkhāsahagatā*		
9.	"	*somanassasahagatā*	*ñāṇasampayuttā*	
10.	"	"	"	*sasaṅkhārena*
11.	"	*somanassasahagatā*	*ñāṇavippayuttā*	
12.	"	"	"	*sasaṅkhārena*
13.	"	*upekkhāsahagatā*	*ñāṇasampayuttā*	
14.	"	"	"	*sasaṅkhārena*
15.	"	"	*ñāṇavippayuttā*	
16.	"	"	"	*sasaṅkhārena*

B. *akusalavipākā*

1.-4.	*cakkhuviññāṇaṃ—jivhāviññāṇaṃ*	*upekkhāsahagataṃ*
5.	*kāyaviññāṇaṃ*	*dukkhasahagataṃ*
6.	*manodhātu*	*upekkhāsahagatā*
7.	*manoviññāṇadhātu*	"

C. *kiriyā*

1. *manodhātu*	*upekkhāsahagatā*		
2. *manoviññāṇadhātu*	*somanassasahagatā*		
3. "	*upekkhāsasahagatā*		
4. "	*somanassasahagatā*	*ñāṇasampayuttā*	
5. "	"	"	*sasaṅkhārena*
6. "	"	*ñāṇavippayuttā*	
7. "	"	"	*sasaṅkhārena*
8. "	*upekkhasāsahagatā*	*ñāṇasampayuttā*	
9. "	"	"	*sasaṅkhārena*
10. "	"	*ñāṇavippayuttā*	
11. "	"	"	*sasaṅkhārena*

However, before we attempt to explain these descriptions we must first deal with another preliminary question. A cursory glance reveals immediately that there is a curious difference between the sections concerning the *kusalā* and *akusalā dhammā* and the section that treats the *avyākatā dhammā*. Whereas the first two sections mention the *cittaṃ* only, the last section distinguishes between the five sense cognitions—*cakkhuviññāṇaṃ* to *kāyaviññāṇaṃ*, *manodhātu,* and *manoviññāṇadhātu*. This has no objective foundation. It is not obvious for example, why an indeterminate process of cognition which represents the maturation of a previous good or evil process of cognition should be described in different terms to this previous process of cognition that has given rise to it. It would seem rather that the third section that deals with the *avyākatā dhammā* is a more advanced and finely elaborated psychology than the first two sections. The way the third section includes and deals with the concepts of the *kiriyā* and the *vipāko* also points to a far more advanced state of doctrinal development. It is not as if these concepts were superfluous in the first two sections, either; good and evil processes of cognition are, after all, also *kiriyā*. Thus here it is not *cittaṃ* which should be discussed in general but, as in the third section, *manodhātu* and *manoviññāṇadhātu*. The enumeration of *rūpārammāṇaṃ* to *phoṭṭabbārammāṇaṃ* would thus be superfluous. Only *dhammārammāṇaṃ* should be given, and so on.

This leads to the conclusion that the first two sections belong to an earlier age, in which psychological concepts were not as thoroughly thought through and developed, whereas the third section represents a later stage of doctrinal development and was not added to the other two sections until later. In itself, this is by no means improbable. In terms of the moral contemplation of things the first and obvious distinction to be made is between good and evil. The inclusion of the category of the morally indeterminate premises more thorough and systematic thought. A good example of this is provided by the doctrine of the roots of good and evil. The *kusalamūlāni—alobho, adoso* and *amoho*, and the *akusalamūlāni—lobho, doso,* and *moho*, are paired as natural opposites from the beginning and are also to be found as such in the old canon.[58] The *avyākatamūlāni—alobho, adoso,* and *amoho*—are merely a poor imitation of the *kusalamūlāni* and were an inadequate solution when the category of the morally indeterminate was taken into account. They also appear at a late stage.

Nevertheless, this distinction between an earlier and a later part in the Cittakaṇḍa has mapped out the path we are to take in our investigation. We must of course deal with each part and attempt to characterize it separately. It is best to begin with the older part which treats the *kusalā* and *akusalā dhammā*.

Any explanation of this text, however, comes up against a number of difficulties. We shall have to rely mainly on the text itself, since later commentators are to be consulted only with caution. Often their explanations are demonstrably wrong. It should also be borne in mind that a period of five hundred years lies between this text and, say, Buddhaghosa. We know nothing about the conditions of transmission during this time. The text itself, however, displays all the weaknesses of the Abhidharma texts. It is based on given concepts of which the most important are not explained. Their application in all imaginable cases follows in tedious prolixity. In terms of actual content, the text is meagre. Any attempt therefore to interpret the text is in many cases dependent on conjecture. The present interpretation can thus only be regarded as an attempt. This attempt must nevertheless be made. Only afterwards will we have a clear picture of all the problems involved and will it then be possible to make gradual progress.

As we have already noted, the *cittaṃ* is the focus of the description of the good and evil elements in this text. It is briefly determined with regard to its respective nature and then all the elements that accompany it are enumerated. Of the determinants of the *cittaṃ*, it is either *somanassasahagataṃ*, *domanassasahagataṃ*, or *upekkhāsahagataṃ*, which is given first. However, since these determinants, apart from *domanassasahagataṃ*, appear in good as well as evil mental processes, they are not characteristic of these processes and we will therefore disregard their explanation for the present. It is rather the determinants listed in second place which are characteristic: *ñāṇasampayuttaṃ* and *vippayuttaṃ* in the good processes, *diṭṭhigatasampayuttaṃ* and *vippayuttaṃ*, and *paṭigha-*, *vicikicchā-* and *uddhaccasampayuttaṃ* in the evil processes. Of these, *ñāṇaṃ* is ambiguous. But in the case of *diṭṭhigataṃ*, *paṭigho*, *vicikicchā*, and *uddhaccaṃ* there can be no question. They are evil elements which determine the evil character of the process of cognition involved.

However, doubt arises immediately. It is normally the *akusalamūlāni*, *lobho*, *doso*, and *moho*, on which the evil character of a process of cognition is based. And these are in fact present here. But they occur in the middle of the enumeration of the elements that accompany the *cittaṃ*. Now it seems to me to be unthinkable that if the author of the psychology of the Cittakaṇḍa wanted to allocate them a decisive role that he did not assign them a different position. Rather, the order he actually places them in clearly shows that for him, *diṭṭhigataṃ*, *paṭigho*, *vicikicchā*, and *uddhaccaṃ* were the decisive elements. It is probable that the *akusalamūlāni* did not originally belong to the list of elements accompanying the *cittaṃ*. This could be unobtrusively supplemented and expanded at any time, as was indeed the general tendency in the Abhidharma.

The group consisting of *diṭṭhigataṃ*, *paṭigho*, *vicikicchā*, and *uddhaccaṃ* is not otherwise common in the Pāli Abhidharma. It is true that *paṭigho*, *diṭṭhi*, and *vicikicchā* are found in the old group of the 7 *anusayā*.[59] In the commentaries on the Dhammasaṅgaṇi, *vicikicchā* appears under the 3 *saṃyojanāni* (§ 8, 9, 105 and 107), *paṭigho*, *diṭṭhi*, and *vicikicchā* under the 10 *saṃyojanāni* (§ 42), *uddhaccaṃ* and *vicikicchā* under the 6 *nīrvaraṇāni* (§ 66) and *diṭṭhi*, *vicikicchā*, and *uddhaccaṃ* under the 10 *kilesā* (§ 97). But the four do not occur as a group in their own right. Thus, the assumption would appear to be justified that it was the author of the psychology in the Cittakaṇḍa who singled out these four elements because they seemed to him to be particularly important and in order to assign to them this decisive position in his doctrine.

However, if it is *diṭṭhigataṃ, paṭigho, vicikicchā,* and *uddhaccaṃ* which condition the evil character of the *akusalā dhammā,* one would correspondingly expect in the case of the *kusalā dhammā* the elements to be given on which their good character is based. There, however, only *ñāṇaṃ* is given. This is at first surprising, but, as will become apparent, *ñāṇaṃ* frequently plays an important role in the Pāli Abhidharma.[60] Moreover, if we consider the importance accorded to ignorance, *avijjā,* in earliest Buddhism, it is understandable how the author of this doctrine could give *ñāṇaṃ* a special position as well. Here, of course, it cannot stand for the individual cognition but for knowledge in its higher sense.

At this point, however, another question arises. It is said that the *cittaṃ* can be associated and not associated both with *ñāṇaṃ* and *diṭṭhigataṃ*. But how can a knowledge condition the good character of a process of cognition and a false view condition its evil character if they are not associated with it? An answer to this question may be found in Kathāvatthu XI, 4 (2). This is an attack on the idea that one cannot say of somebody in whom ignorance has waned, during a process of cognition in which knowledge is not present, that he is knowing *(aññāṇe vigate ñāṇavippayutte citte vattamāne na vattabbaṃ ñāṇīti).* The opposite opinion is then propounded. The author of the doctrine we are at present considering was evidently of the same opinion. For him, knowledge is effective whether it is present in a particular process of cognition or not. The same is true of false views. Thus, he can say of both that the *cittaṃ* is good or evil, whether it is *cittasampayuttaṃ* or *vippayuttaṃ*. However, he seems only to claim this for *ñāṇaṃ* and *diṭṭhigataṃ*: in the case of *paṭigho, vicikicchā,* and *uddhaccaṃ,* only their being associated with *cittaṃ* is mentioned. What caused him to make this distinction cannot be deduced from the text. We would at best only be able to offer suppositions. However, the little that we have reveals the author of this doctrine as a thinker of such clarity and originality that there is no reason why he should not be thought capable of making differentiations of this kind in his doctrine.

We now come to the second determinant of the *cittaṃ* as *somanassa-, domanassa-*, and *upekkhāsasahagataṃ. Somanassaṃ* is usually translated by joy *(Freude, gaieté), domanassaṃ* by melancholy *(Kummer, tristesse)*. This corresponds to the usual meaning of these words in Pāli. Nonetheless, this seems to me to be entirely beside the point. Why should joy and melancholy be characteristic concomitant phenomena of good or evil processes of cognition? Are, for example, false views accompanied by joy or feelings of hatred by melancholy? But this passage must deal with things which are relevant to good and evil processes of cognition, otherwise the author of this doctrine would not have placed them together with *ñāṇaṃ, diṭṭhigataṃ* etc., next to the *cittaṃ* as decisive determinants. I would therefore like to propose a different interpretation derived from the Sanskrit, namely, that *somanassaṃ* and *domanassaṃ* stand for good and evil attitude. These are, after all, of decisive importance in the case of good and evil acts. This would also be compatible with the distribution of these determinants among the various processes of cognition. A false view can also be held with a good attitude. Hatred is of necessity accompanied by an evil attitude. The determination as *upekkhāsahagataṃ* also becomes understandable in this way. Good processes of cognition are also possible without a specific attitude, i.e. in the case of indifference. False views can also be held without a specific attitude. Indifference is impossible in the case of hatred. On the other hand, doubt and arrogance[61] are unintentional and thus *upekkhāsahagataṃ*.

One word remains to be explained. After the determination of *cittaṃ* as *ñāṇasampayuttaṃ* and *vippayuttaṃ*, and *diṭṭhigatasampayuttaṃ* and *vippayuttaṃ* there is in each case a variant with the addition *sasaṅkhārena*. However, the text fails to provide an explanation of its meaning. Since—apart from this addition—the wording of these variants is unchanged, there are no clues as to the meaning of the addition. We must therefore leave it unexplained for the time being.

So much for the first part of the Cittakaṇḍa. The doctrine it contains is idiosyncratic and in some respects old-fashioned. Nonetheless, viewing the doctrine in its idiosyncratic nature leads to a further realization. The elements which condition the evil character of the mental processes here are *diṭṭhigataṃ, paṭigho, vicikicchā,* and *uddhaccaṃ*. In the path of meditation that we discussed first, the propensities whose elimination brings liberation are *diṭṭhigataṃ, kāmarāgo, vyāpādo, rūparāgo, arūparāgo, māno, uddhaccaṃ,* and *avijjā*. Both are completely incompatible and only allow the conclusion that the path of meditation and the psychology of the Cittakaṇḍa originally had nothing to do with one another and that the path of meditation was a secondary incorporation into the other text only.

We now come to the second part of the Cittakaṇḍa, which deals with the *avyākatā dhammā*. Here the situation is much simpler. Nonetheless, we must clarify a preliminary question here as well. For the extant text is subject to serious doubt.

As I have already said [see p. 72], the most characteristic feature of this text is that it does not merely speak of *cittaṃ* but that different types of cognition are distinguished: *cakkhu-, sota-, ghāna-, jivhā-, kāyaviññāṇaṃ, manodhātu,* and *manoviññāṇadhātu*. These variants are discussed in turn both in the case of the *kusalavipākā* and the *akusalavipākā avyākatā dhammā*. In the case of the *kusalavipākā*, two types of *manoviññāṇadhātu* are distinguished additionally, according to whether they are *somanassa-* or *upekkhāsahagatā*.

Thus far everything is clear and intelligible. However, in the case of the *kusalavipākā avyākatā dhammā*, the *manoviññāṇadhātu* is again taken up and once more distinguished as *somanassa-* or *upekkhāsahagatā*, and moreover in each case whether it is *ñāṇasampayuttā* or *vippayuttā* and also whether it is *sasāṇkhārena* or not. One wonders why this has been taken up here again and what the point of this further distinction is. Above all, if our interpretation of *ñāṇasampayuttā* and *vippayuttā* is correct, these determinants make no sense here at all.

This paragraph with all its subdivisions corresponds exactly to the description of the *kusalā dhammā* in the first part of the Cittakaṇḍa. It has obviously been taken from there and transferred. In order to adjust it to the *avyākatā dhammā, alobho avyākatamūlaṃ,* and *adoso avyākatamūlaṃ* have been added on to the end. These determinants are otherwise missing and are furthermore unnecessary, since all *vipākā dhammā* are in themselves *avyākatā* but seemed appropriate here in view of the correspondence with the description in the case of the *kusalā dhammā*, which is in other respects complete. Furthermore, here in the second part of the Cittakaṇḍa the list of the *arūpino dhammā* which are enumerated in the case of each process of cognition is given here in a shortened form ending with *jīvitindriyaṃ* (no. 26 in our list).[62] In the paragraph under consideration, the complete list up to *avikkhepo* (no. 86) is suddenly presupposed, whereas in the discussion of the *akusalavipākā dhammā*, the shortened version of the list immediately appears again. The complete list was thus automatically transferred when this paragraph was incorporated. I therefore believe that this paragraph is a secondary interpolation for which the redactors of the Abhidhammapiṭaka were probably responsible.

The same situation obtains with those *avyākatā dhammā* that are *kiriyā*. *Manodhātu* and *manoviññāṇadhātu* are *kiriyā*. These two are discussed and in the case of *manoviññāṇadhātu* a distinction is made as to whether it is *somanassa-* or *upekkhāsahagatā*. Here, too, the *manoviññāṇadhātu* is taken up again and a distinction made not only as to whether it is *somanassa-* or *upekkhāsahagatā,* but also whether it is *ñāṇasampayuttā* or *vippayuttā* and *sasaṅkhārena* or not. The longer list of the *arūpino dhammā* up to *avikkhepo* is also given here and *alobho avyākatamūlaṃ* and *adoso avyākatamūlaṃ* are also added on to the end. We thus have the same later interpolation here as in the case of the *vipākā dhammā*.

Finally, extending the *avyākatā dhammā* into the realm of the higher spheres, i.e. to the realm of meditation, also seems dubious. Is it meaningful to assume that meditation can also occur as *vipāko* and that as *kiriyā* it is not only *kusalā* but also *avyākatā*? Or do all these assumptions owe their origin merely to the prevailing tendency in the Abhidharma to extend the doctrines it propounds to all conceivable cases? It is in any case striking that the path of meditation here appears with its latest supplements and additions such as the 20 *mahānayā* and the distinction between *chandādhipateyyaṃ, viriyādhipateyyaṃ, cittādhipateyyaṃ,* and *vīmaṃsādhipateyyaṃ*. Significantly, the list of the *arūpino dhammā* also appears here again in its longer form up to *avikkhepo*.

In this part of the Cittakaṇḍa, therefore, I consider only those portions which remain after the removal of all these additions to be old. This includes the beginning of the *kusalavipākā dhammā* (nos. 1–8 in the survey given above), the *akusalavipākā dhammā* and the beginning of the *kiriyā dhammā* (nos. 1–3 in the survey).

Of fundamental import for the doctrine contained in this part is the distinction between the various kinds of *cittaṃ*. This is based on the canonical doctrine of the *ayatanāni* and the *dhātuyo*, from which it takes the relevant concepts, and is modelled on the Dhammahadaya where the *cittaṃ* is categorized in the same fashion and 7 *cittāni* are distinguished. What is remarkable here is the attempt to consider this doctrine in further detail and elaborate it. Thus, for example, lust and pain are only attributed to the *kāyaviññāṇaṃ*. This is premised by a fairly advanced stage in the doctrine of karma. It forms the basis for the fundamental distinction between *vipāko* and *kiriyā*, whereby *kiriyā* is limited to *manodhātu* and *manoviññāṇadhātu*. All this is foreign to the first part of the Cittakaṇḍa.

This concludes our survey of the Cittakaṇḍa. To sum up, it can be said that in essence it is made up of three constituent parts: an archaic system of psychology in the first part which confines itself to good and evil mental processes; this is supplemented in the second part by the introduction of morally indeterminate processes, which presupposes a more advanced stage both of psychological concepts and of the doctrine of karma; finally an originally separate and idiosyncratic form of the paths of meditation and liberation has been incorporated. Each of these constituent parts are an interesting testimony of the development of the doctrine in the Pāli school and have come down to us through their being incorporated into the Dhammasaṅgaṇi by the redactors of the Abhidhammapiṭaka. The fact that it is overrun with the usual formalism of the Abhidharma does not diminish its importance.

[b. Rūpakaṇḍa]

We now come to the later parts of the Dhammasaṅgaṇi, the Rūpakaṇḍa and the two commentaries on the *mātṛkā* of the Dhammasaṅgaṇi. Since the Rūpakaṇḍa also consists of a *mātṛkā* with a commentary, I will begin with a few words about the nature of these commentaries in general.

Closer examination of these commentaries shows that their authors hold particular views to which they substantially adhere throughout the whole work. Side by side with this, however, we find deviations and occasionally even contradictions. This can be explained as follows. As the *mātṛkāḥ* are old, a certain amount of old material which had in the interim become meaningless was also taken over with the explanations. Above all, however, the *mātṛkāḥ* are a patchwork of different materials and have furthermore been arbitrarily and unsystematically extended. For their commentators, therefore, they contain much that was not of interest or contradicted their ideas but which nevertheless had to be dealt with. Thus, one finds odd material again and again in these commentaries. Frequently one can see how this material has been forcibly bent into shape in order to accommodate it to the commentators' views.

Nevertheless, it is relatively easy to disentangle the most important views held by the various commentators. What hinders an understanding of these views is rather the truncated and disconnected form in which they are given. Everything is formulated concisely and whenever a topic is mentioned again, the same formulations are repeated without any change. No explanations are given. Thus, much remains unclear and must be left open if one is to avoid getting lost in vague speculation.

We will now turn to the individual texts. The first of these, the Rūpakaṇḍa, was evidently included as a counterpart to the Cittakaṇḍa. A somewhat artificial link between the two texts is established by means of a connecting paragraph (p. 147,1–5). The following description is entirely independent.

This description contains a fairly advanced form of the doctrine of matter *(rūpaṃ)*. It begins with an enumeration of all the material elements, which is subsequently referred to repeatedly (p. 160, 5–176, 11). This enumeration takes the following form: first, a distinction is made between secondary *(rūpaṃ upādā)* and primary matter *(rūpaṃ no upādā)* and then follows the enumeration and explanation of the enumerated concepts.

Secondary matter is given as (p. 160, 5–12):

1. *cakkhāyatanaṃ*
2. *sotāyatanaṃ*

13. *kāyaviññatti*
14. *vacīviññatti*

3. *ghānāyatanaṃ*
4. *jivhāyatanaṃ*
5. *kāyāyatanaṃ*
6. *rūpāyatanaṃ*
7. *saddāyatanaṃ*
8. *gandhāyatanaṃ*
9. *rasāyatanaṃ*
10. *itthindriyaṃ*
11. *purisindriyaṃ*
12. *jīvitindriyaṃ*
15. *ākāsadhātu*
16. *rūpassa lahutā*
17. *rūpassa mudutā*
18. *rūpassa kammaññatā*
19. *rūpassa upacayo*
20. *rūpassa santati*
21. *rūpassa jaratā*
22. *rūpassa aniccatā*
23. *kabaḷīkāro āhāro*

The primary matter listed is (p. 175,1–5 and 176,9–10):

I. *phoṭṭhabbāyatanaṃ*
 1. *paṭhavīdhātu*
 2. *tejodhātu*
 3. *vāyodhātu*
 4. *kakkhaḷaṃ*
 5. *mudukaṃ*
 6. *saṇhaṃ*
 7. *pharusaṃ*
 8. *sukhasamphassaṃ*
 9. *dukkhasamphassaṃ*
 10. *garukaṃ*
 11. *lahukaṃ*

II. *āpodhātu*
 1. *āpo*
 2. *āpogataṃ*
 3. *sineho*
 4. *sinehagataṃ*
 5. *bandhanattaṃ rūpassa*

The distinction between primary and secondary matter has a prototype in the old canon where the four great elements *(cattāri mahābhūtāni)*, namely, *paṭhavīdhātu, āpodhātu, tejodhātu,* and *vāyodhātu* and matter derived from them *(catunnaṃ mahābhūtānaṃ upādāya rūpaṃ)* are distinguished.[63] Even though the four elements do not here constitute primary matter on their own, they are nevertheless the most important and are therefore accordingly placed first. The new form of categorization may have been chosen in order to incorporate by means of the *phoṭṭhabbāyatanaṃ* primary matter into the *āyatanāni* as well, which are the focus of the secondary matter. Perhaps it also seemed important to separate the *āpodhātu* from the other elements. The elements are further supplemented by a number of other material elements.

There is a large number of these material elements *(rūpino dhammā)* in the case of the secondary matter. They start with the material *āyatanāni*, i.e. the sense organs and sense objects. Three sense faculties are then mentioned: *itthindriyaṃ, purisindriyaṃ,* and *jīvitindriyaṃ*. The other sense faculties, which together with the latter constitute the canonical 22 sense faculties, we have already encountered in the mental elements of the Cittakaṇḍa. The *jīvitindriyaṃ* occurs twice. This was explained by saying that one was the *jīvitindriyaṃ* of the *arūpino* and the other that of the *rūpino dhammā*.[64] However, this explanation could have been devised afterwards in order to justify the double incorporation of the one *jīvitindriyaṃ* that had been transmitted. The lists of the Cittakaṇḍa and the Rūpakaṇḍa were, it is true, created on the basis of the same notions, but they do not constitute a unified or coordinated creation. This is also demonstrated by the following: the Rūpakaṇḍa list gives *rūpassa lahutā, rūpassa mudutā,* and *rūpassa kammaññatā*, while the Cittakaṇḍa list gives *kāya-* and *citta-lahutā, kāya-* and *cittamudutā,* and *kāya-* and *cittakammaññatā*. The fact that *kāyo* is here included among the *arūpino dhammā* while the *kāyāyatanaṃ* belongs to the *rūpino dhammā* is inexplicable. An attempt was made to explain *kāyo* here as *vedanā-, saññā-,* and *saṅkhārakkhando*. However, that is little more than an awkward makeshift solution.

Especial attention should be paid to the *kāya-* and *vacīviññatti* in this list since they play an important role in development of the doctrine of karma. Like the four elements, the *ākāsadhātu* has been taken from the canonical list of the 6 *dhātuyo*.

The discussion by means of a *mātṛkā* of the material elements which follows their enumeration and explanation in the lists mentioned is largely without significance, yet it also contains some interesting material, for example, the discussion of the relation of the individual elements to the *cittaṃ*.

[c. The Commentaries]

The Rūpakaṇḍa is followed by two further sections which, as we have already said, contain commentaries on the *mātṛkā* on which the Dhammasaṅgaṇi is based. However, before we examine these commentaries in more detail, we must once again clarify a preliminary question.

The *mātṛkā* on which the Dhammasaṅgaṇi is based is divided numerically and consists of a dyad and a triad *mātṛkā*. The dyad *mātṛkā* is itself divided into two sections, the first designated as Abhidhammadukamātikā, the second as Suttantadukamātikā. These names are appropriate, since the members of the second section have been taken from sūtras, in this case, mainly from the Saṅgītisuttanta; they even appear in almost the same order. It is notable, as we have already seen, that the Suttantadukamātikā is only treated in the first of the two commentaries. It is missing in the second. This could be interpreted such that it was later added as the last section of the whole *mātṛkā* and that the commentary that deals with it is thus the later of the two, while the other commentary which does not mention it derives from the time before it belonged to the *mātṛkā*. However, I do not think this assumption is valid. If we examine the commentary which includes the Suttantadukamātikā in its entirety, it reveals a curious discontinuity. The commentary works with certain fixed basic concepts which are rigidly adhered to and which occur repeatedly. This changes abruptly with the beginning of the Suttantadukamātikā. Suddenly these basic concepts disappear. Simultaneously the whole character of the commentary changes. It now consists of simple explanations of the concepts named in the *mātṛkā*, often in the old form of paraphrase and frequently in imitation of passages in the old canon. However, this is the same type of commentary, albeit in a simpler form, that one finds in the Sarvāstivādin's Saṅgītiparyāya, the commentary on the Saṅgītisūtra. Occasionally there are even extensive correspondences between the two texts. I therefore believe that the Suttantadukamātikā together with its commentary did not originally belong to the Dhammasaṅgaṇi but rather derives from a work of the Pāli school that corresponded to the Saṅgītiparyāya of the Sarvāstivādin, and that it was the redactors of the Abhidhammapiṭaka who incorporated it at this point.

As far as the commentaries themselves are concerned, it should be borne in mind that the *mātṛkā* of the Dhammasaṅgaṇi is essentially an attribute-*mātṛkā* which can be used as such with various subjects which are discussed with the aid of this *mātṛkā*. In the present case, the subject of both commentaries is related, since both are based on the same doctrine, but in particular details there are a number of differences.

In the case of the first of the two commentaries, the basic concepts which are constantly used are as follows.[65] The *khandhā* are enumerated as the fundamental elements; these are usually only the four mental *khandhā*, since it is the mental processes which are the focal point of interest here, i.e. *vedanā-, saññā-, saṅkhāra-,* and *viññāṇakkhandho*. These extend to all three spheres, i.e. they are *kāmāvacarā, rūpāvacarā,* and *arūpāvacarā*. They can, however, also be transmundane *(lokuttarā)* and not included in the spheres *(apariyāpannā),* in this case as *maggā*. The 4 *maggaphalāni (sāmaññaphalāni)* and the *asaṅkhatā dhātu* are also transmundane and not included in the spheres.

The moral character of the elements is accorded especial importance. This is based on the 3 *kusalamūlāni, alobho, adoso,* and *amoho*, the 3 *akusalamūlāni, alobho, adoso,* and *amoho* and the 3 *avyākatamūlāni, alobho, adoso,* and *amoho*, which are enumerated under the *hetū*. Beside the *akusalamūlāni*, moreover *(tadekaṭṭhā),* are the *kilesā*. If the mental *khandhā*, i.e. *vedanā-, saññā-, saṅkhāra-,* and *viññaṇakkhando*, are connected *(taṃsampayuttā)* with the *kusalamūlāni*, then they are also *kusalā*. If they are connected with the *akusalamūlāni*, then they are *akusalā*. Similarly, the karma that issues from them—i.e. *kāyakammaṃ, vacīkammaṃ,* and *manokammaṃ*—is good if it issues from the good *khandhā* and evil when it issues from the evil *khandhā*. This karma gives rise to new mental *khandhā* as maturations *(vipākā),* which belong to all three spheres and can also be transmundane, but which are morally indeterminate *(avyākatā)*. Also indeterminate is every *kiriyā* that is not good, evil or the maturation of a karma, all matter and the *asaṅkhatā dhātu*.

For our present purposes we can disregard the failings and contradictions of this doctrine. In the way it is presented here, it makes a well-rounded, consistent impression. However, it contains a number of strange features. It is unimportant and understandable when on occasion the *āyatanāni* are mentioned in place of the *khandhā* (§ 22). However, it is entirely out of place when the *kāya-, vacī-,* and *manokammaṃ* are sometimes abruptly replaced by *kāyaviññatti* and *vacīviññatti* (§ 82–84). These belong to the Rūpakaṇḍa, insofar as they have not in fact been taken over from another school. Some of these extraneous features are conditioned by the *mātṛkā*, for example, the distinction between *cittaṃ* and *cetasikā dhammā*. The Dhammasaṅgaṇi generally uses the term *arūpino dhammā*. The *mātṛkā* forms the base for the discussion of the groups of *āsavā, saññojanā, ganthā, oghā, yogā, nīvaraṇā* and *parāmāsā* (§ 36–76). The author of the commentary had little or nothing to say about most of these groups, but was obliged to discuss them as traditional canonical material.[66] The influence of other doctrines also makes itself felt, for example in the distinction between *dassanena pahātabbā* and *bhāvanāya pahātabbā dhammā* (§ 8 and 105), which has no foundation in the Pāli Abhidharma. Characteristic is the artificial manner in which the three *saññojanāni* are incorporated into the normal scheme of the *akusalā dhammā*.[67]

So much for the first commentary. With the second, the most significant feature is that instead of the *khandhā*, the mental processes *(cittuppādā)* discussed in the Cittakaṇḍa here constitute the basic concepts to which the *mātṛkā* is applied. This takes the form of the *kāmāvacarā cittuppādā* being treated down to the last detail together with all their variations as given in the Cittakaṇḍa. The only exception to this is the treatment of the *rūpāvacarā* and *lokuttarā cittuppādā*, which confines itself to discussing the 4 and 5 *jhānāni*. Besides the *cittuppādā*, which constitute the core of the description, *rūpaṃ* and *nibbānaṃ* are mentioned whenever all the elements are enumerated. The *cittuppādā* extend into all three spheres and are, moreover, as *maggā*, transmundane *(lokuttarā)* and not included in the spheres *(apariyāpannā)*. Besides the 4 *maggā*, the 4 *sāmaññaphalāni*, and the *nibbānaṃ* are also transmundane and not included in the spheres.

The karma and the maturation of the karma are not discussed separately here since they have already been treated with the *cittuppādā*, in accordance with the Cittakaṇḍa. Accordingly, the *kusala-, akusala-*, and *avyākatamūlāni* also retreat into the background. They are, it is true, enumerated as *kusalahetū* under the *hetū* (§ 23), but with the individual processes of cognition they only appear beside those elements which in the Cittakaṇḍa determine the moral character of these cognitional processes, and are of far less importance than them. And in the discussion of the *dassanena* and *bhāvanāya pahātabbā dhammā* they are only mentioned beside the corresponding elements from the Cittakaṇḍa, *diṭṭhigatāni* etc. (§ 8–9 and 105–108). In any case, their status here is completely different to that in the first commentary.

Alien influences also make themselves felt here, mostly due to the *mātṛkā*. For example, when the question is asked according to the *mātṛkā* of which *dhammā* are *cittaṃ* and which are *cetasikā* (§ 78–87), suddenly the *cittuppādā* are replaced by the *khandhā*. And in the middle of all this (§ 82), a long series of material elements taken from the Rūpakaṇḍa is enumerated. It is furthermore significant that *kāya-* and *vacīviññatti* reappear here as well.

In conclusion, I should like to add a few words about the relationship between the two commentaries. The second commentary, as we have seen, presupposes a connection with the Cittakaṇḍa. The first commentary, on the other hand, represents the pure Dhammasaṅgaṇi tradition, which was retained beside it. It is therefore valuable in that it represents a line of transmission of its own, preserving many interesting doctrines which would otherwise have been lost.

7. Kathāvatthu

In the case of the Dhammasaṅgaṇi, it was necessary to go into detail. With the next work, the Kathāvatthu, however, where the individual works will only be characterized and their significance for the development of the doctrine pointed out, we can be brief. As is well known, the Kathāvatthu contains a treatment of dissenting doctrines. As L. de La Vallée Poussin has shown,[68] its oldest parts display points of contact with the Vijñānakāya of the Sarvāstivādin and probably go back to the 3rd century B.C. The date of its later parts is uncertain and would have to be determined individually in each case. A work of this kind was particularly prone to being added to and extended whenever new controversies arose. Since additions of this kind did not change the character and structure of the work as a whole, they were possible even after the redaction of the Abhidharmapiṭaka.[69] A close examination should be made of the attribution of the controversial doctrines to the various schools. The commentary in which it is contained dates from a late period. It is also hard to believe that the transmission regarding the original opponents of the polemic was preserved over the centuries out of antiquarian interest. It is perfectly conceivable, indeed perhaps even likely, that the individual polemics were later related to contemporary schools. This still needs to be clarified.

8. Paṭisambhidāmagga

We now come to the Paṭisambhidāmagga, the last work of the Abhidharma to be included in the canon, albeit only in the Khuddakanikāya. In its transmitted form, the work consists of 3 parts, each with 10 sections. However, this apparently even structure is merely the work of the redactors, who arbitrarily contrived sections and parts out of disparate material. In reality, this work is a loose sequence of longer and shorter texts which deal with very different doctrinal concepts.

In most cases, a sūtra is first presented and then explained. Thus, for example, at the beginning of the second part, the Yuganaddhasutta[70] of the Aṅguttaranikāya is quoted in its entirety and then explained. The explanation is generally conducted in the typical manner of the Abhidharma by means of distinguishing between and discussing numerous variants. Sometimes the sūtra merely provides as it were the key word which then forms the basis for further discussion. Thus, in II, 10 (p. 436ff.), the Suññatalokasutta[71] of the Saṃyuttanikāya is cited, in which the Buddha speaks of the voidness of the world following a question from Ānanda. Following this, 25 kinds of voidness are enumerated and discussed. Frequently it is merely single sentences from the sūtras which serve as a point of departure for the discussion. Thus, in II, 9 (p. 425ff.), the 5 *balāni* are introduced in the form of a sūtra.[72] This provides the starting point for distinguishing between and then discussing 68 *balāni*. Sometimes the subject is given by the author of the text himself, as for example, in II, 8 (p. 423f.), where all the *lokuttarā dhammā* are enumerated without any reference to a sūtra being given. The only exception here is the first section of the first part, which bears the name Ñāṇakathā. It is in any case exceptional by virtue of its size, since it constitutes more than a quarter of the total work. It is based on a *mātṛkā* which enumerates the 73 kinds of knowledge *(ñāṇaṃ)*, which are then commented on. It is thus a short work in its own right after the fashion of the

Puggalapaññatti.[73] This work differs from the Ñāṇavibhaṅga[74] in that its *mātṛkā* already consists of a simple list, whereas the Ñāṇavibhaṅga *mātṛkā* is artificially structured on a numerical order, using a large number of different attributes. The commentary conforms to the usual pattern of the Paṭisambhidāmagga.

As we have already said, the method of commenting in the Paṭisambhidāmagga consists as a rule in distinguishing between and discussing all the possible variants of the individual doctrinal concepts treated. However, in some cases, this format is extended: the questions *ken' aṭṭhena? kati lakkhaṇāni?* are asked as well as *kati ākārehi?* Sometimes these questions are placed at the head of a section and the subject of the section dealt with accordingly. Thus, at the beginning of the Iddhikathā (III, 2), for example, it says: *kā iddhi? kati iddhiyo? iddhiyā kati bhūmiyo, kati pādā, kati padāni, kati mūlāni?* The Diṭṭhikathā (I, 2) is introduced with the following questions: *kā diṭṭhi? kati diṭṭhiṭṭhānāni? kati diṭṭhipariyuṭṭhānāni? kati diṭṭhiyo? kati diṭṭhābhinivesā? katamo diṭṭhiṭṭhānasamugghāto?*

One could see this procedure as a striving towards greater objectivity and a more systematic approach and consequently representing a step forward compared to the older Abhidharma. The Paṭisambhidāmagga also differs in other respects from the latter, to its advantage. Several "excrescences" of the "method" which are so unpleasantly obtrusive in the old Abhidharma are missing here: the excessively extended *mātṛkāḥ*, the mechanical application of attribute *mātṛkāḥ*, appropriate or inappropriate by turn, the endless stringing together of all the different combinations of elements which hardly say anything about the nature of things, and so forth.

However, these positive features are counterposed by strongly negative characteristics. The systematic structure as such is purely superficial. Under the surface an often alarming void predominates. Pointless explanations of words are strung together endlessly. Thus, with the explanation of the word *lokuttarā* (p. 423, 5ff.), it says: *lokaṃ tarantīti lokuttarā, lokaṃ uttarantīti lokuttarā, lokato uttarantīti lokuttarā, lokamhā uttarantīti lokuttarā, lokaṃ atikkamantīti lokuttarā*. In this fashion there follow 66 explanations of this one word. This is not an isolated case. The variants distinguished between are mostly meaningless. It is sufficient to look at the list of 68 *vimokkhā* (p. 273f.), where everything possible is interpreted as *vimokkho* and attached to the canonical *vimokkhā*—it is those sections which follow the old sūtras that still make the best impression here.

In addition, the attempts at treating larger complexes of problems systematically, signs of which we have already seen in the Dhammasaṅgaṇi in particular, were not continued here. There is nothing that goes beyond the pedantic treatment of the individual doctrinal concepts. Isolated attempts at treating certain problems independently such as the Kammakathā (I, 7) or the Abhisamayakathā (III, 3) do not amount to much. One has the feeling that here the Abhidharma is silting up and dessicating.

Nonetheless, is this not a rather overhasty judgment? Is it possible to come to any clear conclusion at all, in view of the fact that the transmission is more than inadequate and even failed for a long period?

[9. Vimuttimagga and Visuddhimagga]

In order to answer this question it would be best to look at the later period, which produced a wealth of commentaries and for which the name of Buddhaghosa may stand. This period created one great work, which attempts to fuse the traditional doctrine into a unified whole and which has come down to us in Upatissa's Vimuttimagga and Buddhaghosa's Visuddhimagga. Since this work provides a good picture of how the old canonical doctrine lived on in later times, I shall use it as a base for the present investigation.[75]

The work has the following structure. It consists of three parts which treat *sīlaṃ, samādhi,* and *paññā* respectively as follows:[76]

1. *sīlaṃ*	ch. I–II	= p. 3–67
2. *samādhi*	ch. III–XIII	= p. 68–368
3. *paññā*	ch. XIV–XXIII	= p. 369–612

Of these, the second part, a description of the path of meditation, is the most extensive. It is based on the path of meditation in the Dhammasaṅgaṇi. This is particularly evident from the position of the *kasiṇāni* or the role of the *jhānāni,*[77] which is clearly revealed in formulations such as *paṭhamaṃ jhānaṃ adhigataṃ hoti paṭhavīkasiṇaṃ*. It is not surprising that in the attempt to create the most comprehensive compilation of the doctrine possible, it was this path of meditation that was used. As we have seen, it is the only case in the old Abhidharma where a part of the doctrine has been systematically developed into a larger, coherent whole.

This path of meditation is here extended into a path of liberation. This has been achieved by premising a section representing the preparatory moral behavior and also adding a further section treating of the cognition attained through meditation. What is more, the path of meditation itself has been altered in some respects. This is understandable; between the path of meditation of the Dhammasaṅgaṇi and that of Buddhaghosa's Visuddhimagga lies a considerable number of centuries. We shall now proceed to examine these additions and changes and see how they compare with the old Abhidharma, whether they are only based on known works or whether we can infer a derivation from works that have been lost but which would perhaps alter our picture and opinion of the old Abhidharma.

I shall begin with the second section. It is the most instructive of the three sections because things are clearest there. Like the other two sections, it begins with a number of questions, the answers to which constitute the description. These are: *ko samādhi? ken' aṭṭhena samādhi? kān' assa lakkhaṇarasapaccupaṭṭhānapadaṭṭhānāni? katividho samādhi? ko c' assa saṅkileso? kiṃ vodānaṃ? kathaṃ bhāvetabbo? samādhibhāvanāya ko ānisaṃso?* This method of treating a subject is the same as was developed at the time of the Paṭisambhidāmagga. The way in which the explanations are given—by enumerating the many variants and their subsequent elucidation—also corresponds to the style of the latter work. This formalistic method naturally had its disadvantages. Each question and each variant given had to be commented on, even if there was nothing or very little to say about it. This led to an accumulation of unessential and insignificant material. If we disregard all this, it is in particular the answers to two questions which bring up important aspects: the question *kathaṃ bhāvetabbo* (Ch. III, 27–XI, 199 = p. 72–311) and the question *samādhibhāvanāya ko ānisaṃso?* (Ch. XI, 120–XIII, 129 = p. 311–368). The answer to the first question leads to the discussion of the levels of meditation and the answer to the second to the discussion of the miraculous powers attained through meditation.

The levels of meditation are described in the following manner. First the preparation for the meditation exercises is briefly discussed. This is followed by a description of the exercises themselves. They are classified according to the objects that the meditation focuses on *(kammaṭṭhānāni)*. 40 kinds of meditation are distinguished, namely,

10 *kasiṇā*	ch. IV,21–V,42	= p. 99–144
10 *asubhā*	ch. VI,1–94	= p. 145–161
10 *anussatiyo*	ch. VII,1–VIII,251	= p. 162–243
4 *brahmavihārā*	ch. IX,1–124	= p. 244–270
4 *āruppā*	ch. X,1–66	= p. 271–284
1 *āhāre paṭikkūlasaññā*	ch. XI,1–26	= p. 285–290
1 *catudhātuvavatthānaṃ*	ch. XI,27–117	= p. 290–311

If we compare this list of levels of meditation with the path of meditation in the Dhammasaṅgaṇi, there are considerable differences. The *abhibhāyatanāni, vimokkhā,* and *lokuttarajhānāni* have been omitted. On the other hand, the *anussatiyo, āhāre paṭikkūlasaññā,* and the *catudhātuvavatthānaṃ* have been added. There are also individual differences in detail. In place of the well-reasoned number of eight *kasiṇāni* in the Dhammasaṅgaṇi the number of ten has been reestablished here. What led to these changes remains to be seen. In any case, they were not always felicitous. This is evident in the undecided placing of the *āhāre paṭikkulasaññā* and the *catudhātuvavatthānaṃ,* either before or after the *āruppā.*[78] However, it was the duplication with the *āruppā*, which had arisen due to the restoration of the ten instead of eight *kasiṇā ni,* that caused especial problems. Attempts were made to deal with these either by omitting the first two *āruppā* or by reinterpreting the last two *kasiṇāni* as *ālokakasiṇaṃ* and *paricchinnākāsakasiṇaṃ.* However this might be, we can in any case say that the author of this new work, whether it was Upatissa or one of his predecessors, was working with old, familiar material, apart from the *catudhātuvavatthānaṃ.* And there is nothing to indicate that he used any works of the old Abhidharma other than those which we know of and are extant.

There is little to say about the miraculous powers attained through meditation and the section dealing with them is correspondingly short. It is based on a list of the 5 *abhiññā, iddhividhaṃ, dibbasotaṃ, cetopariyañānaṃ, pubbenivāsānussati,* and *dibbacakkhu* or *cutūpapātañāṇaṃ.*[79] The discussion bases itself on old sūtra texts. Furthermore, in the case of the *iddividhaṃ*, the description from the Iddhikathā of the Paṭisambhidāmagga has largely been used (Ch. III, 2 = p. 467–477). Thus there is also nothing here that would indicate knowledge of lost works of the old Abhidharma.

One would imagine that otherwise unknown material would be most likely to occur in the third part of the work, which deals with the *paññā*, that is, the cognition attained through meditation (Ch. XIV–XXIII = p. 369–612), since this section demanded new material, there being no model for this in the path of meditation of the Dhammasaṅgaṇi. However, this expectation is delusive.

Let us first examine the structure of this part of the work. Again, it begins with a series of questions. However, the only thing of importance here is the answer to just one of these questions, namely, *kathaṃ paññā bhāvetabbā*, which takes up almost the whole of this section. This entire section is in turn divided into two parts. The first of these (Ch. XIV–XVII = p. 375–502) treats the *khandhā, āyatanāni, dhātuyo, indriyāni, saccāni,* and the *paṭiccasamuppādo*; the second (Ch. XVIII–XXII = p. 503–600) discusses a series of cognitional processes, which Buddhaghosa calls *visuddhiyo.*[80]

This structure is odd, and one wonders what the reason for it was. I believe this can be answered in the following way. In the Dhammasaṅgaṇi, the path of meditation ends with the *lokuttarajhānāni*, which lead to the liberating cognition and with this to liberation itself, and which therefore form the natural conclusion to the path of meditation. These *lokuttarajhānāni* are omitted here and replaced by the *paññā*. Buddhaghosa expressly attests that the *paññā* is substituted for the *lokuttaro samādhi,* and he adds by way of an explanation *paññāya hi bhāvitāya so bhāvito hoti* (Ch. III, 27). I believe the reason why the *lokuttarajhānāni* were replaced by the *paññā* can be found in the following.

The work present in the form of the Vimuttimagga and the Visuddhimagga demonstrates visibly the effort to give the most comprehensive account possible of the whole of the traditional doctrine. However, this was far more than could be accommodated within the frame of the traditional path of meditation of the Dhammasaṅgaṇi. To solve this problem, all the rest of the doctrinal material that was to be stated was presented as a cognition attained through meditation. For this purpose, the *lokuttarajhānāni* were replaced by the section on the *paññā*. All the important basic doctrinal concepts are treated in this section, from the *khandhā* to the *paṭiccasamuppādo,* that is, the subjects which in the other systems constitute the doctrine of the principles. However, this alone was not enough. Something was needed that could serve as the conclusion of the path of meditation and could fittingly represent the *lokuttarajhānāni*.

It was the Paṭisambhidāmagga which provided the appropriate material. As we have already seen, this work begins with the Ñāṇakathā, a short text which was originally a work in its own right and in which the numerous kinds of cognition are enumerated and discussed. As is the case with most enumerations of this kind, it also incorporates a number of small, preexisting groups. Thus, at the beginning of the whole enumeration, we find the following series:

1. *sutamaye ñāṇaṃ*
2. *sīlamaye ñāṇaṃ*
3. *samādhibhāvanāmaye ñāṇaṃ*
4. *dhammaṭṭhitiñāṇaṃ*
5. *sammasane ñāṇaṃ*
6. *udayabbayānupassane ñāṇaṃ*
7. *(bhaṅgānupassane paññā) vipassane ñāṇaṃ*
8. *(bhayatupaṭṭhāne paññā) ādīnave ñāṇaṃ*
9. *(muñcitukamyatāpaṭisaṅkhāsantiṭṭhanā paññā) saṅkhārupekkhāsu ñāṇaṃ*
10. *gotrabhuñāṇaṃ*
11. *magge ñāṇaṃ*
12. *phale ñāṇaṃ*
13. *vimuttiñāṇaṃ*
14. *paccavekkhaṇe ñāṇaṃ*

This is a coherent, consistently constructed series of cognitions which lead from the preparation for meditation via meditation itself to the highest level of the arhan and thus to liberation. This offered itself as suitable material for forming an appropriate conclusion to the path of meditation in the Vimuttimagga and the Visuddhimagga. This is in fact what happened. The authors took from this series what seemed useful for their purposes, recast it where necessary and incorporated it into their texts.[81] And so this not only provided the section on the *paññā* with a suitable conclusion, but also neatly rounded off the work as a whole.

However, all this indicates that this part of the work is also based on familiar older material and that it does not presuppose the existence of older Abhidharma works that are otherwise unknown. The section dealing with the basic concepts only summarizes what the old Abhidharma had to say about them, and the second section is based, as we have seen, on the Paṭisambhidāmagga. Thus, we are confirmed in our conclusion that the old Pāli Abhidharma, after a few modest attempts at elaborating and developing the doctrine such as are to be found in the Dhammasaṅgaṇi, ossified into a barren formalism.

In conclusion, I would like to say a few words about the work represented by the Vimuttimagga and the Visuddhimagga. As we have seen, this work essentially belongs to the tradition of the old Abhidharma. Formally and in terms of its explanations, it is most closely related to the Paṭisambhidāmagga. In this, it represents the most comprehensive collection of the transmitted material and one could thus see it as a conclusion and an attempt at the development of a system. However, with regard to the latter, the weaknesses of this work also become evident. There is no underlying structure, as one would expect with the formation of a system. The path of meditation forms the sole framework. We have already seen in the case of the Dhammasaṅgaṇi path of meditation how the attempt was made by transforming the type of meditation transmitted in the canon by altering the status of the *jhānāni* and introducing the *lokuttarajhānāni* to establish uniformity and inner coherence. Here, by contrast, we find the material has been merely collected and loosely strung together, which virtually amounts to a step backwards when compared to the latter work. This can hardly be described as a proper system as such. Only a few of the Buddhist schools created systems that were of equal rank to those of the philosophical schools. And the Pāli school was not among their number.

However, that does not imply that this work does not contain material which is both new and interesting, particularly in the case of the later version, the Visuddhimagga. But it is a new spirit and a different focus of interest which is expressed in this new material. I refer to the wealth of examples and similes with which the basic material is explained and to the wide-ranging practical instructions and advice given to the aspiring disciple.[82] What is particularly interesting is the way in which the attempt is made to explain and account for the progressive stages on the path of meditation in psychological terms. However, as I have said, this is the expression of a new spirit and a different age. And that goes beyond the limits of this study.

IV

The Śāriputrābhidharma

The Śāriputrābhidharma, which was translated into Chinese between A.D. 407 and 414 by the Buddhist monks Dharmayaśas and Dharmagupta,[1] is in all probability the Abhidharma of the Dharmaguptaka school.[2] According to indications in the Sseu fen liu, the Vinaya of the Dharmaguptaka, its Abhidharma consisted of the following 5 parts:[3] 1: Sapraśnaka, 2. Apraśnaka, 3. Saṃgraha, 4. Saṃprayoga, and 5. Prasthāna.[4] This corresponds to the structure of the work in question, and A. Bareau has demonstrated exhaustively that the doctrines it contains correspond most closely to those ascribed to the Dharmaguptaka by the doxographers.

The contents of the work are as follows:

1. Sapraśnaka

1. the 12 *āyatanāni*	(a)[5]	p. 525c5–526c11
	(b)	p. 526c11–534b3
2. the 18 *dhātavaḥ*	(a)	p. 534b9–535a18
	(b)	p. 535a19–542c28
3. the 5 *skandhāḥ*	(a)	p. 534a5–545c8
	(b)	p. 545c8–552c7
4. the 4 *āryasatyāni*	(a)	p. 552c13–554c3
	(b)	p. 554c4–560a2
5. the 22 *indriyāṇi*	(a)	p. 560a8–561a12
	(b)	p. 561a13–568a19
6. the 7 *bodhyaṅgāni*	(a)	p. 568a25–568b28
	(b)	p. 568b29–570a28
7. the 3 *akuśalamūlāni*	(a)	p. 570b1–570b27
	(b)	p. 570b27–571a14

8. the 3 *kuśalamūlāni*	(a)	p. 571a16–571b18
	(b)	p. 571b18–572c15
9. the 4 *mahābhūtāni*	(a)	p. 572c17–573a18
	(b)	p. 573a19–573c8
10. the *upāsakaḥ*		p. 573c10–
a) its 5 *saṃvarāḥ*	(a)	p. 574a7–574c24
	(b)	p. 574c25–575b1

2. Apraśnaka

1. *dhātuḥ*	p. 575b7–579b23
2. *karma*	p. 579b25–584c9
3. *pudgalaḥ*	p. 584c15–589c2
4. *jñānam*	p. 589c8–606a12
5. the *pratītyasamutpādaḥ*	p. 606a18–612b20
6. the 4 *smṛtyupasthānāni*	p. 612b26–616c7
7. the 4 *samyakprahāṇāni*	p. 616c9–617a20
8. the 4 *ṛddhipādāḥ*	p. 617a22–619c18
9. the 4 *dhyānāni*	p. 619c24–624c24
10. *mārgaḥ*	p. 625a5–646a1
11. *akuśalā dharmāḥ*	p. 646a7–661a9

3. Saṃgraha

a) Enumeration and explanation of the elements to be discussed	p. 661a15–666a5
b) in which *skandhāḥ, dhātavaḥ,* and *āyatanāni* these elements are contained	p. 666a6–671b22

4. Saṃprayoga

a) Enumeration and explanation of the mental elements to be discussed	p. 671c5-673c21
b) in which *skandhāḥ, dhātavaḥ,* and *āyatanāni* these elements are contained	p. 674a5–679a18

5. Prasthāna

1. the 10 *pratyayāḥ*	679b5–687b17
2. the *hetavaḥ*	p. 687b19–689a18
3. *nāmarūpam*	p. 689a20–690a29
4. the 10 *saṃyojanāni*	p. 690b2–694b10

5. the *kāya-, vāk-,* and *manaścaritam*	p. 694b12–694c11
6. *sparśaḥ*	p. 694c13–697b16
7. *cittam*	p. 697b18–700a11
8. the 10 *akuśalāḥ karmapathāḥ*	p. 700a13–700c7
9. the 10 *kuśalāḥ karmapathāḥ*	p. 700c9–701a29
10. *samādhiḥ*	p. 701b6–719a21

Before we go on to examine the composition and structure of this work, we shall briefly review what our investigation of the other works of the Abhidharma, especially that of the Pāli Abhidharma, has established.

First we established the existence of an ancient core, consisting of *mātṛkāḥ* with commentaries, in the Vibhaṅga, the Dhātukathā, and in the older parts of the Dhammasaṅgaṇi. However, here we were forced to conclude that the *mātṛkāḥ* had been subjected to various changes during the course of time and that the commentaries reflect a late stage of development from the time when the texts had undergone their final redaction. It is furthermore characteristic for the Dhātukathā that the concepts of the *mātṛkā* are discussed according to *saṅgaho* and *sampayogo*.

Next to these ancient *mātṛkāḥ* are those which enumerate and explain countless variations of a particular subject and which I shall therefore refer to as single-*mātṛkāḥ*. When they attain a certain length, they appear as a work in their own right, an example being the Puggalapaññatti. If they were too short to form a work in their own right, the redactors of the Abhidharma added them to other works, such as the Ñāṇavibhaṅga to the Vibhaṅga, and the Ñāṇakathā, which was added to the Paṭisambhidāmagga. These single-*mātṛkāḥ* are as a rule meager in content and have no significance for the development of the doctrine. The question of their age is also doubtful, since they could be compiled easily at any time, whereby the material borrowed for this purpose resulted in a wealth of different connections.

Works in which subjects of any kind are discussed in broad detail on the basis of a certain framework of questions, such as the Yamaka and Paṭṭhāna, represent a special case of their own. They unite a minimum of content with an excessively broad presentation, from which the small amount of valuable material they contain must be extracted.

A special position is also occupied by the examination of deviating doctrinal opinions. This is only present to a limited extent in the Sarvāstivāda, namely, in the Vijñānakāya. This discussion was continued in the Pāli Abhidharma, where it has been preserved in the form of the Kathāvatthu.

The first steps towards the development of the traditional doctrine are particularly significant in that they represent an attempt to think through and further extend individual themes of the doctrine. Here the presentation is partially given by means of a *mātṛkā*, as in the Rūpakaṇḍa of the Dhammasaṅgaṇi, and partially in free form, as in the Cittakaṇḍa. These developments occur relatively late[6] and have only been preserved to the extent that the redactors of the Abhidharma incorporated them into the traditional works of the Abhidharma. Moreover, the doctrines they contain were also used in the final redaction of the commentaries on the old *mātṛkāḥ*.

Considering things from this point of view, the question arises of where the Śāriputrābhidharma fits into the picture.

As far as its original core is concerned, the predominant connections with the Vibhaṅga were demonstrated a long time ago.[7] In fact, the situation is as follows.

As I have shown earlier on in this investigation,[8] the *mātṛkā* in the Vibhaṅga consists of three parts, the first containing a list of general basic concepts; the second a list of doctrinal concepts concerning the path of liberation; while the third forms the Kṣudravastuka. Furthermore, we established that the first two parts also form the basis for the Dhātukathā.

The first part of the Śāriputrābhidharma, the Sapraśnaka, begins with the discussion of the following concepts:

1. 12 *āyatanāni*
2. 18 *dhātavaḥ*
3. 5 *skandhāḥ*
4. 4 *āryasatyāni*
5. 22 *indriyāṇi*

This corresponds to the first part of the Vibhaṅga *mātṛkā*, with only the *pratītyasamutpādaḥ* missing. This is to be found in the second part of the Śāriputrābhidharma, the Apraśnaka, in fifth place. It is followed by:

6. 4 *smṛtyupasthānāni*
7. 4 *samyakprahāṇāni*

8. 4 *ṛddhipādāḥ*
9. 4 *dhyānāni*
(10. *mārgaḥ*)

This is the beginning of the second part of the Vibhaṅga *mātṛkā*. Thus, a major part of the first two sections of this *mātṛkā* is to be found in the same order in the Śāriputrābhidharma. Moreover, if we consider that these two sections (as we have already seen) serve as a basis for the discussion of the *saṅgaho* and *sampayogo* in the Dhātukathā, then we may also see a correspondence in the following two sections of the Śāriputrābhidharma, the Saṃgraha and the Saṃprayoga.

It would thus appear that large sections of the Śāriputrābhidharma are based on an ancient inherited body of material which is common to both works, despite the fact that much has been changed and expanded. However, we have encountered changes of this kind in the Abhidharma of the other schools as well and they may be considered as natural during the course of such a long separate development.

If we now look briefly at these changes, we find that the first part of the old *mātṛkā* in the Sapraśnaka, which consists of five members, has been extended by the addition of five further members. This is in itself unremarkable. Additions were bound to be made over the course of time, especially in the case of an Abhidharma which consisted of one single work and where any new ideas had thus to be inserted into this work and arranged to suit the transmitted body of material.

The first four members in the next section, the Apraśnaka, which are placed in front of the second part of the old *mātṛkā*, are remarkable. However, this circumstance can be explained if we consider the nature of these members. They consist of single-*mātṛkāḥ*, that is, they are small, independent works which did not need to be joined to others of the same kind but could be inserted as required into existing works. The fact that they were not counted as belonging to the first section and that the division was made before them may have been due to a wish (so rightly emphasized by A. Bareau) to produce sections of roughly similar length. Incidentally, the two final members of the Apraśnaka also display the characteristic features of single-*mātṛkāḥ*.

If we now turn to the body of old material again, we see that the first part of the old *mātṛkā* in the Sapraśnaka has been preserved virtually unchanged. The fact that it starts with the *āyatanāni* instead of the *skandhāḥ* is not significant.[9] It is only strange that the 7 *saṃbodhyaṅgāni* have been taken from the second part of the old *mātṛkā* and added to the first part as its sixth member.

It is striking that in the Apraśnaka it is only the beginning of the second part of the old *mātṛkā* that has been preserved. However, this is not wholly incomprehensible. Early oral transmission had tended to preserve the beginnings of texts rather more reliably than the rest. In the case of an early text which had lost its relevance in the course of time, it was not unnatural that the end should eventually disappear completely. If we take the incorporation of the *saṃbodhyaṅgāni* in the first section into account, it is in fact only three members that are missing here. The last member, the *mārgaḥ*, has been reworked in the form of a single-*mātṛkā*. This led to the addition of a similarly composed passage on the *akuśalā dharmāḥ*.

There remains one important question: why have the two parts of the old *mātṛkā* been separated in the Śāriputrābhidharma and contrasted as Sapraśnaka and Apraśnaka? The answer to this question lies in the different treatment of the two parts in the two different sections. In the Sapraśnaka, the individual members of the *mātṛkā* are first of all explained briefly and then discussed according to an attribute-*mātṛkā*. In the Apraśnaka there is no question of this; the discussion of the individual members is limited to a detailed explanation with the aid of sūtra passages. The former treatment is also to be found in the Vibhaṅga. Besides the discussion of the individual members of the *mātṛkā* in the form of the Suttantabhājanīya and the Abhidhammabhājanīya, there is the Pañhāpucchaka in third place, where the discussion is pursued with the aid of an attribute-*mātṛkā*. The name Pañhāpucchaka can be explained in that this is done in the form of question and answer.[10] This is the same procedure as in the Sapraśnaka and this name can therefore be explained in the same way. By contrast, the Apraśnaka explains the members of the *mātṛkā* in the same way as the Suttantabhājanīya and its separation from the Sapraśnaka is thus understandable and justified.

The following picture has thus emerged: the first two parts of the Śāriputrābhidharma are based on the first two parts of the Vibhaṅga *mātṛkā*. The changes and additions are of the sort which typically occurred in the Abhidharma over the course of time and they do not alter the nature of the text. The Śāriputrābhidharma differs from the Vibhaṅga and the Dharmaskandha, the corresponding texts in the Abhidharma of the Pāli school and the Sarvāstivādin, in that its first part is only treated in the style of the Pañhāpucchaka, and the second in the style of the Suttantabhājanīya, which corresponds to the method of the Dharmaskandha.

Since the first two parts of the *mātṛkā* of the Vibhaṅga form the basis for the discussion of *saṅgaho* and *sampayogo,* as the Dhātukathā shows, here, where in contrast to the Vibhaṅga and the Dharmaskandha there is no third part between them, the Saṃgraha and Saṃprayoga follow on immediately. Both display the usual changes we have encountered above all in the Dhātukāya.

In the case of the Saṃgraha, it is the *mātṛkā* providing its basis which has been changed. Only the first part of the Vibhaṅga *mātṛkā,* i.e. the *mātṛkā* of the Sapraśnaka has been used. This has, however, been expanded in a variety of ways. First of all, the various elements connected and not connected to the Four Noble Truths are discussed (p. 661a20–b1). There then follows the *mātṛkā* of the Sapraśnaka itself, in the same expanded form as in the Śāriputrābhidharma with all ten members (p.661b1–c11). Finally, the attribute-*mātṛkā* of the Sapraśnaka is added on (p.661c11f.).[11] The discussion of includedness confines itself to asking in how many *skandhāḥ, dhātavaḥ,* and *āyatanāni* the elements of the *mātṛkā* are contained or not contained. The fact that further questions were intended is evident from the introduction to this section (p. 661a15–19). However, this was not carried out.

The section on the Saṃprayoga displays more fundamental changes. The old *mātṛkā* has been wholly abandoned and replaced by a long list of mental elements, and the question dealt with here is with which elements the elements of this list can be connected. At a first glance, this would seem to represent a complete break with tradition. However, this is not an isolated occurrence. We have already encountered something very similar in the Dhātukāya of the Sarvāstivādin.[12] In that work, the old *mātṛkā* was also replaced by a list of mental factors and not only the Saṃprayoga, but also the Saṃgraha referred to this list. Nevertheless, there is naturally no question of a direct relation of dependence. Both the lists, that of the Śāriputrābhidharma and that of the Dhātukāya, are completely different. It is rather a case of the same developmental tendency being at work in both cases. At a certain period, interest was directed towards the nature of the mental elements. Attempts were made to comprehend these elements in all their diversity by analyzing their constituent parts. This resulted in various lists of mental elements, which naturally differed from school to school. A further question was asked as to which of these mental elements could be connected with the various mental processes. It seemed logical to answer this question within the frame of the old Saṃprayoga. This is in fact what happened with the Sarvāstivādin and in the Śāriputrābhidharma. However, it was also possible to choose another form for this. An example of this is is to be found in the Cittakaṇḍa in the Dhammasaṅgaṇi of the Pāli school, which is ultimately based on the same question.

As far as the list of mental elements in itself is concerned, we shall return to it later. The Saṃprayoga itself is given relatively brief treatment. It is merely asked with which elements the individual members of the list seem to be connected (p. 677a26–679a18). However, here too the introduction indicates (p. 671c5–13) that a more detailed treatment was planned but not carried out.

With this, we have discussed the core of old transmitted material in the first four parts of the Śāriputrābhidharma. We have seen that these parts all have their basis in old, transmitted material, even though much has been changed and extended. But what is the situation with the Prasthāna, the fifth part?

In the case of this part, too, it was shown at an early date that the beginning, which deals with the various kinds of conditions, displays points of contact with the Paṭṭhāna of the Pāli Abhidharma.[13] The question here is whether these are merely superficial similarities or whether the two works derive from a common source. To assume a common source would seem problematic, since this part of the Śāriputrābhidharma is merely a short text of a few pages, as opposed to the Pāli Abhidharma, where we find an extensive work of several volumes. However, on closer examination these reservations disappear. First, we have seen other cases in the Saṃgraha and Saṃprayoga where texts which were given broad treatment in other schools have only a rudimentary form in the Śāriputrābhidharma. In addition, the Paṭṭhāna represents a special case. It is the Pāli school work in which the "method" that was so popular in this school found its most intemperate expression, in that an intrinsically simple formulation of a question is applied to innumerable individual cases, to which all possible variants are then added, so that the whole swells to massive size.[14] Nevertheless, this is all based on a relatively simple core. Naturally, it is only this core that could possibly be derived from the old transmitted material.

What does this core look like in both cases? Both begin with an enumeration of the various conditions, which are then subsequently explained. In the Śāriputrābhidharma there are 10 conditions (p. 679b6–680b13) and in the Paṭṭhāna 24 (p. 3,1–11,22).

In the Śāriputrābhidharma this is followed by a discussion of the relationship of the various conditions to each other in the following manner. It is possible, for example, for something to be simultaneously *hetupratyayaḥ* and *anantarapratyayaḥ*. It is possible that something is *hetupratyayaḥ* but not *anantarapratyayaḥ*. Furthermore, it is possible that something is not *hetupratyayaḥ* but *anantarapratyayaḥ*. Finally, it is possible that something is neither *hetupratyayaḥ* nor *anantarapratyayaḥ*. This relationship of each condition to all the other conditions is demonstrated (p. 680b13–687a27). This is followed by a brief discussion of good, evil and indeterminate elements and of how they can arise from each other individually or in various combinations (p. 687a28-b17).

The presentation in the Paṭṭhāna on the other hand is as follows. Here the possibility of good, evil, or indeterminate elements arising individually or in various combinations with one another is discussed. However, the causal relation is taken into account right from the beginning, with all 24 conditions considered. In addition, all the possible different combinations are considered, that one causal relation exists and a second one at the same time, that neither the one nor the other exists, that the first exists but not the second, that the first does not exist but the second does, i.e. *siyā . . . dhammo uppajjeya hetupaccayā ārammaṇapaccayā, na hetupaccayā na ārammaṇapaccayā, hetupaccayā na ārammaṇapaccayā, na hetupaccayā ārammaṇapaccayā*. Finally, the same possibilities are considered with an arbitrary number of conditions. All of this is presented in the form of questions (p. 11,23–19,18). Then the answers are given at length (p. 20,1–63,21).[15]

A comparison of these two versions demonstrates very clearly how the transmission alternates between exaggerated breadth and extreme abbreviation, a state of affairs which is very typical for the early Abhidharma. A common source is contained in the enumeration of the conditions. The tendency towards exaggerated breadth of treatment shows itself particularly in the Paṭṭhāna, especially in the juxtaposition of variants such as *anantara-* and *samanantara-paccayo, nissaya-* and *upanissayapaccayo,* and in the linking of contrasting pairs such as *purejāta-* and *pacchājātapaccayo, sampayutta-,* and *vippayuttapaccayo* and so forth. In the discussion of the effect of the individual conditions, the various possibilities are listed on both sides of how good, evil, and indeterminate elements arise either individually or in combination with one another. However, in the Śāriputrābhidharma this is only mentioned very briefly near the end of the work. What is most striking is that it is not said which kind of conditions are effective. This is, however, imperative. Otherwise this does not fit into a section which is supposed to deal with the various conditions. Thus, the transmission is distorted here. On the other hand, the relation of the individual conditions to one another is discussed in great detail in the Śāriputrābhidharma, in almost more detail than in the Paṭṭhāna, where it is eclipsed by the rest of the presentation. In the latter work, however, the discussion of this relation is expanded to include groups of conditions as well. And this is missing in the Śāriputrābhidharma. However, I feel inclined to assume that this is a case of excessive proliferation in the Paṭṭhāna.

To sum all of this up: there is an abundance of differences and it is these differences which initially determine the general impression. However, closer examination forces us to conclude that these differences—where they are not due to the transmission—merely concern the exposition. The material treated and the underlying ideas are the same in both works. It can therefore be assumed that in this respect the Śāriputrābhidharma and the Paṭṭhāna derive from a common body of ancient material.

There is one more small piece of this ancient material in this part of the Śāriputrābhidharma, namely, in the next section which deals with the causes (*hetavaḥ*). This section also begins with an enumeration and explanation of all the causes (p. 687b21–c3 and 687c4–688b28). However, what is presented here is of precious little significance. The first ten causes are merely imitations of the ten conditions (*pratyayāḥ*), created simply by substituting *-hetuḥ* for *-pratyayaḥ* everywhere. What follows are virtually only the members of the *pratītyasamutpādaḥ* which are described as causes here. Finally, the negations of these causes are presented. All in all, this is an extremely insignificant compilation.

However, this is followed by a passage of a wholly different character (p. 688b29–689a18). In this passage causes and classes of causes are compiled as pairs of four and discussed. These are: elements which are a cause but which do not have a cause, elements which have a cause but which are not a cause; elements which are a cause and which have a cause and elements which are neither a cause nor have a cause; then follow elements which are a cause but are not connected to a cause, elements which are connected to a cause but which are not a cause; elements which are a cause and are connected to a cause, and elements which are neither a cause nor connected to a cause. Similar pairs of four are then formed out of past and concurrent, past and future and concurrent and future causes.

None of this has anything to do with the beginning of this passage, with the enumeration and explanation of the causes. The concepts used here are not taken from there. However, they recall similar material in the Abhidharma of other schools. In the *mātṛkā* of the Dhammasaṅgaṇi, for instance, it says among other things: *hetū ceva dhammā sahetukā ca, sahetukā ceva dhammā na ca hetū, hetū ceva dhammā hetusampayuttā ca, hetusampayuttā ceva dhammā na ca hetū* (v. nos. 23–28; p. 6,1–12). Similar passages are also to be found in the 6th chapter of the Prakaraṇa, the *mātṛkā* of which displays other points of contact with the *mātṛkā* of the Dhammasaṅgaṇi as well (v. Nos. 63–66; T 1541, p. 644c4–6 = T 1542, p. 711c7–8). Evidently the redactors of the Śāriputrābhidharma added a seemingly appropriate piece of old transmitted material to the newly written passage on the causes.

However, this is the only thing from the body of old transmitted material in this part of the Śāriputrābhidharma. What follows no longer has anything to do with it. Passages of very different content follow in arbitrary order. To all appearances, these are pieces which were available to the redactors of the Abhidharma and which they wanted to include. It was therefore the simplest and most natural thing to add them here at the end of the work.

This concludes our discussion of the ancient transmitted material which forms the core of the Śāriputrābhidharma. Summing up the essential points briefly, we can say that the main part of the work is based on the same material as the Vibhaṅga and the Dhātukathā of the Pāli canon and as the Dharmaskandha and the Dhātukāya of the Sarvāstivāda. What has been used here are the first two parts of the Vibhaṅga *mātṛkā,* that is, the same parts on which the Dhātukathā is also based. The manner of commentation used here is strange. It is not the same in both parts, as was the case in the Pāli school and with the Sarvāstivāda; here these parts have been separated, with the first being explained in the manner of the Pañhāpucchaka in the Vibhaṅga and the second in the manner of the Suttantabhājanāya. Immediately after this follow the Saṃgraha and the Samprayoga, which correspond to the discussion according to *saṅgaho* and *sampayogo* in the Dhātukathā. To this main part of the work which forms a unit in itself is added a brief presentation of the doctrine of causes. This has the same origin as the ancient core of the Paṭṭhāna, the material from which this huge work was later spun.

It is on this ancient material that the Śāriputrābhidharma as a whole is based. The manner in which its constituent parts are linked is the reason why the Abhidharma is here constituted by a single work. None of the material added later changed this structure in any way.

We shall now turn to those parts of the work which were added to the ancient core. Some of these no doubt contain old material, especially those sections based on single-*mātṛkāḥ*. Correspondences have long been pointed out between the third section of the second part, which deals with the *pudgalaḥ,* and the Puggalapaññatti of the Pāli Abhidharma. Similar correspondences exist between the fourth section, which deals with *jñānam,* and the Ñāṇavibhaṅga. However, as we have already seen, correspondences of this kind could easily result from the treatment of the same subject in single-*mātṛkāḥ*. Otherwise the school of the Śāriputrābhidharma seems to have had a predilection for treating subjects in the form of single-*mātṛkāḥ*. The first two sections of the second part, which deal with *dhātuḥ* and *karma,* are also based on *mātṛkāḥ* of this type. Perhaps this method of treating *dhātuḥ, āyatanam,* etc. was also considered in the Pāli Abhidharma.[16] But here we find the same procedure in the tenth and eleventh section as well, in the discussion of the *mārgaḥ* and the *akuśalā dharmāḥ,* and in addition to this in the tenth section of the fifth part, in the discussion of the *samādhiḥ*. Nonetheless, all of these sections are essentially compilations of material devoid of fertile thought, their great size mainly resulting from the fact that the relevant sūtras are quoted at full length.

As contrasted with the single-*mātṛkāḥ*, which occur more frequently in the Śāriputrābhidharma than in the Pāli Abhidharma, here there are no passages which would correspond to the other component parts of the Pāli Abhidharma. Thus, there is no counterpart to the Yamaka. This not so significant in itself, since the Yamaka is evidently a later creation peculiar to the Pāli Abhidharma. However, there is also no discussion of the ideas of the other schools, such as constitutes the content of the Kathāvatthu and such as we find, at least in a rudimentary form, in the Sarvāstivādin's Abhidharma at the beginning of the Vijñānakāya.[17]

We now come to the doctrinal developments to be found in the Śāriputrābhidharma. We shall consider only the most important developments and disregard the lesser ones.[18]

We have already encountered a development of this kind. In the discussion of the fourth part, the Saṃprayoga, we saw that the Śāriputrābhidharma does not start from the old *mātṛkā* in the question of the combination of the various elements as used in the Dhātukathā of the Pāli school, but replaces this with a list of mental elements, as in the Dhātukāya of the Sarvāstivādin. We have already indicated that this was an important step in the development of the psychological ideas. We shall now examine this list in detail. It takes the following form (p. 671c14–22):[19]

1. 7 *dhātavaḥ*: *cakṣurvijñāna-, śrotravijñāna-, ghrāṇavijñāna-, jihvāvijñāna-, kāyavijñāna-, mano-,* and *manovijñānadhātuḥ.*
2. 10 *saṃsparśāḥ*: *kāya-, citta-, adhivacana-, pratigha-, lobha-, dveṣa-, vidyā-, avidyā-, vidyābhāgīya-,* and *avidyābhāgīyasaṃsparśāḥ.*

3. 5 *indriyāṇi*: *sukha-, duḥkha-, saumanasya-, daurmanasya-,* and *upekṣendriyam.*
4. 27 *caitasikā dharmāḥ*: *vedanā, saṃjñā, cetanā, sparśaḥ, manaskāraḥ, vitarkaḥ, vicāraḥ, kśāntiḥ, darśanam, jñānam, adhimokṣaḥ, alobhaḥ, adveṣaḥ, amohaḥ, śraddhānusāraḥ (?), apatrāpyam, anapatrāpyam, prītiḥ, saumanasyam, cittapraśrabdhiḥ, cittaprāguṇyatā, śraddhā, chandaḥ, apramādaḥ, smṛtiḥ, upekṣā,* and *bhayaḥ (?).*[20]
5. 10 *anuśāyaḥ*: *dṛṣṭiḥ, vicikitsā, śīlavrataparāmarśaḥ, lobhaḥ, dveṣaḥ, īrṣyā, mātsaryam, avidyā, mānaḥ,* and *auddhatyam.*
6. 3 *samādhayaḥ*: *savitarkaḥ savicāraḥ samādhiḥ, avitarko vicāramātraḥ samādhiḥ,* and *avitarko 'vicāraḥ samādhiḥ.*
7. 3 *samādhayaḥ*: *śūnyatā-, animitta-,* and *apraṇihitasamādhiḥ.*
8. 5 *indriyāṇi*: *śraddhā-, vīrya-, smṛti-, samādhi-,* and *prajñendriyam.*

As we have already seen, the Dhātukāya contains a similar list. And the list of mental factors used in the Cittakaṇḍa of the Dhammasaṅgaṇi is of the same type. The list given above is related to these lists but despite this basic relationship it displays characteristic features of its own.

Whereas the Cittakaṇḍa list gives an undifferentiated enumeration, the Dhātukāya list distinguishes between individual groups. In the list given above no distinctions as such are made but the individual groups stand out so clearly from one another that we can take them as such. Thus, in this respect, it is closer to the Dhātukāya.

Of these individual groups, the *caitasikā dharmāḥ,* the group of mental elements in a narrower sense, is of especial importance, since it embodies the actual progress made in psychological conceptions. Thus, it was later included together with the *anuśayāḥ* in the psychology of the school. However, whereas in the Dhātukāya a distinction is also made here between *mahābhūmikā dharmāḥ, kleśamahābhūmikā dharmāḥ* etc., the list above merely confines itself to an enumeration, and thus in this respect displays a point of contact with the list in the Cittakaṇḍa.

Some of the other groups also correspond to groups in the Dhātukāya. The latter also gives *saṃsparśāḥ* and *indriyāṇi.* However, it gives five *saṃsparśāḥ* and here we have ten. And only the first of the two groups of *indriyāṇi* that we find here has a counterpart in the Dhātukāya. The two groups of *samādhayaḥ* also have no correspondence.

As far as the origin of the individual groups is concerned, the 7 *dhātavaḥ* are taken from the canonical group of 18 *dhātavaḥ* and represent, as is occasionally also the case in the Pāli Abhidharma, the *cittam,* which is followed by the *caitasikā dharmāḥ*. The groups of *indriyāṇi* and the *samādhayaḥ* also derive from the old canon.

The group of 10 *saṃsparśāḥ* is a later creation. In this form, it is unique to the Śāriputrābhidharma, which moreover gives the *saṃsparśāḥ* a section of their own (V, 6), in which not only the ten *saṃsparśāḥ* are given but also a large additional number of *saṃsparśāḥ* are enumerated and explained. Incidentally, the Śāriputrābhidharma is not alone in this. The Abhidharma of the Sarvāstivādin also names and discusses a group of 16 *saṃsparśāḥ* in the Jñānaprasthāna.[21]

Finally, the other feature of especial importance here is the group of 10 *anuśayāḥ* or *kleśānuśayāḥ,* due to the role they play in the doctrine of liberation. They are not the only item in this doctrine, however, being accompanied by the *saṃyojanāni.* But because it is only they that are *caitasikāḥ,* while the *saṃyojanāni* belong to the *cittaviprayuktāḥ saṃskārāḥ,* only they are given here in the enumeration of the mental elements. Otherwise, the *anuśayāḥ* have the same relationship to the *saṃyojanāni* as the *anuśayāḥ* to the *paryavasthānāni* in the other schools.[22] I shall not go any further into the associated problems here since this would demand a more detailed examination, which will be given elsewhere in due course. [Frauwallner never returned to this issue.]

The *saṃyojanāni* also constitute the subject of one of the few sections in the Śāriputrābhidharma (V, 4) which deserves mention because it contains new, valuable, and unique material. However, as is so often the case in works of the Abhidharma, the essence of what this has to say, especially as far as the relationship to the *anuśayāḥ* is concerned, is confined to a few sentences at the beginning of the section (p. 690b6–14). The rest of the section is concerned with the discussion of the *saṃyojanāni* from various points of view in the manner of an attribute-*mātṛkā*.

In connection with this, mention should be made of a section (V, 7) which, albeit only briefly, touches on an interesting and controversial problem, namely, the question of the nature of the *cittam.* The old canon already contains the assertion that the mind is naturally pure and is only defiled by external impurities.[23] This statement is repeated here at the beginning of the section (p. 697b18–22) almost word for word. However, this is all there is. It is followed in the usual manner by the lengthy enumeration and explanation of varieties of *cittam.* However, it does declare the position of the Śāriputrābhidharma on this important question.

Finally, we shall look briefly at the commentary on the old *mātr̥kā,* or rather at that part of it which is most important in terms of content, the commentary on the *mātr̥kā* of the basic general concepts (I, 1–5). For, as we have often said, the commentaries reflect the state of development that the doctrine had attained at the point in time when they were finally fixed, which, in this case, was the time of the redaction of the Abhidharma. Thus, important information can be inferred from the commentaries about the contemporary state of doctrinal development.

In the present case, with the commentary on the *mātr̥kā* of the basic general concepts, it turns out that it mainly derives from old transmitted material. This is evident from a comparison with the Abhidharma of the other schools, in particular with the Vibhaṅga and the relevant sections of the Rūpakaṇḍa of the Dhammasaṅgaṇi.[24]

Let us start by looking at the first two sections which deal with the *āyatanāni* and the *dhātavaḥ.* Here we find a correspondence not only generally in terms of content and method but also partly in the phrasing. With the explanation of *cakṣurāyatanam,* for example (p. 525c9–20), several explanations are juxtaposed just as they are in the Rūpakaṇḍa. The introductory words *cakkhu catunnaṃ mahābhūtānaṃ upādāya pasādo attabhāvapariyāpanno* are identical in both cases. The two variants with *passati* and *paṭihaññati* reappear in both cases (p. 160,16 = p. 525c13f. and p. 160,24 = p. 525c16). The concluding words *cakkhuṃ petaṃ cakkhāyatanaṃ petaṃ cakkhudhātu pesā cakkhundriyaṃ petaṃ loko peso dvārā pesā samuddo peso* etc., also correspond (p. 160, 16–20 = p. 525c16–20). There is the same kind of correspondence, albeit with more pronounced differences in detail, in the explanation of the *rūpāyatanam* etc. (Vibhaṅga p. 86,6–17 = p. 526a25–b4).[26] The only innovation is the inclusion of *karma* and *vipākaḥ* (p. 526a28, b7, etc.).

The discussion of the *skandhāḥ* is also entirely traditional. In the case of the *rūpaskandhaḥ* (p. 543a6–23), we find the familiar determination as *catvāri mahābhūtāni catvāri ca mahābhūtāny upādāya rūpam*. Next to this is a division into three according to whether the *rūpam* is *sanidarśanaṃ sapratigham, anidarśanaṃ sapratigham,* or *anidarśanam apratigham*. The *vijñānaskandhaḥ* (p. 545b9-c8) is explained as the 6 *vijñānakāyāḥ* and the 7 *vijñānadhātavaḥ*. The *vedanā-* and *saṃjñāskandhaḥ* (p. 543b14–545b3) are treated in greater detail. Here, as in the Abhidhammabhājanīya of the Vibhaṅga (p. 20–45) and also in the Dharmaskandha (T 1537, p. 501a2–b16), all possible kinds of variants are listed in numerical gradation and discussed. And all this concludes with the canonical description[26] which serves as the basis for the Suttantabhājanīya of the Vibhaṅga.

Thus, it is evident that the commentary on the old *mātṛkā* in the Śāriputrābhidharma, as we said at the beginning, is entirely in the thrall of the old tradition. In one case only, with the explanation of the *dharmāyatanam*, the *dharmadhātuḥ*, and the *saṃskāraskandhaḥ* (p. 526c2–11, p. 535a9–18 and p. 545b4–8), do we come across an exception and encounter something completely new.

This explanation goes as follows, beginning with the *dharmāyatanam*. First of all, the question is asked as to what the *dharmāyatanam* is. The answer is given that it consists: 1. of three *skandhāḥ*, 2. of invisible and non-resistant matter (*anidarśanam apratighaṃ rūpam*) and 3. of the unconditioned (*asaṃskṛtam*). Then the question is repeated and all the elements that belong here are enumerated as follows:

1. a) *vedanā, saṃjñā, cetanā, sparśaḥ, manaskāraḥ, vitarkaḥ, vicāraḥ, darśanam, jñānam, adhimokṣaḥ, alobhaḥ, adveṣaḥ, amohaḥ, śraddhānusāraḥ (?), apatrāpyam, anapatrāpyam, prītiḥ, saumanasyam, cittapraśrabdhiḥ, cittaprāguṇyatā, śraddhā, chandaḥ, apramādaḥ, smṛtiḥ, samādhiḥ, upekṣā, vicikitsā,* and *bhayaḥ (?)*.
   b) *jātiḥ, jarā, maraṇam, jīvitam, saṃyojanāni, asaṃjñisamāpattiḥ, phalapratilābhaḥ,* and *nirodhasamāpattiḥ*.

2. *kāyavāgasaṃvarāvijñaptiḥ, sāsravā kāyavāksaṃvarāvijñaptiḥ, sāsravā kāyapraśrabdhiḥ, sāsravā kāyaprāguṇyatā, samyagvāk, samyakkarmāntaḥ, samyagājīvaḥ, samyakkāyapraśrabdhiḥ,* and *samyakkāyaprāguṇyatā.*
3. *pratisaṃkhyānirodhaḥ, apratisaṃkhyānirodhaḥ, niyāmaḥ, dharmasthitatā, pratītyasamutpādaḥ, ākāśānantyāyatanam, vijñānānantyāyatanam, ākiñcanyāyatanam,* and *naivasaṃjñānāsaṃjñāyatanam.*

The same explanation and enumeration is given in the discussion of the *dharmadhātuḥ.* Only the discussion of the *skandhāḥ* differs somewhat. For *vedanā* and *saṃjñā* are *skandhāḥ* in their own right and the *anidarśanam apratighaṃ rūpam* is, of course, classified under the *rūpaskandhaḥ.* Only the *asaṃskṛtam* is missing. Apart from this, however, the same material has been used.

As to the composition of this enumeration, which appears unstructured in the text, it emerges partially as a result of the answer to the preceding question. It is easily understood in terms of content and I have therefore already divided it up accordingly in the passage given above. It starts (1a) with the *caitasikā dharmāḥ* or *cittasaṃprayuktāḥ saṃskārāḥ,* the mental elements which accompany the processes of cognition. This is followed by (1b) the conditioned elements not associated with mind, the *cittaviprayuktāḥ saṃskārāḥ.* As the contrast to what has gone before, the list concludes (3) with the unconditioned, the *asaṃskṛtam.* Between these two categories are (2) those kinds of *rūpam* which could not be accommodated under the rest of the *āyatanāni* and *dhātavaḥ.*

It is easy to see the purpose of this enumeration. It was intended to fit into the scheme of the *āyatanāni, dhātavaḥ,* and *skandhāḥ* both the concepts that had been newly created and canonical concepts that had not been taken into account until then. As we have already seen, the *cittasaṃprayuktāḥ saṃskārāḥ* had been newly created when the Saṃprayoga was newly adapted. The adoption of the *anidarśanam apratighaṃ rūpam* was mainly the result of the development of the doctrine of karma. And the group of *cittaviprayuktāḥ saṃskārāḥ* and the *asaṃskṛtam* was created on the model of the Pañcavastuka, in which a first attempt had been made to set up a systematic compilation of all the elements independently of all traditional classifications, and which had later had a major influence. For despite a general disinclination to break with tradition in this way, these innovations gave rise to decisive impulses.[27]

However, all this shows that at the time when the commentary on the old *mātṛkā* was written, the doctrine of the Śāriputrābhidharma school had already reached an advanced stage of development. The great number of newly adopted elements indicate a considerable widening of the field of vision. The new arrangement and the creation of the group of the *cittaviprayuktāḥ saṃskāraḥ* and so forth indicates a better insight into the peculiar nature of the various elements. Moreover, the development of the doctrine of karma and the creation of the concept of *avijñaptiḥ* arose from a more advanced understanding of the problems involved and from remarkably serious attempts at solving them.

However, the Śāriputrābhidharma is not alone in this. A similar state of affairs also obtained in the other schools known to us. Thus, this is another case of the general course of development gradually taking effect in the various schools and leading to similar and yet differing solutions. In the Dharmaskandha of the Sarvāstivāda school, which contains a commentary on the same old *mātṛkā*, a similar enumeration is given with the *dharmāyatanam* and the *saṃskāraskandhaḥ* (T1537,p. 500c17–22 and p. 501b16–23), as in the part of the Śāriputrābhidharma we have discussed. Nonetheless, the lists from Pañcavastuka have been taken over unchanged. This can be explained in that the Pañcavastuka arose in the province of the Sarvāstivāda and therefore had most influence there. It is in Asaṅga's Abhidharmasamuccaya, which is based on a Hīnayāna Abhidharma, that we find a free and independent development comparable to that in the Śāriputrābhidharma. Initial signs of development are present in the Pāli Abhidharma, although these were not consistently elaborated. Some features in the latter work bear close resemblance to the Śāriputrābhidharma. Thus the discussion of the *dharmāyatanam* (Vibhaṅga p. 87,23–88,22; cf. p. 111,4–112,9), for example, is introduced by the question: *tattha katamaṃ dhammāyatanaṃ?* The answer is: *vedanākkhandho, saññākkhandho, saṅkhārakkhandho, yaṃ ca rūpaṃ anidassanaappaṭighaṃ dhammāyatanapariyāpannaṃ, asaṅkhatā ca dhātu.* However, the enumeration is different.[28]

This concludes our general survey of the Śāriputrābhidharma. It emerges as an interesting text of idiosyncratic character. While mainly based on old transmitted material, even this is organized in a different way as compared with the other schools that we have discussed. It contains little in the way of innovation or doctrinal evolution.[29] However, we should not forget that it is the only work of the Abhidharma of this school to have survived. Moreover, the little that it does contain deviates from the doctrines of the other schools in several important respects. Thus, it gives us a picture of a separate, individual evolution and contains material that is not only interesting in itself but which helps us to avoid the one-sided judgments that exclusive observation of the Abhidharma of the other schools might otherwise lead us into making.

Part 2

The Development of Buddhist Philosophical Systems

V

The Origin of the Buddhist Systems

The Buddhist systems are among the major achievements of the classical period of Indian philosophy. Nevertheless our knowledge of them, especially as regards their origin and development, is still fragmentary. This is especially true of the Hīnayāna systems, and it is precisely these which are of special interest. The Mahāyāna systems certainly produced great, even daring flights of thought. However, for an understanding of the development of the philosophical systems in general, it is the Hīnayāna systems which are of paramount importance. They are the older systems and as such form the basis for later development. With them,the actual process of the creation of the philosophical systems first took place. Thus, wherever the Mahāyāna schools had progressed to the creation of a system, as for instance with the Yogācāra school under Asaṅga and Vasubandhu, they did so under the influence of the Hīnayāna systems.

Given these circumstances, why is it that so little research has been done on the Hīnayāna systems? The reason lies partly in the course that research in general has taken, and partly in the nature of the material itself.

As far as the former is concerned, it was largely determined by the accessibility of the sources and progressed broadly as follows. The first material to come to light was the Buddhist manuscripts preserved in Nepal, which (partly in the original, partly as copies) found their way into Indian and European libraries through the offices of the British Resident, Brian Houghton Hodgson. These formed the basis for the work of, for example, Eugène Burnouf, probably the most important scholar of that time. However, these manuscripts contained works from the late period of Buddhism and as yet the necessary prerequisites for an understanding of these texts were lacking. The turning point came with the work carried out on the writings of Ceylonese Buddhism, first by George Turnour and later above all T. W. Rhys Davids and the Pāli Text Society, which he himself had founded. These writings went back to the time and personality of the Buddha himself, and understandably from then on scholarly interest centered above all on this early period. In this field, the pioneering achievements of Hermann Oldenberg were of the utmost importance. However, this all meant that the later period retreated into the background again, a state of affairs which did not change until the Chinese sources became known. These go back much further than the Tibetan translations and provide a wealth of material which for many centuries is the only really important material available. The Belgian scholar Louis de La Vallée Poussin did outstanding work here, above all with his translations of Vasubandhu's Abhidharmakośa in 1923–31 and of the Vijñaptimātratāsiddhi in 1928–29. With the translation of the Abhidharmakośa, one of the great Hīnayāna systems had been made known for the first time and it was as if a new world had opened up. However, it also demonstrated how fragmentary our knowledge was and just how much research still remained to be done. A wide gulf separates the comprehensive and finely developed system of the Abhidharmakośa from the ancient and simple teachings of the Buddha. The distance in time between them is also immense since the Buddha died in c. 480 B.C. and the Abhidharmakośa was written in A.D. c. 450, almost a thousand years later. It thus became the task of future research to bridge this gap, a task which still remains largely incomplete even today. Work has been done in some areas and a variety of material supplied, yet exactly how the development occurred and what in particular determined the course it took, is on the whole still unclear.

If one is enquiring about the origins of the Buddhist systems, it would seem logical to seek an answer in the more recent layers of the Buddhist canon. As is well known, the Buddhist canon consists of three parts: the collection of precepts, Vinayapiṭaka, the Buddha's sermons, Sūtrapiṭaka, and a collection of systematic doctrinal concepts, Abhidharmakośa. The last is a comparatively late work, and displays considerable differences from school to school; it was in fact only fully developed by a few schools. One could therefore expect to find here the beginnings of a later development which subsequently led to the formation of the systems. On first inspection, however, the extant material is disappointingly unpromising. It is deficient in content, dry and dull in form, and seems at first to yield little in the way of useful information.

The Buddhist Abhidharma evolved from simple lists *(mātṛkāḥ)*. One of the older sūtra (DN 33) recounts how, while the Buddha was still alive, the death of his great contemporary Vardhamāna, the founder of Jainism, was followed shortly afterwards by quarrels among his disciples as to the correct interpretation of his teachings. To prevent similar occurrences among the followers of the Buddha, one of his most trusted disciples, Śāriputra, compiled a long list of all his important doctrinal concepts which he used to recite to the other disciples.

However apocryphal this account may be, it is known that a need for a summary of the Buddha's teachings was felt very early on. The essential pronouncements of the Buddha are all contained in a small number of doctrinal statements, as for instance, the Four Noble Truths and the doctrine of dependent co-arising. However, besides these there is also a wealth of specific teachings scattered among the Buddha's numerous sermons. The reason is obvious: the Buddha attained enlightenment in the thirty-sixth year of his life and lived to the age of 79. During his lifetime, he was ceaselessly engaged in advising and teaching his disciples. He drew their attention to the weaknesses and faults they would have to overcome, gave them advice, showed them which stage they had reached in their efforts towards liberation, what goal they should next direct their efforts towards, and so on. However, none of this was taught systematically; advice was given piecemeal as and when the occasion arose. It was therefore only natural that the wish should arise to collect together the essential content of these scattered teachings. As in the sūtra mentioned above, this led to compilations in the form of lists, where the most important doctrinal concepts were enumerated. These were then complemented (at first orally) by the necessary commentaries.

Soon there was an almost infinite variety of such lists. Besides comprehensive lists which included everything without discrimination, shorter lists containing related doctrinal concepts were also compiled. Lists of attributes were made, according to which the given concepts were discussed. They enumerated which of the items listed occur together, which are mutually included in each other and so on.

Soon, however, degeneration also set in. The lists, especially those enumerating attributes, were extended almost limitlessly. Not only the association of single things with one another and their mutual inclusion were discussed but also the diversity of interrelations existing between them. Then, after a detailed exposition and dicussion of a given topic, variations on the theme were contrived and the whole process was repeated from the beginning. By this means a minimum of content could be stretched to fill volume after volume. The only possible justification for this activity was that in composing these works the authors believed that they were accruing religious merit.

Thus, it is not surprising that these works, uninviting in the circumstantiality of their form and the meagreness of their content, did not exactly encourage further study and that scholars gave up hope of finding anything useful in them. The general impression was that it would be virtually impossible to obtain from the works of the Abhidharmapiṭaka a coherent picture of the origins and development of the doctrines which eventually led to the establishment of the great systems of Buddhist philosophy.

Yet one should not be put off by the unfortunate form of these works, since closer examination reveals rather more profitable aspects. To take some of the works of the Pāli Abhidharma: one of the oldest of these is the Vibhaṅga, which is based on a list well-attested by plural transmission.[1] There are two sections in this work which are not accounted for in the list and the question arises of what they are doing here. The answer, however, is easy if we subject these passages to closer inspection. The first, called the "Ñāṇavibhaṅga," discusses the various kinds of knowledge *(ñāṇāṃ)*. They are listed numerically and then discussed, which is the treatment normally accorded to topics elsewhere in the Abhidharma. A text of this kind could have appeared as an independent work in its own right, a good example of which in the Pāli Abhidharma being the Puggalapaññatti, where this method is employed to discuss the different types of persons. However, the Ñāṇavibhaṅga is substantially shorter.The redactors of the Pāli Abhidharma clearly considered it too short for inclusion as a separate work in its own right and so, in compiling the Abhidhammapiṭaka, they incorporated it into a larger work, the Vibhaṅga. The Abhidhammapiṭaka did not of course develop as an organic whole; texts were collected and edited. This example demonstrates how they went about including and preserving texts that were too short to constitute independent canonical works.

The second section in the Vibhaṅga of interest to us here, the Dhammahadavibhaṅga, represents a similar case. It, too, has no connection with the original Vibhaṅga list; it is a short, separate work in its own right, actually a first attempt at systemization. A series of the most important doctrinal concepts are set out and elucidated and this is followed by a discussion of the spheres in which these elements occur and to which beings they apply. The text is slightly longer than that of the Ñāṇavibhaṅga, but here again the redactors of the Abhidhammapiṭaka clearly considered it too short for inclusion as a separate work and it was therefore added to the Vibhaṅga.[2] The important point to be noted here is that works that already represented a further development of the old doctrine were available to the redactors of the Abhidhammapiṭaka as well as texts belonging to the old, transmitted basis of the Abhidharma.

The Vibhaṅga is, however, not the only work in the Abhidhammapiṭaka that contains insertions of this kind in addition to the basic stock of texts. Texts of this kind also occur elsewhere, above all—leaving aside other, minor texts—in the Dhammasaṅgaṇi. This also basically consists of an old list with accompanying commentary and in this case the commentary is even given twice. However, in between the list and the commentary two further texts have been inserted, the Cittakaṇḍa and the Rūpakaṇḍa. The former is only superficially connected to the old list and the latter possesses its own list, which clearly indicates that both of these are insertions. The Rūpakaṇḍa contains an advanced theory of the elements which goes far beyond anything in the old canon. The Cittakaṇḍa contains a fully developed psychology that establishes which mental processes are good, evil, or morally indeterminate, what the basis for this moral distinction is, and lists the mental elements that accompany the respective mental processes. In addition, the Cittakaṇḍa contains a description of the path of meditation and liberation which summarizes the old canonical doctrines and further develops them.

In the Pāli canon we thus find side by side with the old tradition of the Abhidharma widely differing attempts at a development of the old canonical doctrines in various interpolated texts.

However, this is the case not only with the Pāli Abhidharma: the same is true of the Sarvāstivāda school, whose Abhidharma has also come down to us complete. Here the texts cannot be so easily disentangled as in the case of the Pāli Abhidharma, but the relevant doctrines can be clearly recognized from the way in which they are, as it were, reflected and refracted in the text.

Here we find the recognizable beginnings of systemization in the so-called Pañcavastuka dealing with the most important basic concepts[3] following the five groups *(skandhāḥ)* which, according to the Buddha's doctrines, form the personality. The beginnings of a psychology are incorporated into the Dhātukāya, where diverse mental elements are enumerated and grouped, above all those which accompany every mental process and those which determine good and evil actions.[4] Here we also find a further development of the canonical theory of liberation which goes far beyond that of the Pāli school.[5] The doctrine of causality contained here should also be mentioned. While it is limited to essentials—in contrast to the formalistic prolixity of the Paṭṭhāna in the Pāli Abhidharma—it does provide a lucid exposition.[6]

Here we have essentially the same situation as in the Pāli canon, however much the details may vary. It is thus obviously not an isolated phenomenon but rather a general trend of development. One can say that in the Abhidharma, before the final editing of the Abhidharmapiṭaka, an attempt was made not merely to record and transmit the traditional doctrinal concepts or at most to give them application to the widest possible range of cases, but rather to follow them through in their individual contexts and, where necessary, reformulate and develop them.

A date for the beginning of this tendency can be established within defined limits. Both schools—the Pāli school in Ceylon and the Sarvāstivāda school in the extreme northwest—owe their foundation to the missions which were sent out under King Aśoka around the middle of the third century B.C. Since both schools have a common core in the old, basic stock[7] of their Abhidharma, it is obvious that this core predates the missions and was thus brought to the mission countries as a common heritage. It is, however, equally obvious that the development and transformations of the doctrines we are here dealing with, while treating the same problems, attempt quite different solutions and represent individual developments in the respective schools. This process must, therefore, have taken place after the foundation of these schools, that is, after Aśoka's missions. Yet since, on the other hand these texts predate the redaction of the Abhidharmapiṭaka in which they were included, I would like to assign them a date of between 250–50 B.C.

This is, however, relatively late and means that more than two centuries had passed since the death of the Buddha before any attempt was made at developing his teachings. This is not improbable if we imagine how matters stood: it is not uncommon for the influence of an outstanding personality to continue to hold sway for a considerable period of time after his death, until it eventually weakens and new movement begins. In the case of the Buddha the following factor also has to be taken into account: his pronouncements were limited to a few central tenets—the Four Noble Truths, dependent co-arising *(pratītyasamutpādaḥ)* and the description of the path to liberation. Otherwise he flatly rejected all theoretical speculation as diverting attention from what he saw as the most essential element: the practical striving on the path towards liberation. It is hardly surprising that the attitude he had adhered to so unswervingly throughout the decades when he was teaching should have prevailed for such a long time after his death. In this context, it is indicative that the cause of the first dispute in the community of which we have reliable accounts and which was debated at the so-called second Council of Vaiśālī was not theoretical in nature but occasioned by the lax conduct of a certain group of monks. This took place about a hundred years after the death of Buddha. It was not until some years later that differences of opinion arose that led to an actual schism in the community. Even then it concerned questions of an internal, practical nature, namely, the position of the perfect saint or arhan.[8] Further decades were to pass before a dispute over any important theoretical problem occurred, and when it did—concerning the existence and nature of a personality, the *pudgalaḥ*—there was a special reason for it. The question of the self, the *ātmā,* had been an issue of central interest ever since the beginnings of Indian philosophy in the Upaniṣads. The Buddha, however, had avoided committing himself on this question because he knew that it would only lead to endless theoretical disputes. He therefore confined himself to explaining that the factors that form the visible earthly personality, that is, the five groups *(skandhāḥ)*, do not represent the self. In general, this avoidance of a clear definition prevailed and proved its worth. In the end, however, it was inevitable that the question of the Self would reemerge. About 200 years after the Buddha's death, a teacher named Vātsīputra appeared and claimed that there existed a personality, the *pudgalaḥ*, besides the five groups, and founded a school whose teachings included this doctrine. This broke the ice so to speak, and from then on other problems were subjected to reconsideration, and, if it was held to be necessary, the traditional teachings were further developed or transformed. This was probably how the beginnings of the new teachings that we find in the Abhidharmapiṭaka evolved. An additional factor could also have been that all this was contemporaneous with the origin of the oldest philosophical systems; the general climate of thought at that time must have been conducive to this sort of development.

While this would explain the new attempts at transformation and development of the old canonical doctrines in the Abhidharma, it does not explain the development of the later systems since, as has already been established, this was only the beginning: there was a long way to go before fully developed systems were created.

Here one must also consider that these new formulations have no connection with one another. They occur in isolation and are often mutually contradictory. To cite only a few examples: in the Sarvāstivāda school, the psychology of the Dhātukāya has no group which would correspond to the ten propensities *(anuśayāḥ)* of the doctrine of liberation. This group was obviously unknown or disregarded when this psychology was formulated. With the doctrine of liberation of the Pāli Abhidharma in the first section of the Dhammasaṅgaṇi, the propensities that are to be eliminated one after the other on the path to liberation are: *diṭṭhi-gatāni, kāmarāgo, vyāpādo, rūparāgo, arūparāgo, māno, uddhaccaṃ,* and *avijjā*. The propensities named in the discussion of the evil mental processes *akusalā cittuppādā*, whose elimination one would expect above all others on the path to liberation, are *diṭṭhi-gatāni, paṭigho, vicikicchā,* and *uddhaccaṃ*; that is, fewer in number and to some extent different. The Rūpakaṇḍa of the Dhammasaṅgaṇi postulates a duality in the karma doctrine: *kāyaviññatti* and *vacīviññatti*. The commentary on the basic list of the same work deals with a triad: *kāyakammaṃ, vacīkammaṃ,* and *manokammaṃ*. In the Sarvāstivāda school, the Vijñānakāya presents a doctrine of causality which differentiates between four conditions: *hetupratyayaḥ, samanantarapratyayaḥ, ālambana-pratyayaḥ,* and *adhipatipratyayaḥ*. The Jñānaprasthāna teaches six causes: *saṃprayuktakahetuḥ, sahabhūhetuḥ, sabhāgahetuḥ, sarvatragahetuḥ, vipākahetuḥ,* and *kāraṇahetuḥ*. Both doctrines are based on differing philosophical perspectives and are mutually exclusive, despite all later attempts at harmonization.

There is thus in the Abhidharmapiṭaka a motley collection of doctrines which are unrelated to each other and sometimes even mutually contradictory. This is not in itself remarkable: the men who evolved these doctrines were not trying to create a new system. They were themselves part of a tradition of pronouncement which contained all that was necessary for its disciples. Only when some point in the traditional doctrine seemed unclear or unsatisfactory was it developed or transformed. However, as the evidence indicates, this happened independently, without any attempt being made to take other doctrines into account and it resulted in these differing, often contradictory attempts at systematic development.

In summary, we can say that the Abhidharma texts bear witness to a new movement in the doctrinal tradition of Buddhism in the third century B.C. Traditional doctrines, such as the doctrine of liberation or psychology, were transformed and developed. Individual attempts at systematic development were also made, such as in the Dhammahadaya and the Pañcavastuka, but only in isolated, unrelated cases. A uniform organization and synthesis which could have formed the basis for the formation of a system, did not take place.

This is what can be gleaned from the Abhidharma texts: they show us the starting points for later development. However, they leave unanswered the question of the origin of the later philosophical systems. To find an answer to this question we must take later sources into consideration. The best place to begin is with the Sarvāstivāda school.

At the start of my lecture I mentioned Vasubandhu's Abhidharmakośa, which was composed around A.D. 450. This work is a description of the Sarvāstivāda system and is one of the most important descriptions of a Buddhist philosophical system that we possess. It is, however, not entirely new in that it is based on the works of a number of predecessors. The earliest of these works available to us (and probably the earliest of them all) is the Abhidharmasāra of a certain Dharmaśrī, which gives a brief description in verse explicated by an accompanying prose text. This work long enjoyed high standing: new commentaries were repeatedly written and the verse text supplemented and extended until Vasubandhu eventually wrote a new verse text and commentary in his Abhidharmakośa. Yet only the form is completely new: in all essentials he bases his work on that of Dharmaśrī.

It is, of course, obvious that if we want to explain the origin of the Sarvāstivāda system we must start with the earliest work, Dharmaśrī's Abhidharmasāra. This work consists of 10 chapters. Its structure will be clearer if we differentiate between two parts. The first part, consisting of chapters 1 to 7, contains a systematic description of the doctrinal concepts. The second part, chapters 8 to 10, contains all the other transmitted material that Dharmaśrī was unable to accommodate elsewhere in his work. Later, Vasubandhu composed a further chapter on the structure of the world and incorporated this into the systematic description, so that his version comprises 8 chapters. He also integrated the contents of the last three chapters into this description. However, what his work now possessed in compactness, it lacked in clarity and lucidity of exposition.

If we now look more closely at the systematic description in Dharmaśrī's work, the following structure emerges: following the 5 groups *(skandhāḥ)*, he first discusses the constituent elements of which, according to old canonical doctrine, the phenomenal world consists. Proceeding from the realization that things never come into being in isolation, he goes on to discuss the various kinds of mental elements, briefly mentions the theory of atoms and afterwards deals with the different temporal states and the doctrine of causality; that is, the four kinds of conditions *(pratyayāḥ)* and the six causes *(hetavaḥ)*. Vasubandhu subsequently inserted a description of the Buddhist conception of the world as consisting of various spheres. There then follows a discussion of the doctrine of karma; how good or evil actions determine the fate of beings in the cycle of existence. This is followed by the doctrine of liberation, a discussion of the propensities *(anuśayāḥ)* which determine entanglement in the cycle of existence and the knowledge by which these propensities can be eliminated. Finally there is a description of the different kinds of knowledge *(jñānāni)* and concentration *(samādhiḥ)*.

The systematic structure of this description is striking. It begins with a type of theory of first principles. Then follow the conception of the world, the laws which determine the fate of beings in the vicissitudes of the world and finally the doctrine of liberation. The fact that knowledge and concentration are then dealt with separately can be explained in that the idiosyncratic treatment of the doctrine of liberation, to which I have given the name Abhisamayavāda, gives the customary form of these concepts too little emphasis. On the whole, however, we can say that this constitutes a real system which covers all the principal doctrinal concepts and presents them in a consistent, logically connected structure.

Nevertheless, however uniformly constructed and complete this work would seem to be, it is not entirely original. Closer examination reveals that in all essential points it was composed from older material, particularly that from the earlier sections of the Abhidharmapiṭaka mentioned above. The beginning of the theory of principles is based on a Pañcaskandhaka.[9] The discussion of the mental elements is modelled on that of the Dhātukāya. The doctrine of causality takes the four conditions *(pratyayāḥ)* from the Vijñānakāya and the six causes *(hetavaḥ)* from the Jñānaprasthāna. The doctrine of karma is modelled on the 3rd part of the Lokaprajñapti. The doctrine of liberation (at least in its first part) can be attested in the Prakaraṇa in the doctrine of the propensities *(anuśayāḥ)* and elsewhere, and the sections on knowledge and concentration are again based on the Jñānaprasthāna.

In the light of all this, one could see the Abhidharmasāra as a compilation, and so it is to a certain extent. However, it is not a compilation in the same sense as many of the sections of the Abhidharma, which are little more than a dull accumulation of material. Here a scholar with an appreciation of logical connections and an understanding of systematic thought has built up an edifice and thus a real philosophical system.[10] His work also stood the test of time: as I have pointed out, all later standard descriptions of the Sarvāstivāda system, up to those of Vasubandhu and Saṃghabhadra, are based on this work.

Thus, we have seen one example of how a philosophical system came into being. In this case, the decisive factor was the work of a scholar who was able to collate the extant attempts and skillfully to assemble them to form a whole. But what was the situation in the case of the other schools? It would be too much of a coincidence for the right man to be born at the right time in the right place in every case.

Unfortunately the material fails us here. There is only one other school besides the Sarvāstivādin where a major part of the Abhidharma literature has been preserved, namely, the Pāli school in Ceylon. Only faint traces of the other schools have come down to us. Nevertheless, some details emerge to complete the picture given by the Abhidharma of the Sarvāstivādin.

The Pāli school presents an entirely different case. There exists no work similar to the Abhidharmasāra, and I am aware of only one great comprehensive work, extant in Upatissa's Vimuttimagga, "The Path of Liberation", and in a later, enlarged form in Buddhaghosa's Visuddhimagga,[11] "The Path of Purification". As the name tells us, it is a description of the path to liberation. The elaboration of the path to liberation already constitutes one of the most important continuations of the doctrine in the Dhammasaṅgaṇi of the old Abhidharma that we find here, and the same form of the path to liberation is also used in the above mentioned works.

It is, moreover, prefaced by a detailed discussion of moral behaviour *(sīlaṃ)* as the precondition for the successful practice of meditation. Finally there is a description of the insights gained by meditation *(paññā)*. Even if it does not qualify as a system, it is at least a complete description of Buddhist teaching. The fact that the path to liberation is the central point of interest merely corresponds to the spirit of Buddhism.

However, if we compare this description with the Abhidharmasāra a stark contrast becomes apparent. In the former we find a doctrinal system, theoretical considerations and clear, systematic thought. In the latter we have a path to liberation, practical considerations and a good deal of imagination. The style of presentation is also different: in the Vimuttimagga and the Visuddhimagga there are numerous examples and similes interspersed in the text. Unfortunately the less pleasing features of the style of the old Abhidharma also live on here. Again and again we come across enumerations of countless variations and subdivisions. The whole description proceeds supported only by the crutches of an outward device whereby the treatment in every section is laid out according to certain paragraphs. It is hardly surprising that there was no stimulus for any future development in these works and that with Buddhaghosa's work everything rigidified, while Dharmaśrī's creation was continually built on and developed.

The Pāli school demonstrates that the process of development in the Sarvāstivāda was by no means the rule and that things could take quite a different course. There are yet other sources, however, which indicate that the form taken by the systematic development in the Sarvāstivāda was not unique; similar processes also took place in other schools.

Of the Mahāyāna schools, it was especially that of the Yogācāra which attempted to develop its doctrines into a system modelled on those of the Hīnayāna schools. This can be seen above all from one of its earliest and most important representatives, Asaṅga (A.D. c. 315–385). His work clearly displays his efforts to go beyond the achievements of his teacher Maitreyanātha and to create a system. His indebtedness to the Hīnayāna systems is equally apparent. A work has come down to us under his name which is obviously based on the Abhidharma tradition of the Hīnayāna, the Abhidharmasamuccaya. The extant version is of course a product of the Mahāyāna school. It contains a wealth of material originating from the Mahāyāna tradition, and the style of presentation, the ponderous breadth with which it attempts to lend its doctrines weight and prestige, is mainly that of the Mahāyāna. However, the Hīnayāna model is unmistakable.

The work begins with a discussion of the old basic canonical concepts: the five groups *(skandhāḥ)*, the twelve spheres *(āyatanāni)*, and the eighteen elements *(dhātavaḥ)*, with the five groups forming the focus of interest. The latter are first explained in turn (p. 3,12ff.).[12] Then they are discussed with the aid of a list of attributes, an attribute-*mātṛkā* (p. 15,19ff.). This is the old form of the Pañcaskandhaka which Dharmaśrī also used as a basis for his description, and the list used here contains a very ancient core.

Next follows a discussion according to the categories of includedness *(saṃgrahaḥ)*, association *(saṃprayogaḥ)*, and accompaniedness *(samanvāgamaḥ)* (p. 32,5ff.). This also goes back to models in the old Abhidharma works of the Hīnayāna, despite the strongly Mahāyānistic character of individual features of the elaboration.

There then follows a long section divided according to the Four Noble Truths (p. 36–77). Under the truth of suffering, the structure of the world *(bhājanalokaḥ)* and the birth of beings into the various spheres are discussed (p. 36,4ff.). Under the truth of the origin of suffering, the defilements *(kleśāḥ)* and the acts *(karma)* are dealt with in detail (p. 43,9ff.). The cessation of suffering is treated briefly (p. 62,4ff.). In contrast to this, the path to the cessation of suffering is treated in depth (p. 65,10ff.).

In order to be able to assess this section correctly, it is necessary to compare it with a Hīnayāna work from another school, Harivarman's Tattvasiddhi,[13] of which parts have been preserved. It is a rather late work, as Harivarman is not much earlier than Asaṅga, but it goes back to an old tradition. The major part of this work (p. 260–373) is also divided into sections corresponding to the Four Noble Truths. The five groups *(skandhāḥ)* are discussed under the truth of suffering (p. 260ff.), and the acts *(karma)* and defilements *(kleśāḥ)* (p. 289ff.) are discussed under the origin of suffering. The section dealing with the cessation of suffering is brief and of little significance. The section treating the path to the cessation of suffering deals with concentration *(samādhiḥ)* and knowledge *(jñānam)* (p. 334ff.).

If we recall the subjects on which Dharmaśrī bases the main part of his description in the Abhidharmasāra, namely, acts *(karma*, Ch. 3), propensities *(anuśayāḥ*, Ch. 4), the path to liberation *(mārgaḥ*, Ch. 5), knowledge *(jñānam*, Ch. 6), and concentration *(samādhiḥ*, Ch. 7), we see that they are the same topics treated in almost the same order, even if the the exposition differs completely in detail.

Here one should bear the following in mind: some Hīnayāna systems may have evolved independently. In particular, the Sarvāstivāda texts as extant would support the view that there was an independent, consistent development. On the other hand it would have been natural, once one important system or other became common knowledge, for other schools to attempt their own version. Similarly it would have been natural in such a case to attempt to give their own doctrines a systematic form. This is what seems to have happened here. The effective external framework is provided by the venerable Four Noble Truths. It is not as natural a structure as Dharmaśrī's, but it is nonetheless impressive. To fill in the framework, the material was subsumed into groups similar to those that Dharmaśrī had used in his Abhidharmasāra. Thus, a sound system of doctrines was created, one that would stand comparison with other systems.

Now, Asaṅga also organizes one of the most important and comprehensive sections in his Abhidharmasamuccaya according to the Four Noble Truths and distributes the material amongt them in a similar way. Since, as Harivarman's Tattvasiddhi indicates, this structure was available in works of the Hīnayāna, and when we see that the previous sections of the Abhidharmasamuccaya are based on Hīnayāna models, it seems justified to assume that Asaṅga was using the Abhidharma of a Hīnayāna school as a model here too. As we know for certain that he converted to Mahāyāna from the school of the Mahīśāsaka, it could have been the Abhidharma of this school.

However, this is to enter the realms of speculation. Unfortunately, the poverty of the material here only admits of speculation for the present. Speculation can, however, serve to clarify the problems and the various possible solutions.

To recapitulate, it can be said that the formation of the Buddhist philosophical systems did not progress as in other philosophical systems, where the fundamental, motivating ideas are gradually elaborated and extended to form a system. Here, the basis consisted of the transmitted teachings of the Buddha, which for its part was limited to a small number of precepts forming the basis for the path to liberation and was not a system as such. Only gradually were attempts made at solving individual problems. A proper system only came into being if there was a personality capable of assimilating these initial attempts into a unified whole, as happened in the case of the Sarvāstivāda school. Under the influence of models such as these, other schools then gave their doctrines—if only outwardly—a systematic form. This seems to have been the case with Harivarman's Tattvasiddhi and Asaṅga's Abhidharma-samuccaya. However, it could also happen, as we have seen in the case of the Vimuttimagga and the Visuddhimagga of the Pāli school, that the form of the pure doctrine of liberation was retained and whatever they had to say on the subject was compressed into this framework.

VI

Pañcaskandhaka and Pañcavastuka

The first two chapters in Vasubandhu's Abhidharmakośa, covering the doctrine of principles, seem at first glance to be clearly structured. The elements with which the Sarvāstivāda constructs his conception of the world are clearly set out and discussed. The unconditioned elements *(asaṃskṛtāḥ)* are dealt with first, followed by the conditioned elements *(saṃskṛtāḥ)*. Matter *(rūpam)* is dealt with straight away in the first chapter. The second chapter deals with the mind *(cittam)*, the mental factors *(caittāḥ)*, and the conditioned factors not associated with mind *(cittaviprayuktāḥ saṃskṛtāḥ)*. This is a very common structure and one which we find time and again. Following this, all the elements are divided according to 5 categories *(vastūni)*, namely, *rūpam, cittam, caittāḥ, cittaviprayuktāḥ saṃskārāḥ* and *asaṃskṛtam*. Vasubandhu has altered the usual order only to the extent of putting the unconditioned elements in first place.

However, if we examine his presentation more closely, things are not as simple as they seemed at first. The fact that he occasionally interposes other material is in itself of little significance: in the old texts of the Abhidharma, many subjects were treated which were insignificant for the system as a whole but which had to be included in a complete description of the dogmatics. Thus, we find insertions of this kind in the Abhidharmakośa, an example being the discussion of the senses *(indriyāṇi)*, which Vasubandhu interpolates between *rūpam* and *cittam* at the beginning of the 2nd chapter. However, quite apart from this, there are all kinds of stumbling blocks. In order to understand and explain these, we must first examine the course of Vasubandhu's description in detail.[1]

He begins by assigning all the elements to the categories of undefiled *(sāsravaḥ)* or defiled *(anāsravaḥ)*.[2] Since the unconditioned elements *(asaṃskṛtāḥ)* are undefiled, it is these which are first discussed in detail.[3] Following this Vasubandhu goes on to discuss the conditioned elements *(saṃskṛtāḥ)*,[4] not, however, treating matter as such, but beginning with a discussion of the 5 groups *(skandhāḥ)* in the usual order, matter receiving the most detailed treatment. After a linking discussion of the spheres *(āyatanāni)* and the elements *(dhātavaḥ)* and their relationship to the groups, there follows a long section which fills the rest of the 1st chapter.[5] Here Vasubandhu enumerates a series of attributes, in each case debating which of the 18 *dhātavaḥ* to assign them to. The last of these questions leads into a discussion of the 22 sense faculties *(indriyāṇi)*, the detailed treatment of which comprises the first section of chapter 2.[6] Vasubandhu then breaks off and raises the question of whether the elements already discussed arise independently, or if certain of them necessarily arise together.[7] In this context, he then classifies all the elements according to the 5 categories, *rūpam, cittaṃ, caittāḥ, cittaviprayuktāḥ saṃskārāḥ,* and *asaṃskṛtam*. Using this classification, he proceeds to answer his own question, starting with *rūpam*, where he speaks of atoms which only occur in conglomerations. Having dealt with this,[8] he continues with the remark that *cittaṃ* and *caittāḥ* necessarily arise together and goes on to discuss these two. However, he here abandons the question of simultaneous or non-simultaneous arising and he discusses the *caittāḥ* and *cittaviprayuktāḥ saṃskārāḥ* respectively without referring to it again. A treatment of the doctrine of causality concludes the description.[9]

Thus, the following picture emerges: the discussion of the 5 categories of *rūpam, cittaṃ, caittāḥ, cittaviprayuktāḥ saṃskārāḥ,* and *asaṃskṛtam* certainly constitutes the main content of Vasubandhu's description; however, it is not structured around them. The 5 categories are in fact introduced much later, by means of a rather artificial link, and only part of the material is then treated. Matter *(rūpam)*, apart from the theory of atoms, is discussed in another context. That which is unconditioned *(asaṃskṛtam)* is also presented in another place and within a different framework. However, this means that Vasubandhu did not base his description on the structure most obviously suited to a systematic description of this kind. He rather took it into consideration to a certain degree in retrospect. This is striking, and all the more so for the fact that this arrangement of the material was not new. One work, the Pañcavastuka,[10] has come down to us in a Chinese translation, for example, which must have possessed considerable standing and which is of a much earlier date than Vasubandhu's work, since it was first translated into Chinese around the middle of the 2nd century A.D. This work—as the name tells us—is based on the same framework.

The most obvious explanation for this is that he was bound by tradition; his material had been transmitted in a set form from which he was unwilling to depart. This is confirmed if we recall the structure of the first chapter. Its main subject is a discussion of the 5 *skandhāḥ*. This organization of the material, however, is one which goes back to the oldest tradition. The discussion of the attributes of the *dhātavaḥ* that follows is also of particular interest. Here Vasubandhu employs a list of attributes or *mātṛkā*, which contains very old parts,[11] thus again constituting a link with ancient tradition. The treatment of this material according to the oldest methods of the Abhidharma is in fact a gross anachronism in Vasubandhu's work which in form and spirit belongs to quite another age. All of this gives grounds to suppose that Vasubandhu's description of the doctrine of principles was determined by a model that organized the material within the framework of the 5 *skandhāḥ* and then discussed the attributes of the subject matter presented according to an ancient method, that is, using a *mātṛkā*. He completed this description, which, in its antiquated framework, no longer corresponded to the stage of development of a later age, along the lines of a Pañcavastuka.

There are other observations which support this supposition. First, however, it can be shown that the completion of the description of the 5 *skandhāḥ* by additional material from a Pañcavastuka had taken place before Vasubandhu's time. This is significant, for otherwise it would be difficult to understand why a late author such as Vasubandhu the Younger (A.D. c. 400–480) should make the basis of his work an outdated and inadequate description based on the 5 *skandhāḥ*, followed by a discussion according to a *mātṛkā*.

As we know, the best comprehensive account of the Sarvāstivāda dogmatics before Vasubandhu's Abhidharmakośa is Dharmaśrī's Abhidarmasāra. It is well known that Vasubandhu relied heavily on the older work in his choice and arrangement of the material. If we now examine the beginning of the Abhidharmasāra, the following picture emerges.

After treating the necessity of recognizing the nature of the elements *(dharmāḥ)* and the role played by the defiled *(sāsravāḥ)* elements, Dharmaśrī starts to discuss the 5 *skandhāḥ*[12] and explains their relationship to the *dhātavaḥ* and the *āyatanāni*. He then discusses the attributes of the *dhātavaḥ*,[13] using a list which corresponds with the first half of the list in Vasubandhu's work. This takes up the remainder of the 1st chapter. In the 2nd chapter, Dharmaśrī discusses the origin of the elements. First he remarks[14] that the elements can only originate in connection with one another and not alone and by means of their own faculties. He does this with the examples of mind *(cittaṃ)* and the mental elements *(caittāḥ)*[15] and takes the opportunity to enumerate and briefly discuss the latter. He also discusses how many mental elements accompany each good or evil moment of cognition in the various spheres. He then turns to matter and demonstrates how many atoms arise together in each case.[16] Then he discusses the conditioned factors not associated with mind *(cittaviprayuktāḥ saṃskārāḥ)* which accompany the origin of all things, that is, the defining characteristics *(lakṣaṇāni)*, birth, duration, age, and transience.[17] The rest of the chapter is taken up with a discussion of the causes *(hetavaḥ)* and conditions *(pratyayāḥ)*, that is, the doctrine of causality. The following chapters in the Abhidharmasāra correspond to the 4th to the 8th chapters of the Abhidharmakośa. However, Dharmaśrī does not stop here but supplements his work with addenda, the second of which is of interest to us.[18] Dharmaśrī begins by stating his intention of treating collectively all the elements discussed so far. He thus enumerates the attributes that *cittam* and *caittāḥ* have in common: they have an object *(sālambanaḥ)*, are associated *(samprayuktaḥ)*, have an appearance *(sakārāḥ)*, and a support *(sāśrayaḥ)* and so forth. He then goes on to discuss the *cittaviprayuktāḥ saṃskārāḥ*[19] and the *asaṃskṛtam*,[20] enumerating them and adding brief explanations. The rest is of no special interest to us here.

I have gone into more detail than is perhaps strictly necessary for the question that concerns us here. However, the comparison with Dharmaśrī gives a very clear picture of Vasubandhu's working method. He goes much further than Dharmaśrī in terms of the wealth of the material he uses and in the profundity of his treatment of it. But the structure of his work is based on pure scissors-and-paste methods. Leaving aside for a moment the fact that he places his treatment of the unconditioned *(asaṃskṛtam)* first, he begins as Dharmaśrī does with a discussion of the 5 *skandhāḥ* and their relation to the *āyatanāni* and *dhātavaḥ*. Similarly, he discusses the attributes of the *dhātavaḥ* with the aid of the same *mātṛkā*, simply making it twice as long. With the discussion of the sense faculties *(indriyāṇi)* he introduces a heterogeneous item, but returns to Dharmaśrī's order again with the discussion of the mental elements *(caittāḥ)*, which also occurs at the beginning of Dharmaśrī's 2nd chapter. He has also taken over the introductory idea that *cittam* and *caittāḥ* must necessarily originate together, while discarding the context in which all this is treated in Dharmaśrī's work, that is, the problem of the origin of the elements. The subsequent discussion of the conditioned factors not associated with mind *(cittaviprayuktāḥ saṃskārāḥ)* is taken from a later chapter of Dharmaśrī's work, and here again Vasubandhu takes over the introductory enumeration of the common attributes of the *caittāḥ*. Given these circumstances, the reason why Vasubandhu concludes his 2nd chapter with a discussion of the doctrine of causality is surely that Dharmaśrī also ends his 2nd chapter in this way.

The extent to which Vasubandhu depends for the structure of his description on Dharmaśrī's work and how much he borrowed from him is thus evident. If we now turn to the differences and determine the reasons for them, it is apparent that it was due to the incorporation of the themes of the Pañcavastuka. Dharmaśrī was also familiar with these and took them for granted. However, he treats the *cittaviprayuktāḥ saṃskārāḥ,* and the *asaṃskṛtam*, the two subjects which had no place within the old framework of the 5 *skandhāḥ* and could only have been introduced artificially, in an appendix. Vasubandhu incorporates them into his description of the doctrine of principles, putting *asaṃskṛtam* first as *anāsravam*, where the *anāsravam* also has its place in Dharmaśrī's work. He puts the *cittaviprayuktāḥ saṃskārāḥ* in the same place as in the Pañcavastuka, namely, after the *caittāḥ*. It is evident that this was a conscious and intentional decision, since he felt it necessary to emphasize the five categories *(vastūni)*[21] precisely at the point where he leads into the new arrangement, namely, after his excursion on the sense faculties. It thus also becomes clear why, in contrast to Dharmaśrī, he discusses the simultaneous origination of the atoms before the simultaneous origination of *cittam* and *caittāḥ*, since this is the sequence of the 5 categories he has just enumerated. It also becomes clear why the question of simultaneous origin ceased to be of primary importance for him. In contrast to Dharmaśrī, he develops the 1st and 2nd chapter of his work into a homogeneous description of the doctrine of principles by incorporating the themes of the Pañcavastuka. Hence the detailed and systematic discussion of the *caittāḥ* and the treatment of all the *cittaviprayuktāḥ saṃskārāḥ* at this point. This would, however, have been incompatible with the subject of Dharmaśrī's 2nd chapter, the question of the origin of the elements, and Vasubandhu therefore omits this. Only in the incorporation of isolated passages from Dharmaśrī's work have some of the latter's themes been carried over into Vasubandhu's work.

However, let us return to the problem in hand. We have seen that Vasubandhu bases his description in the first two chapters of his Abhidharmakośa on an old-fashioned treatment of the material which divides it according to the 5 *skandhāḥ*, and that he supplemented it according to the themes of the Pañcavastuka. We have now seen that this is also the case with his predecessor Dharmaśrī, the difference being that with Dharmaśrī the supplementary material from the Pañcavastuka is merely added on as it were externally, whereas Vasubandhu incorporated it to a greater extent. With Dharmaśrī, we are thus confronted with the same problem as in the case of Vasubandhu, and we can try applying the same explanation here, namely, that his description was determined by an influential ancient model and that he supplemented its antiquated description in accordance with the subject matter of the Pañcavastuka. However, this again raises the question of whether there is any further proof for this supposition, and above all whether the existence of an ancient model of this kind can be proved or at least assumed to be probable. The only difference is that Dharmaśrī belongs to a much earlier period, at least two and a half centuries before Vasubandhu's time.[22]

In order to answer this question we should first look at Ghoṣaka's Abhidharmāmṛtaśāstra (A-p'i-t'an kan lou wei louen).[23]

The author is one of the teachers whose views are repeatedly mentioned in the Mahāvibhāṣāśāstra. The work itself was translated into Chinese between A.D. 220 and 265; that is, at a time not so far removed from that of Dharmaśrī. It is the 5th chapter of this work that is of most interest to us.[24] It begins with a few words about the defiled *(sāsravaḥ)* elements followed by a discussion of the 5 *skandhāḥ*[25] and then treats the 12 *āyatanāni* and the 18 *dhātavaḥ*.[26] A contrived, rather infelicitous link is used as an opportunity to make brief mention of the *caittāḥ*.[27] Then the attributes of the 18 *dhātavaḥ* are discussed, as to which of them are good *(kuśalaḥ)*, which are bad *(akuśalaḥ)*, and which are indeterminate *(avyākṛtaḥ)*[28] and so forth. This takes up the rest of the chapter. The fact that in terms of both content and structure it is virtually identical to the 1st chapter of Dharmaśrī's Abhidharmasāra is immediately apparent. Thus, we have here further evidence of the influence of the same model, which for reasons of brevity I shall henceforth call Pañcaskandhaka, as the counterpart to the Pañcavastuka.

Kātyāyanīputra's Jñānaprasthāna[29] contains evidence which is not so clear but all the more important. This work is very much a part of the old Abhidharma tradition. It treats its material in the traditional manner, sometimes even to an exaggerated extent. The old Abhidharma tended to work with lists *(mātṛkāḥ)*. A list of attributes was composed and a topic was discussed with reference to these attributes.Sometimes a list of doctrinal concepts was composed and these were discussed one after the other with reference to the list of attributes. This is the same procedure which survives in the Pañcaskandhaka, in the discussion of the attributes of the 18 *dhātavaḥ*. The Jñānaprasthāna also works with lists of this kind.

Two of these lists are of particular importance. The first can be found at the beginning of the 2nd Skandhaka.[30] It consists of 16 doctrinal concepts which are all connected with the doctrine of the *anuśayāḥ*. These 16 doctrinal concepts are enumerated, briefly explained and then discussed as to their attributes. The second list can be found towards the end of the same Skandhaka.[31] It contains a total of 42 doctrinal concepts, which are simply enumerated without further explanation. This is followed by the discussion.

The commentators of the Jñānaprasthāna attached great importance to these two lists. The authors of the Mahāvibhāṣāśāstra, who—to their credit—regarded thorough and searching discussion as more important than the scholasticism of the Jñanaprasthāna, gave a far more comprehensive explanation of the individual items of these lists than those given by Kātyāyanīputra. Thus, the explanation of the second list in the Mahāvibhāṣāśāstra, for example, covers 72 pages in the Taishō edition, whereas the commentaries that follow are dealt with in a mere 37 pages. The most extreme example is Che-t'o-p'an-ni's Vibhāṣā (T 1547), which limits itself almost exclusively to the explanation of the two lists.

Of these two lists it is the second which is of importance to us here. Closer examination reveals that it is composed of several parts. It begins (Nos. 1–6) with the 22 *indriyāṇi*, 18 *dhātavaḥ*, 12 *āyatanāni*, 5 *skandhāḥ*, 5 *upādānaskandhāḥ,* and 6 *dhātavaḥ*, followed by a set of attributes (Nos. 7–16). It continues with a number of numerically ordered doctrinal concepts (Nos. 17–23) concerned with meditation. Next 8 *jñānāni,* 3 *samādhayaḥ,* and *trividhāḥ samādhayaḥ(?)* are listed in no particular connection (Nos. 24–26). Finally (Nos. 27–42), there begins a longer series of doctrinal concepts, again numerically ordered, which is identical to the first list of the Jñānaprasthāna mentioned above. The different parts of which this list is composed thus stand out clearly from one another.

Here, it is remarkable that this second series of attributes is essentially identical to the list of attributes used by Dharmaśrī to discuss the *dhātavaḥ* in the first chapter of his work that corresponds to the Pañcaskandhaka. Furthermore, the fact that it is preceded by an enumeration of the *dhātavaḥ, āyatanāni,* and *skandhāḥ* suggests that the first two parts of this list were taken from a Pañcaskandhaka. The fact that the *dhātavaḥ, āyatanāni,* and *skandhāḥ,* which appear interconnected in the Pañcaskandhaka, are here enumerated in succession, is after all in the nature of a list. Added to this are the 22 *indriyāṇi* and the 6 *dhātavaḥ*. However, the latter are also treated after the discussion of the relationship between *dhātavaḥ, āyatanāni,* and *skandhāḥ* in the 1st chapter of Vasubandhu's Abhidharmakośa. This, and the fact that the 22 *indriyāṇi* are treated at the beginning of Vasubandhu's 2nd chapter, would seem to suggest a close link with an older model. However, if this part of the list from the Jñānaprasthāna goes back to a Pañcaskandhaka, this means that we have arrived at a very early period indeed, even if the Jñānaprasthāna is the latest of the canonical Abhidharma texts of the Sarvāstivādin.

Before we go on to consider other sources, we should take a look at the list of attributes used to discuss the *dhātavaḥ* in the Pañcaskandhaka. Changes will of course have occurred in lists of this kind in the course of time; it is only natural that they should have been added to and extended. However, it could also have happened that older material came to be regarded as obsolete and was thus omitted. The list in the Jñānaprasthāna comprises ten items and appears in the following form:

1.	*rūpi*		*arūpi*
2.	*sanidarśanam*		*anidarśanam*
3.	*sapratigham*		*apratigham*
4.	*sāsravam*		*anāsravam*
5.	*saṃskr̥tam*		*asaṃskr̥tam*
6.	*atītam*	*anāgatam*	*pratyutpannam*
7.	*kuśalam*	*akuśalam*	*avyākr̥tam*
8.	*kāma-*	*rūpa-*	*ārūpya-pratisaṃyuktam*
9.	*śaikṣam*	*aśaikṣam*	*naivaśaikṣanāśaikṣam*
10.	*darśana-*	*bhāvanā-*	*a-prahātavyam*

If we compare this with Dharmaśrī's list, we find essentially the same attributes. He omits 1, 6, 9, and 10 and adds:

savitarkaṃ savicāram	*avitarkam avicāram*
sālambanam	*anālambanam*
upāttam	*anupāttam*

Ghoṣaka's list[32] differs from that of Dharmaśrī in that he additionally omits 2 and 3. He adds:

adhyātmāyatanasaṃgr̥hītam	*bāhyāyatanasaṃgr̥hītam*

Vasubandhu took over all the attributes given by Dharmaśrī and Ghoṣaka and added an even greater number himself. Of the attributes from the Jñānaprasthāna that Dharmaśrī had rejected, he includes only no. 10. However, this particular attribute occurs so frequently that it could equally well derive from a different source. All of this points to a progressive development and moreover indicates that the oldest available form of the Pañcaskandhaka is indeed reflected in the Jñānaprasthāna.

We shall now turn to a wholly different kind of source: Asaṅga's Abhidharmasamuccaya.[33] This work begins with an enumeration and brief explanation of the *skandhāḥ*, *dhātavaḥ*, and *āyatanāni* (p. 1,7–3,11). Then comes a detailed discussion of the *skandhāḥ* (p. 3,12–12,12), followed by a much shorter discussion of the *dhātavaḥ* (p. 12,13–13,13) and the *āyatanāni* (p. 13,14–17), focusing particularly on the relationship of the *dhātavaḥ* to the *skandhāḥ* and that of the *āyatanāni* to the *dhātavaḥ*. Several rather odd discussions follow (p. 13,18–15,18). Then a long series of attributes is enumerated and assigned to the *skandhāḥ*, *dhātavaḥ*, and *āyatanāni* respectively (p. 15,19–31,5). This completes the 1st chapter.

It is immediately clear that this is another example of a Pañcaskandhaka. Indeed, the short work by Vasubandhu, which has come down to us in Chinese and Tibetan translation[34] and which is in actual fact nothing more than a free adaptation of this section of the Abhidharmasamuccaya, actually bears the title Pañcaskandhaka.[35] There are, however, some remarkable differences compared to the works already discussed here. In particular, the *dhātavaḥ* and *āyatanāni* are treated independently, although the *skandhāḥ* are discussed in much broader terms. Furthermore, the additional material from the Pañcavastuka has been fully integrated into the description. Both the *cittaviprayuktāḥ saṃskārāḥ* and the *caittāḥ* are treated under the *saṃskāraskandhāḥ* (p. 10, 15–11, 24), and the *asaṃskṛtā dharmāḥ* under the *dharmadhātuḥ* (p. 12,17–13,11).

The reason behind these differences lies in the fact that all of the sources we have been looking at belong almost exclusively to the Sarvāstivāda school. The exception is Asaṅga. It is true that he associates himself strongly with the Hīnayāna tradition—as I have demonstrated elsewhere, one of his most important achievements was to develop the system of the Yogācāra by appropriating and integrating the dogmatics of the Hīnayāna so that it could in every respect be considered the equal of the great Hīnayāna schools of that time.[36] However, the Hīnayāna school that he followed was not that of the Sarvāstivādin but that of the Mahīśāsaka. The first chapter of his Abhidharmasamuccaya—disregarding certain additions and adaptations—thus represents the Pañcaskandhaka tradition of a different Hīnayāna school.

The relationship of this tradition to that of the Sarvāstivādin is demonstrated by the following characteristic: if we examine the list of attributes that concludes the Pañcaskandhaka section of the Abhidharmasamuccaya, we see at first that it has been considerably extended. Significantly, it concludes with the remark that this process could be continued indefinitely (p. 31,5). However, if we examine it more closely and compare it with the lists we have found in the Sarvāstivādin texts, it is obvious that all 10 items from the Jñānaprasthāna list appear here again and in the same order (p. 17,8–18,10; 19,5–15; 21,8–26,11). Thus, although later than Dharmaśrī and Ghoṣaka, Asaṅga is closest not to them but to the Jñānaprasthāna. That is, he is part of a tradition which from quite an early date runs parallel to that of the Sarvāstivādin, but which remained unaffected by the changes taking place in the latter.

If we summarize the findings we have so far arrived at, the following picture emerges. At an early period of Buddhism, at the time of the old Abhidharma, we find a standard form being used to represent comprehensively the elements of being that were the material of the dogmatics. The canonical lists of the *skandhāḥ*, *āyatanāni,* and *dhātavaḥ* serve as a framework, with the emphasis, however, on the *skandhāḥ*. The *āyatanāni* and the *dhātavaḥ* are treated at the end and only in relation to the *skandhāḥ*. First the *skandhāḥ* are enumerated and briefly explained. Then they are discussed with reference to a *mātṛkā,* a list of attributes. This form of description seems to have been fairly widespread; it was in any case not confined to one school alone.

Later a form of description evolved which summarized all the elements of being far more comprehensively, was completely independent of the old form, and organized according to the 5 categories *(vastūni)*: the Pañcavastuka.[37] This new description signified an important advance, but had little influence. The Pañcaskandhaka, the old form of description, which was based on the framework of the five *skandhāḥ,* was already too deeply rooted in the tradition. The innovations in the Pañcavastuka which could not simply be ignored, were therefore taken over but not so much incorporated as forced into the framework in any way possible. Thus, the old form of the Pañcaskandhaka prevailed until the end of the Abhidharma period and the last, authoritative reworking of the dogmatics in the works of Vasubandhu the Younger.

What is the significance of all this? To understand this we must first bring to mind what the creation of the Pañcavastuka meant. In its essence, the Pañcavastuka represents an attempt to record exhaustively all the elements of being and order them systematically. Attempts of this kind are not, however, isolated phenomena in the history of Indian philosophy. It is rather a phenomenon characteristic of philosophy in the early classical period, a time when the older doctrines were being developed into complete philosophical systems. The process consisted of systematically collecting all the elements of which a given world view was composed and putting them so to say programmatically at the forefront of the description of the system. This happened, for example, in an antiquated form in the Sāṃkhya, in the form of the doctrine of evolution and in a more developed and systematic form in the list of categories of the Vaiśeṣika.

Now, judging by its structure, the Pañcavastuka also belongs to this stage of development. However, it can hardly be assumed that Buddhism played a leading role in this, considering that its interests lay in quite a different direction. It is far more likely to have been the great philosophical systems that provided the impulse for the creator of the Pañcavastuka. However, in terms of chronology this would mean that the Pañcavastuka was written around the year A.D. 0, or at any rate not much earlier.

And what about the time before this? How should we imagine the development prior to this? It is important to remember that the systematic development of the philosophical systems was also a gradual process. It was preceded by attempts at systematically collecting the basic elements that constituted a given world view. However, these attempts were confined to what was near at hand and more easily accessible. One example of this is the ancient epic text of the Sāṃkhya, which I regard as being of preeminent importance for the history of the Sāṃkhya and which I have therefore called the epic basic text. It begins with an enumeration of the elements, describes everything that originates from them, above all the objects of the senses and the sense organs, mentions the mental factors and their effects, and only then goes on to the rest of the topics. The Pañcaskandhaka corresponds to this. It begins with a discussion of matter, that is, the elements and derived matter *(upādāyarūpam)*, above all the sense organs. This is followed by a treatment of the most important mental elements.

Thus, the whole course of the development was roughly as follows: when the oldest Abhidharma began to deal methodically with the philosophical problems confronting it, it turned at first to the central concern of Buddhism, the doctrine of liberation. In the later course of development, the elements of being, which are a precondition for the doctrine of liberation, were systematically ordered, including matter with the sense objects and sense faculties on the one hand and the mental elements on the other. The framework was provided by the canonical concepts of the *skandhāḥ, āyatanāni,* and *dhātavaḥ*. The *skandhāḥ* seemed to have assumed more importance as the fields of matter and the mental elements can thus be more easily distinguished. I believe it is also possible that even at this early stage of development, matter was dealt with fairly extensively. This is possibly how the first Pañcavastuka came into being. Its description was to remain prevalent and authoritative until, with the general development under the influence of the philosophical systems that had grown up in the meantime, a new and much more comprehensive attempt was made in the Pañcavastuka to evolve a systematic doctrine of principles.

Whatever form this development took in detail, there are already two distinct stages of development apparent in the dogmatics of the early Abhidharma. The initial stage, which found expression in the Pañcaskandhaka, is a first attempt at philosophical systematics. The second, represented by the Pañcaskandhaka, is an attempt at a comprehensive and systematic doctrine of principles. From this important conclusions can be drawn. I regard the creation of the Pañcavastuka as the most important step on the way from Buddhist dogmatics to a philosophical system. However, before we follow this line of thought, it is necessary to cast our net further and examine the early period of the Abhidharma. [Cf. chapters I–IV]

VII

The Abhisamayavāda

1. Introductory remarks

Our investigation of the canonical Abhidharma works of the Sarvāstivāda school has shown how inadequate and unreliable this material is [cf. chapter II]. A brief recapitulation of the most important features reveals the following picture.

First of all, the material is by no means as extensive as it initially seems. A body of voluminous works has, it is true, been preserved; however, in consideration of the fact that these are distributed over a period of several centuries, the number is not in fact that great. In addition, there is the prolix treatment of the material: not content with stating something in general, valid terms once and for all, it repeats it for a whole series of cases in the same words. Furthermore, in all kinds of cases, numerous variants, in themselves unimportant, are differentiated. *Mātṛkāḥ*, spun out to extremes, are applied in a senseless, mechanistic fashion, leading to any number of indifferences and irrelevancies being discussed in tedious detail. The result of all this is that the real content of these works amounts to only a fraction of their bulk.

In addition to this, these texts by no means offer a complex systematic description of the Abhidharma. This or that topic is treated arbitrarily, almost at random. Furthermore, not everything is included in the canon of each school. In the Sarvāstivāda canon, for example, there is no work which corresponds to the Puggalapaññatti in the Pāli canon.[1] By turn, the Pāli Abhidharma does not contain a description of the structure and process of the world, such as the Lokaprajñapti. A number of topics treated are only mentioned in passing or dismissed in a formula, as, for example, with *karma* and *kleśāḥ* in the treatises of the Pāli Abhidharma.

The way the material is presented for long stretches in the question and answer form of the catechesis is also unfortunate. It all too easily results in clinging to purely superficial features. The question is discussed of how many elements of this or that kind exist, what relationship they have to one another and so forth. However, the question of why this is so is not examined and one searches in vain for an answer. The various combinations of the individual elements are discussed in tedious detail: fundamental questions remain as a rule untouched.

On top of all this, we have the unreliability of the transmission. The earliest Abhidharma consisted of lists (*mātṛkāḥ*) which were learnt by heart and to which oral explanations were given, similar to the Brahminical sūtra. And just as the latter were adapted and augmented in the course of time and did not have a fixed form until the advent of the written commentaries, and just as the explanations continuously adapted to the progressive development of the relevant system, it is also likely that a similar development took place in the Buddhist Abhidharma. Thus, we find new and old side by side in its texts. And in the earliest works there are explanations which correspond to a much later stage of development. However, this precludes for us the possibility of distinguishing the course of development from the sequence of these works.

Taking all of these factors into consideration, it will be clear that working with this fragmentary and questionable material is very different to the work on other texts. In order to clarify the origin and earliest development of the system of the Sarvāstivādin, the system which was brought to perfection by the great works of Vasubandhu and Saṃghabhadra and can be counted among the most important achievements of ancient Buddhism, we must employ different methods. I believe the following method to be the best. I intend to go forward in time until we reach the point where with the beginning of written transmission, reliable and usable sources start to appear. I shall take the stage of doctrinal development indicated by these sources as my point of departure and attempt to elucidate the beginnings and early stages of development with the aid of the Abhidharma works in particular, but also using all the other sources preserved from this early period.

There need be no fear of going too far forward, so that a gap emerges between the works of the Abhidharma and the written sources being used. For the origin and development of the Abhidharma texts goes forward to the time when the written transmission begins. And there were other works treating similar subjects in an independent form which originated alongside the latest Abhidharma texts. That they were not included in the canon is due to the fact that this only happened with those works which displayed the—by this time—venerable form of the Abhidharma texts. This period also saw the beginning of comprehensive, systematic works of philosophy and the first signs of independent philosophical thought. For the purposes of this investigation, the whole period from the beginnings of the Abhidharma to the emergence of the written transmission can thus safely be regarded as a unit in itself.

Turning now to the question of which of the works from the earliest period of written transmission are suited to be taken as the point of departure for an investigation and simultaneously serve to demarcate the period treated, I feel that the following qualify: Kātyāyana's Jñānaprasthāna, the Pañcavastuka by Vasumitra, and Dharmaśrī's Abhidharmasāra. The Jñānaprasthāna is the latest of the canonical Abhidharma texts of the Sarvāstivāda school. This is already apparent from the fact that it was not recognized by a part of the school known as the Ābhidharmika, which accepted only the six-membered Abhidharma.[2] Compared to the older works of the Abhidharma, it represents progress in so far as it attempts to collect and systematically organize the mass of material according to the most important concepts. The Pañcavastuka, as I have shown elsewhere,[3] is an exhaustive attempt to collect and order all of the elements of being, independently of the old canonical categorization of all elements according to the *skandhāḥ, āyatanāni,* and *dhātavaḥ*, and one which was obviously influenced by the earliest philosophical systems. It is brief and consists chiefly of enumerations and would therefore have to be supplemented by commentaries.[4] The Abhidharmasāra, finally, represents the earliest dogmatics of the Sarvāstivāda. It unites the most valuable doctrinal material created in the time of the early Abhidharma, forming a great edifice. It was an unsuccessful and perhaps impossible attempt, however, to forge a whole from everything contained in the early Abhidharma texts, and the last chapters present the material that could not be incorporated as appendices. Yet the foundations of this doctrinal edifice had been laid and they stood as long as the school itself existed. We may therefore say that it was not Vasubandhu but Dharmaśrī who was the great dogmatician of the Sarvāstivāda.

As for the chronology of these works, I believe Vasumitra's Pañcavastuka to be the oldest, as Dharmaśrī adopted the most characteristic doctrines regarding the *cittaviprayuktasaṃskārāḥ* and the *asaṃskṛtam* in his Abhidharmasāra. However, since he did not incorporate them directly into his system but added them on as a sort of appendix,[5] the distance between the two was perhaps not so great. The Abhidharmasāra itself would seem to be older than the Jñānaprasthāna. In Tao-yen's foreword to the translation of Buddhavarman's Vibhāṣā, it is related that after the Buddha's death, the monk Dharmaśrī wrote the Abhidharmasāra in 4 books and then Kātyāyanīputra the Abhidharma in 8 books.[6] Here I would like as it were to assert the principle of *lectio difficilior*. It would have been very natural to assume that a non-canonical work was younger than a famous canonical text. The opposite assertion would surely only have been made if a relevant tradition was known. This is by no means contradicted by the fact that the most extensive dogmatic work of the later school, the Mahāvibhāṣā, bases its commentary on the Jñānaprasthāna, since a work of canonical authority would naturally have been chosen for this purpose.

Out of all these works it is the Abhidharmasāra that constitutes the best starting point for our investigation, since, as we have already seen, it contains all the most important material created in the earlier period. However, before we begin, I should like to make a few introductory remarks about the nature of this work.

Seen as a whole, the Abhidharmasāra is divided into two parts, of which the first, constituting the first 7 chapters, contains the actual description of the system. The second part consists of appendices which constitute 3 further chapters. The structure of the first part corresponds to Vasubandhu's Abhidharmakośa, which is ultimately nothing but an extended reworking of the Abhidharmasāra, merely omitting an account of the structure and process of the world, such as Vasubandhu presents it in his third chapter.

Dharmaśrī's system is striking in that its individual components frequently not only fail to match but also even contradict each other. The discussion of the mental elements in the second book, for example, does not tally with the doctrine of the *anuśayāḥ* in the fourth book. The doctrine of the 4 *pratyayāḥ* contradicts the doctrine of the 6 *hetavaḥ*. For the subsequent attempts to harmonize them are purely external and do not touch the core of these doctrines. However, this means that Dharmaśrī united older, often contradictory doctrines in his system, but was afraid of altering them arbitrarily. That it was possible for such contradictory doctrines to emerge in the earlier period of the Sarvāstivāda school is understandable if we take into account the conditions under which the representatives of the early Abhidharma created these doctrines. For them it was not important—as it was for the representatives of the philosophical schools—to define the outline of a system and to develop this gradually. They saw themselves rather as part of the transmission of a doctrine which contained everything its disciples needed to lead them to the desired goal, that is, liberation. Only when one of them with a philosophical cast of mind discovered a problem were original views of their own developed. It was Dharmaśrī who first collated all these attempts and created a system as best he could, whereby the contradictions then however became obvious.

The following investigation will take Dharmaśrī's system as its starting point. We shall extract the most important doctrines and attempt to understand what led to their creation and finally to assign them a place in the general course of the development.

2. The principal features of the Abhisamayavāda

On examining the general features of Dharmaśrī's system, it is the doctrine of liberation which stands out as the basic core. This is not surprising for a Buddhist system. The doctrine is contained in chapters 4 and 5 (= Abhidharmakośa 5 and 6). The first chapter treats the *anuśayāḥ* as the cause of entanglement in the cycle of existences. The second chapter deals with the path that leads to their elimination and thus to liberation. We should thus begin with a discussion of the doctrine of the *anuśayāḥ*.[7]

The essence of this doctrine is as follows: 10 *anuśayāḥ* are attached to a human being and these are divided into 98 subtypes according to how they are eliminated and the sphere to which they belong. On the path to liberation, these *anuśayāḥ* are eliminated in a single process of cognition which consists of a beholding of the 4 Noble Truths and is divided into 16 moments, the *darśanamārgaḥ*, and through the contemplation of the 4 Noble Truths, the *bhāvanāmārgaḥ*. Once this has been achieved, the knowledge of the destruction arises, the *kṣayajñānam*, and the knowledge of not arising again, the *anutpādajñānam*—and thus liberation—is attained.

This is entirely new, being alien to the old canon of the sūtras,[8] and it gives rise to the question of what prompted its formulation.

Although it is not actually present in the old canon, the latter does contain a model which it obviously derives from. In the final form of the old path to liberation, which in my opinion goes back to the Buddha himself,[9] the process of liberation is described as follows:

When a disciple, after the necessary preparations, has entered meditation and has attained the fourth level of meditation, he first of all cognizes his previous existences. He then cognizes the fate of beings in general, how they pass away and are reborn according to their works. The following passage then reads:

so evaṃ samāhite citte parisuddhe pariyodāte anaṅgane vigatūpakkilese mudubhūte kammaniye ṭhite ānejjappatte āsavānaṃ khayañāṇāya cittaṃ abhininnāmeti. so idaṃ dukkhan ti yathābhūtaṃ pajānāti, ayaṃ dukkhasamudayo ti yathābhūtaṃ pajānāti, ayaṃ dukkhanirodho ti yathābhūtaṃ pajānāti, ayaṃ dukkhanirodhagāminī paṭipadā ti yathābhūtaṃ pajānāti; ime āsavā ti yathābhūtaṃ pajānāti, ayaṃ āsavasamudayo ti yathābhūtaṃ pajānāti, ayaṃ āsavanirodho ti yathābhūtaṃ pajānāti, ayaṃ āsavanirodhagāminī paṭipadā ti yathābhūtaṃ pajānāti. tassa evaṃ jānato evaṃ passato kāmāsavā pi cittaṃ vimuccati, bhavāsavā pi cittaṃ vimuccati, avijjāsavā pi cittaṃ vimuccati, vimuttasmiṃ vimuttam iti ñāṇam hoti; khīṇā jāti, vusitaṃ brahmacariyaṃ, kataṃ karaṇīyaṃ, nāparaṃ itthattāyāti pajānāti.

The similarity of this description to the doctrine under discussion is unmistakable. In both cases, the subject treated is the decisive process of liberation. The 4 Noble Truths are cognized, upon which the *āsravāḥ* or *anuśayāḥ* respectively disappear. The knowledge is attained that rebirth is destroyed and liberation attained.

It thus seems justified to derive the doctrine we are examining from this canonical model. However, besides these basic similarities, there are numerous and fundamental differences. Even if it is not an entirely new concept, the old canonical doctrine has nonetheless been thoroughly reformulated. Thus, the question we must ask ourselves is this: how and why did this reformulation take place?

To arrive at an answer to this question, we should begin by attempting to clarify why the new doctrine replaced the *āsravāḥ* of the canonical model with the concept of the *anuśayāḥ*. We can get a lead by examining the way the two concepts are used in the canon. To start with the *āsravāḥ*: these are already a terminologically established concept in the old canon and the group of the 3 *āsravāḥ, kāmāsravāḥ, bhavāsravāḥ* and *avidyāsravāḥ* are firmly anchored in the doctrine of liberation. The *anuśayāḥ* represent an entirely different case. In the early period, the word *anuśayāḥ* is mainly used in a general sense to mean a bad inclination. There are only isolated occurrences of a group of 7 *anuśayāḥ* and it only becomes more common at a later date. The canon does not contain a group of 10 *anuśayāḥ*. The group of 10 *anuśayāḥ* contained in the doctrine under discussion came about rather through the expansion of the group of 7 *anuśayāḥ*.[10] However, all of this means that the author of the new doctrine replaced the old concept of the *āsravāḥ* as rigidly determined in the tradition, with a younger, more flexible term which he then reformulated for his own purposes.

The fact that he took a term from the old canon and used it in his own sense instead of choosing a new expression for the new concept he had created can be easily explained. There was always, especially in the earlier period, the endeavor in Buddhism, which despite all change ultimately always claimed to promulgate the word of the Buddha, to continue the transmission and avoid any breaks with tradition. We will therefore encounter similar cases again and again.

What kind of reformulation took place with the doctrine of the *anuśayāḥ*? The old group of the 7 *anuśayāḥ* consisted of the following members: *kāmarāgaḥ, pratighaḥ, bhavarāgaḥ, mānaḥ, avidyā, dṛṣṭiḥ,* and *vicikitsā*. In the group of the 10 *anuśayāḥ*, the distinction between the *kamarāgaḥ* and the *bhavarāgaḥ* has been abandoned. Instead, the *dṛṣṭiḥ* has been replaced by a group of 5 *dṛṣṭayaḥ,* i.e.: *satkāyadṛṣṭiḥ, antagrāhadṛṣṭiḥ, mithyādṛṣṭiḥ, dṛṣṭiparāmarśaḥ,* and *śīlavrataparāmarśaḥ*. The abandoning of the distinction between *kāmarāgaḥ* and *bhavarāgaḥ* is easily explained. The distinction follows the model of the distinction between *kāmāsravaḥ* and *bhavāsravāḥ,* which in turn derives from the distinction between *kāmatṛṣṇā* and *bhavatṛṣṇā,*[11] but which had become meaningless in the meantime. But where do the 5 *dṛṣṭayaḥ* originate from?

It should be mentioned that there was no such group in the old canon. However, there were related concepts or at least related expressions. The *satkāyadṛṣṭiḥ* is frequently mentioned. Furthermore, it occurs together with the *śīlavrataparāmarśaḥ* in the group of the 3 *saṃyojanāni* and the 5 *avarabhāgīyāni saṃyojanāni,* which are both firmly anchored in the doctrine of liberation, since the disciple becomes *srotaāpannaḥ* and *sakṛdāgāmī* with the disappearance of the 3 *saṃyojanāni* and *anāgāmī* (*opapātiko*) with the disappearance of the 5 *avarabhāgīyāni saṃjoyanāni.*[12] The *micchādiṭṭhi* is often mentioned. Furthermore, it is related of a bad monk that he *micchādiṭṭhiko hoti antagāhikāya diṭṭhiyā samannāgato.*[13] And even though the *dṛṣṭiparāmarśaḥ* does not seem to appear in the old canon, the expresson *sandiṭṭhiparāmāsī*[14] occurs frequently. The group of the 5 *dṛṣṭayaḥ* is thus a characteristic creation using older material and it would not be wrong to attribute it to the author of the doctrine of the 10 *anuśayāḥ*.

However, the incorporation of the 5 *dṛṣṭayaḥ* into the old group of the 7 *anuśayāḥ* changed the latter fundamentally. The disappearance of the distinction between *kāmarāgaḥ* and *bhavarāgaḥ* meant that the *dṛṣṭayaḥ* constituted exactly half of the group. This also means, however, that the author of the new doctrine invested them with special significance, otherwise he would not have treated them at such length. Moreover, it seems evident that what was most important to him was what he added to the old doctrine and not what he merely took over from the tradition. With this, however, the 5 *dṛṣṭayaḥ* assume especial importance and it is with them that we must start in any attempt to explain why the old group of the 7 *anuśayāḥ* was expanded and then formed the basis of a whole new doctrine.

I believe that this can be explained as follows. The *dṛṣṭayaḥ* are all false views, that is, errors. According to the teaching of the Buddha, liberation comes about through cognition. However, a cognition can be particularly beneficial if it eliminates errors, the latter being even more fateful than sheer ignorance. In the old path to liberation, it was said that the liberating cognition brought cognition of the 4 Noble Truths, namely suffering, the origin of suffering, the cessation of suffering and the path that leads to its cessation, as well as of the *āsravāḥ*, their origin, cessation and the path that leads to their cessation. This is formulated in general terms. Why the cessation of the *āsravāḥ* occurs and why the mind is liberated from them is not expressly stated. Everything becomes clear, however, when the *āsravāḥ* are replaced by errors which are eliminated by cognition. I would therefore like to state that the new doctrine was created to establish a causal relation between liberating cognition and the disappearance of the *āsravāḥ*, in order to explain and clarify the process of liberation.

The following evidence also supports this view. As was established at the beginning of this essay [p. 154], the 10 *anuśayāḥ* divide into numerous subtypes according to the new doctrine. The basic principle here is the distinction between 5 types (*prakārāḥ*), according to the way each is eliminated. A distinction was made between *duḥkhadarśanaprahātavyāḥ, samudayadarśanaprahātavyāḥ, nirodhadarśanaprahātavyāḥ, mārgadarśanaprahātavyāḥ,* and *bhāvanāprahātavyā anuśayāḥ*. While the distinction between *duḥkha-, samudaya-, nirodha-,* and *mārgadarśanaprahātavyā anuśayāḥ* to a certain extent represents merely a division into subtypes, the distinction between *darśana-* and *bhāvanāprahātavyā anuśayāḥ* derives from a fundamental difference and it is to this that we shall next turn our attention.

Here it can again be demonstrated that the latter are concepts which have been taken from the old canon and given a new interpretation. For this purpose we should enlist the aid of the Sabbāsavasutta in the Majjhimanikāya.[15] There the Buddha speaks of the elimination of the *āsravāḥ* and distinguishes between seven kinds, according to whether they are *dassanā, saṃvarā, paṭisevanā, adhivāsanā, parivajjanā, vinodanā,* or *bhāvanā pahātabbā*. In the first case, with the *dassanā pahātabbā āsavā*, there is a detailed description of how man, by not heeding the elements that should be heeded, and heeding those that should not be heeded in the contemplation of the course of the world, comes to believe in a self, entangles himself in false views and thus becomes subject to the suffering of the cycle of existences. The disciple who has heard the true doctrine, on the other hand, does not heed those elements which should not be heeded and heeds those elements that should be heeded, upon which the *āsravāḥ* disappear, is finally liberated through the cognition of the 4 Noble Truths[16] from the 3 *saṃyojanāni, satkāyadṛṣṭiḥ, vicikitsā,* and *śīlavrataparāmarśaḥ*. In the case of the *bhāvanāpahātabbā āsavā*, according to old usage, *bhāvanā* means "a bringing forth," "practice," that is here the practice of the 7 *bodhyaṅgāni*, the members of enlightenment; once these have been practised, the *āsravāḥ* cannot bring suffering and pain any longer. We can dispense with the explanation of the other kinds here.

It was from this canonical description that the new doctrine obviously took the two concepts of the *darśanaprahātavyāḥ* and the *bhāvanāprahātavyā anuśayāḥ*, but it endowed them with new content. According to this doctrine, the *darśanaprahātavyāḥ* are *anuśayāḥ* which are eliminated by beholding the 4 Noble Truths during the liberating process of cognition. *Bhāvanāprahātavyāḥ* are *anuśayāḥ* which are eliminated by the repeated realization of the knowledge gained, and I therefore translate *bhāvanā* in this sense as "contemplating". Thus, two concepts have been lifted from the canonical description: the first has been given a clearer, more precise definition and the second has been given a new meaning. Everything else has been discarded.

Why this happened and what purpose the distinction between and contrasting of these two concepts served in the new doctrine is immediately clear if we remind ourselves of which *anuśayāḥ* in this doctrine are exclusively *darśanaprahātavyāḥ* and which are simultaneously *bhāvanāprahātavyāḥ*. It is in fact the 5 *dṛṣṭayaḥ* and *vicikitsā*, that is, errors and doubt, which are exclusively *darśanaprahātavyāḥ*. *Rāgaḥ, pratighaḥ, mānaḥ,* and *avidyā*, that is, passions and the ignorance that accompanies them, are also *bhāvanāprahātavyāḥ*. Thus, the distinction rests on the insight that unique processes of cognition such as early Buddhism saw in liberating cognition, can indeed eliminate errors and doubt, but that the elimination of passions demands continuous efforts, the suitable remedy for which was seen in repeated realization of the relevant knowledge attained.

This also confirms the view stated above on the reason for the incorporation of the 5 *dṛṣṭayaḥ* in the circle of the *anuśayāḥ*. For they are, besides the *vicikitsā*, the only *anuśayāḥ* which are eliminated exclusively by the liberating process of cognition. They were thus necessary in order to explain the circumstances of the process of liberation.

Our investigation has, however, led us right into the middle of the train of thought of the new doctrine's creator, and we will now attempt to follow it further. For this purpose it would be best to examine the reason for the subdivision of the *darśanaprahātavyā anuśayāḥ* according to the 4 Noble Truths. Again, the best approach here is from the canonical doctrine.

To recapitulate: the old doctrine held that in the liberating process of cognition, the 4 Noble Truths are cognized first, then the *āsravāḥ* in the same form following which the mind is liberated from the *āsravāḥ*.

This doctrine is impressively presented in the canon. However, as soon as one looks for the causal connection, a wealth of questions arises. The cognition of the 4 Noble Truths and the cognition of the *āsravāḥ* are juxtaposed without any connection. What is caused by the cognition of the 4 Noble Truths when the cognition of the *āsravāḥ* is additionally necessary for the latter's disappearance? And how is the cognition of the *āsravāḥ* effective? A passion such as the *kāmāsravaḥ* does not disappear when it is cognized as such. Similarly, an ignorance like the *avidyāsravaḥ* does not disappear simply by one's becoming conscious of it. And even if the *āsravāḥ* are regarded as errors, these disappear by being corrected, that is, through the correct cognition of what was previously cognized incorrectly, and one is consequently aware of having been entangled in an error. Why then is only the cognition of the *āsravāḥ* mentioned? The canon with its general formulations leaves these questions unanswered.

What the creator of the new doctrine thought about this and how he attempted to solve these questions can be seen from the subdivision of the *darśanaprahātavyā anuśayāḥ* and the connection established thereby of the *anuśayāḥ* with the 4 Noble Truths. This connection was apparently arrived at in the following manner: its point of departure was that liberation results from cognition and that the *āsravāḥ* or *anuśayāḥ* subsequently disappear. What is this cognition? The unconnected juxtaposition of two cognitions—that of the 4 Noble Truths and that of the *āsravāḥ*—was untenable, given his endeavors to investigate the relationships between things. On the other hand, it was impossible for him to discard the cognition of the 4 Noble Truths, since they had been inextricably bound up with the revelations of the Buddha since the Sermon at Benares. Therefore a connection had to be established between the disappearance of the *anuśayāḥ* and the cognition of the 4 Noble Truths, with the former being derived from the latter. This was possible if the *anuśayāḥ* were seen primarily as errors which could be corrected through the 4 Noble Truths. Then the things which had been falsely perceived as a result of the *anuśayāḥ* would be correctly cognized through the Noble Truths and the *anuśayāḥ* would duly disappear.

However, although this idea is apparently simple and clear, various problems remained to be solved in detail. Particular difficulties arose because of conflicting principles of categorization with the 4 Noble Truths and the 10 *anuśayāḥ* respectively. The individual Truths extend over the spheres of several *anuśayāḥ* and most of the *anuśayāḥ* extend over the spheres of more than one Truth. This means, however, that the cognition of one Truth eliminates several *anuśayāḥ* and on the other hand that the same *anuśayāḥ* can only be completely eliminated through the cognition of several Truths. Thus, further differentiation was needed to clarify the processes of the liberating cognition and the disappearance of the *anuśayāḥ*.

The main aim here was to establish a relation between the cognition of the individual Truths and the *anuśayāḥ* which they eliminate. This was achieved in the following way: it was said that each cognition eliminated those *anuśayāḥ* which were directed towards the same object as the cognition itself.[17] This is entirely natural, since each cognition that cognizes an object correctly thereby eliminates those errors which had incorrectly cognized this same object. Accordingly, a differentiation was made with each of the 10 kinds of *anuśayāḥ* as to which of them are focused on the object of a particular Truth and are therefore eliminated through the cognition of this same Truth. Thus the subdivision into *duḥkha-, samudaya-, nirodha-,* and *mārgadarśanaprahātavyā anuśayāḥ* was arrived at.

Had this principle of subdivision been generally applied, it would have resulted in 40 subtypes of *anuśayāḥ*. However, caution was exercised in determining whether it was justified in each case, and the following conclusions were reached: doubt, ignorance and the passions extend over the objects of all the Truths. With the *dṛṣṭayaḥ*, this is only valid for *mithyādṛṣṭiḥ* and *dṛṣṭiparāmarśaḥ*. By contrast, *satkāyadṛṣṭiḥ* and *antagrāhadṛṣṭiḥ* only extend over the object of the Truth of suffering. The *śīlavrataparāmarśaḥ* extends both over the latter and over the object of the Truth of the path. I do not wish to go any further into the reasons for this distinction here, since I intend first to clarify in particular the basic conceptions of the new doctrine. However, it is important to notice that the author of this doctrine—as is obvious here—not only tried to establish the general connections but also paid attention to the differences in individual cases. Taking the latter into consideration resulted, as we have indicated, not 40 but only 32 subtypes of the *anuśayāḥ*, 36 altogether if one counts the 4 *anuśayāḥ* eliminated through contemplation, that is, the passions together with the ignorance that accompanies them.

However, there were other things which seemed worthy of consideration in this respect. The distinction in Buddhism between the 3 spheres of *kāmadhātuḥ, rūpadhātuḥ,* and *ārūpyadhātuḥ* demanded attention, too. For it was held that the 5 subtypes of *pratighaḥ* were not present in the *rūpa-* and *ārūpyadhātuḥ*. Thus, only 31 subtypes of the *anuśayāḥ* are directed towards these spheres. However, with these the enumeration of all the subtypes of the *anuśayāḥ* was complete and the total for all 3 spheres resulted in the sum of 98 *anuśayāḥ* mentioned above [cf. p. 154].

These are the general features of the doctrine of the *anuśayāḥ* in Dharmaśrī's work. As we have seen, it is developed from the doctrine of the old canon by consistent examination of the causal connnections and forms a unified whole. I believe that in all essentials it can be regarded as a conscious and unique creation.

However, it seems that the new doctrine did not confine itself to the creation of the doctrine of the *anuśayāḥ*. As we have already seen, it developed this doctrine with continual regard to the doctrine of the path of liberation. It is therefore natural to assume that it also moulded the latter doctrine according to its intentions. Our next task will therefore be to examine the doctrine of the path of liberation in this light. The doctrine appears as follows in Dharmaśrī's work.[18]

§ 1 After a few words of introduction the description begins with a discussion of the 4 *smṛtyupasthānāni*. The disciple at first contemplates the body (*kāyaḥ*) according to its characteristics as impure, impermanent, suffering, and non-self. He then contemplates the sensations *(vedanāḥ)*, the mind (*cittam*),[19] and the elements (*dharmāḥ*) (v. 3). With the last of these four contemplations, the *dharmasmṛtyupasthānam,* he ultimately unites all these objects and contemplates them as impermanent (because they arise from one another), as void (because they are not self-sustaining), as non-self (because they are not independent), and as suffering (because they are full of misfortune and misery), and in doing so the immaculate eye of insight (*amalaṃ prajñācakṣuḥ*) arises in him (v. 4).

From the *dharmasmṛtyupasthānam* comes a root of good (*kuśalamūlam*) which is called "heat" (*ūṣmānaḥ* or *ūṣmagatam*) because the fire of undefiled insight (*anāsravā prajñā*) it contains is capable of burning up the fuel of all the conditioned factors. Its object are the 4 Noble Truths, which it cognizes in 16-fold form, that is, it cognizes suffering as impermanent (*anityataḥ*) because it arises from causes; as full of suffering (*duḥkhataḥ*) because it is transient; as void (*śūnyataḥ*) because an inward personality is lacking; and as non-self (*anātmataḥ*) because it is not self-sustaining. It cognizes the arising of suffering as cause (*hetutaḥ*) because it produces a similar effect; as an arising (*samudayataḥ*) because it continues itself in the stream (*saṃtānaḥ*); as a becoming (*prabhavataḥ*) because birth and death know no end; and as condition (*pratyayataḥ*) because dissimilar things succeed each other in the stream. It cognizes the cessation of suffering as cessation (*nirodhataḥ*) because it puts an end to all misery; as peaceful (*śāntataḥ*) because it extinguishes the fire of all the defilements (*kleśāḥ*); as preeminent (*praṇītataḥ*) because it surpasses all the elements; and as way out (*niḥsaraṇataḥ*) because it causes birth and death to cease. Finally, it cognizes the path (to the cessation of suffering) as a path (*mārgataḥ*) because it leads to the incomparable (?); as rule (*nyāyataḥ*) because it is not erroneous; as an entrance (*pratipattitaḥ*) because all saints tread it; and as vehicle (*yānataḥ*) because it leads out of the misery of birth and death (v. 5).[20]

After the *ūṣmānaḥ* a further root of good arises in the *kāmadhātuḥ*, called "summits" (*mūrdhānaḥ*) because it surpasses the *ūṣmānaḥ*. After this a third root arises, called "ability" (*kṣāntiḥ*) because of its capability. Both of these have the 4 Noble Truths as their object and both cognize the latter in the 16-fold form described above (v. 6ab).

Finally there arises a last root of good, "the highest worldly elements" (*laukikāgradharmāḥ*), so called because they open the door to nirvana and because they are the most excellent qualities in the mind of the worldly human being (*pṛthagjanaḥ*). They are based on a single moment,[21] because there are no other similar qualities apart from these in the mind of a worldly human being. If there were, these would also open the door to nirvana, which is not the case, however (v. 6 cd). The object of the *laukikāgradharmāḥ* is only the Truth of suffering which they cognize in 4-fold form, as also the first immaculate cognition (*anāsravaṃ cittam*) (v. 7a).

The *laukikāgradharmāḥ* belong to 6 levels of spheres: the *anāgamyam, dhyānāntaram,* and the 4 *mauladhyānāni*; but not to the *kāmadhātuḥ*, because there is no meditation in it, nor to the *ārūpyadhātuḥ*, because this lacks the *darśanamārgaḥ* (v. 7b). The same holds for the *kṣāntiḥ*. By contrast, the *ūṣmānaḥ,* and the *mūrdhānaḥ* can also belong to the *kāmadhātuḥ* if craving has not yet been overcome; otherwise they belong to the *rūpadhātuḥ* (v. 7 cd).

§ 2 From the *laukikāgradharmāḥ* arises an "ability" (*kṣāntiḥ*), which directs itself towards the Truth of suffering. It is called the *duḥkhe dharma(jñāna) kṣāntiḥ* because it is capable of cognizing something which has not previously been cognized. It is the first immaculate (*amalaḥ*) *ānantaryamārgaḥ*. It is followed by a cognition (*jñānam*) which has the same object, namely, the *duḥkhe dharmajñānam*. This is a *vimuktimārgaḥ*. However, both the *duḥkhe dharma(jñāna)kṣāntiḥ* and the *duḥkhe dharmajñānam* direct themselves solely towards the suffering of the *kāmadhātuḥ*

(v. 8). Directed towards the suffering of the higher spheres are a new *kṣāntiḥ* and *jñānam*, which are again *ānantarya-* and *vimuktimārgaḥ*, but which are called "*duḥkhe anvaya(jñāna)kṣāntiḥ*" and "*anvayajñānam*". With these 4 "paths" (*mārgāḥ*), the Truth of suffering is fully cognized. In the same way, four cognitions direct themselves towards each of the other Noble Truths respectively: *dharma(jñāna)kṣāntiḥ* and *dharmajñānam, anvaya(jñāna)kṣāntiḥ,* and *anvayajñānam*. Thus, the entire process of liberating cognition, the insight into the Truth, the *dharmābhisamayaḥ*, encompasses 16 moments of cognition (v. 9).

§ 3a In the first 15 moments of the *darśanamārgaḥ,* the disciple is *dharmānusārī* if his capacities (faith, etc.) are strong (*tīkṣṇendriyaḥ*), and *śraddhānusārī* if they are weak (*mṛdvindriyaḥ*) (v. 10). There are 9 kinds of *anuśayāḥ* (which can be eliminated through contemplation), classified according to whether they are weak-weak, weak-moderate, weak-excessive, moderate-weak, moderate-moderate, moderate-excessive, excessive-weak, excessive-moderate or excessive-excessive. If the disciple who is striving for the fruit of asceticism (*śrāmaṇyaphalam*)—whether he is *śraddhānusārī* or *dharmānusārī*—(while having been *pṛthagjanaḥ*) has not yet eliminated these passions, then he is on the path (*pratipannakaḥ*) to the fruit of the *srotaāpannaḥ*. If he has eliminated 6 of these kinds, he is on the path to the fruit of the *sakṛdāgāmī*. If he has eliminated all 9 kinds, he is on the path to the fruit of the *anāgāmī* (v. 11). At the 16th moment of the *darśanamārgaḥ*, that is, at the moment of the *mārge anvayajñānam*, the disciple finally attains possession of the fruit; he is *phalasthaḥ* and thus *srotaāpannaḥ, sakṛdāgāmī,* or *anāgāmī*. And he is no longer *śraddhānusārī* or *dharmānusārī* but *śraddhādhimuktaḥ* or *dṛṣṭiprāptaḥ* (v. 12).

§ 3b If the *śraddhādhimuktaḥ* or *dṛṣṭiprāptaḥ* has not yet freed himself from the *anuśayāḥ,* which are directed towards the *kāmadhātuḥ* and are eliminated through contemplation, he will be born again a maximum of seven times among the gods and in the world of men (*saptakṛtvaḥparamaḥ*). If he has destroyed 3 kinds of *anuśayāḥ*—those which are excessive-weak, excessive-moderate and excessive-excessive—he is then a *kulaṃkulaḥ*, that is, he will be born again into a maximum of two or three families among the gods and in the world of men and will afterwards enter nirvana. Both the *saptakṛtvaḥparamaḥ* and the *kulaṃkulaḥ* are *srotaāpannaḥ* (v. 13). If the disciple has destroyed 6 kinds of *anuśayāḥ*, those which are excessive and those which are moderate, he is *sakṛdāgāmī*, that is, he will be born again one more time among the gods and then one more time in the world of men, that is, he will return one more time before entering nirvana. If he has destroyed 8 kinds, he is *ekavīcikaḥ* and will only be reborn once. If he has destroyed all 9 kinds of *anuśayāḥ*, he is *anāgāmī* and does not return to the *kāmadhātuḥ* because he has overcome the mire of the cravings (v. 14). However, just as in the *kāmadhātuḥ*, there are also nine 9 kinds of *anuśayāḥ* in the higher spheres, namely, on the 8 levels (*bhūmayaḥ*) of the Brahmalokaḥ, the Ābhāsvarāḥ, the Śubhakṛtsnāḥ, the Bṛhatphalāḥ (?), the *ākāśānantyāyatanam*, the *vijñānānantyāyatanam*, the *ākiṃcanyāyatanam*, and the *naivasaṃjñānāsaṃjñāyatanam*. All of these *anuśayāḥ* can be destroyed on the two paths, that of the *ānantaryamārgaḥ* and that of the *vimuktimārgaḥ* (v. 15).

§ 4 There are two paths (of contemplation); the worldly path (*laukikaḥ*) and the pure path (*anāsravaḥ* = *lokottaraḥ*). Of eight levels—the level of the *kāmadhātuḥ*, the four levels of the *rūpadhātuḥ* and the first three levels of the *ārūpyadhātuḥ*—one can liberate oneself both on the wordly and the pure path. And the *pṛthagjanaḥ* also strives for liberation on the wordly path. The *śaikṣaḥ* who stays on these eight levels free of passions (*vītarāgaḥ*) becomes a *kāyasākṣī* when he attains the *nirodhasamāpattiḥ*, because he touches with his body an element which is like the nirvana (v. 16). The ninth *ānantaryamārgaḥ* of the disciple who is free of passions, which is focused on the level of the *naivasaṃjñānāsaṃjñāyatanam*, bears the name of *vajropamasamādhiḥ*. It is the last *śaikṣaṃ cittam* and bears the name of *vajropamasamādhiḥ* because with it all the *anuśayāḥ* are permanently and thoroughly destroyed and because the whole path of the disciple (*āryaḥ*) is thus completed. The first *aśaikṣaṃ jñānam* to arise next is the knowledge of the destruction (of the *anuśayāḥ*) (*kṣayajñānam*) and the definite cognition arises: "For me, all rebirths are destroyed." From now on, the disciple is a saint (*arhan*) and is liberated from all defilements (*āsravāḥ*) (v. 17).

Dharmaśrī's description is concise and often sketchy. Nonetheless, the essential features are discernible.[22]

The structure of this description is clear and distinct. It begins with § 1 the preparation for the liberating cognition (v. 3–7). Then follows the liberating cognition itself, the *darśanamārgaḥ* (v. 8–9). This is followed by the discussion of the *bhāvanāmārgaḥ*, i.e. § 3a, to the extent that it is practised before the liberating cognition (v. 10–12), and § 3b, to the extent that is practised after the liberating cognition (v. 13–15). The conclusion consists § 4 of the final moments of the path of liberation, the *vajropamasamādhiḥ*, the *kṣayajñānam,* and the *anutpādajñānam* (v. 16–17).

If we now examine this description more closely, it reveals a clear dependence on the doctrine of the *anuśayāḥ*. The distinction between *darśana-* and *bhāvanāmārgaḥ* rests on the distinction between *darśana-* and *bhāvanāprahātavyā anuśayāḥ*. The individual moments of the *darśanamārgaḥ* correspond—as is clearly attested by the later works that are dependent on Dharmaśrī—to the various kinds of *anuśayāḥ* which they eliminate.The classification of the *anuśayāḥ* according to the sphere they are directed towards is also taken into account here. We can thus say that the doctrine of the path of liberation and the doctrine of the *anuśayāḥ* are attuned to one another and represent parts of a compact design.

Thus, an important insight has been gained. However, to judge it merely from the standpoint of the *anuśayāḥ* would result in too one-sided a view of the doctrine of the path of liberation and would neglect essential features. In order to arrive at a precise understanding, one must view the path of liberation as such in its entirety, and above all examine the question of to what extent it is based on canonical models and to what extent it is an original creation. It is, of course, obvious that it is ultimately based on the old canonical path of liberation. However, the latter is limited to a small number of basic facts. The new doctrine, as described by Dharmaśrī, goes far beyond this. It makes not only a number of alterations but above all many new additions. It is the latter to which we must pay especial attention.

Essentially, the old path of liberation as described above,[23] asserts that the disciple, after the appropriate preparations, cognizes (1) the 4 Noble Truths, then (2) the *āsravāḥ* in the same way, by which (3) his mind is liberated from the *āsravāḥ* and he becomes aware of that, and finally he cognizes (4) that the cycle of births is exhausted for him and that he has no further rebirth before him.

The core of the path to liberation described here is constituted by the cognition of the 4 Noble Truths and the cognition of the *āsravāḥ*. These cognitions—as we have already seen in the discussion of the doctrine of the *anuśayāḥ*—are united in one single cognitional process which cognizes the Noble Truths and through this eliminates the *anuśayāḥ*. As we have already seen, two paths are distinguished for their elimination (taking into account the differences of the *anuśayāḥ*): the path of seeing, the *darśanamārgaḥ*, and the path of contemplation, the *bhāvanāmārgaḥ*. This part of the canonical path of liberation thus corresponds to sections §2 and §3 (v. 8–15) in Dharmaśrī's work. However, the latter contain much more material and are presented on much broader lines.

If we first examine section §2 (v. 8–9), which concerns the *darśanamārgaḥ*, we see that the new doctrine as described by Dharmaśrī does not limit itself to 4 cognitions for the 4 Noble Truths, that is, one cognition for each of the Truths, but assumes two cognitions for every Truth, a *darśanajñānam* and an *anvayajñānam*, according to whether this Truth concerns the *kāmadhātuḥ* or the *rūpa-* and *ārūpyadhātuḥ*. Over and above this it also divides each of these cognitions into a *kṣāntiḥ* and the *jñānam* proper. Thus, the cognition of each Truth consists of 4 moments of cognition and the whole liberating process of cognition of 16 moments of cognition.

What is the reason for this division? Dharmaśrī does not give an immediate answer. His presentation is brief and does not contain any explanations. There are, however, clues for discerning what is essential. The distinction between *dharma-* and *anvayajñānam* corresponds to the distribution of the *anuśayāḥ* among the various spheres, that is, it is conditional upon the doctrine of the *anuśayāḥ*. The fact that a cognition of its own is not assumed for each sphere is perhaps connected to the fact that for the disciple who is striving for liberating cognition, the essential thing is whether he is concerned with the sphere he himself belongs to or with higher spheres. Compared to this, the distinction between the higher spheres is less important.

An explanation for the names *dharmajñānam* and *anvayajñānam* can also be found in the old canon. The Saṃyuttanikāya contains a sūtra, the Ñāṇavatthusutta,[24] which describes how the disciple cognizes old age and death, their origin, cessation and the path that leads to their cessation. This cognition is characterized as its *dhamme ñāṇaṃ*. There follows a description of how the disciple concludes on the basis of this cognition that the ascetics and brahmins who have cognized old age and death in the past or will cognize them in the future all cognize them in the same way. And this is his *anvaye ñāṇaṃ*. The same is said of all the other different kinds of objects of cognition (*ñāṇavatthūni*). These two kinds of cognition, *dharmajñānam* and *anvayajñānam*, were united at an early date with two others, the *paracittajñānam* and the *saṃvṛtijñānam* (*pariye ñāṇaṃ* and *sammutiyā ñāṇaṃ*) to form a group of 4 cognitions.[25] However, the fact that a consciousness of their origins had not been lost is demonstrated by the Vibhaṅga, in that it quotes the above-mentioned sūtra for the *anvaye ñāṇaṃ* in the discussion of these 4 cognitions.[26] The author of the new form of the path of liberation now took these two concepts of *dharmajñānam* and *anvayajñānam* from the canonical transmission and used them for his own purposes. Just as in the canon, where the disciple infers similar matters in the past and the future on the basis of his cognition, in this new form, the disciple infers similar matters in higher spheres from his cognition in his own sphere. Thus, we have here yet another case where the author of the new doctrine took up old canonical concepts and expressions and reinterpreted them for his own purposes.

It is less clear what led to the distinction between *kṣāntiḥ* and *jñānam* with the cognition of each of the Noble Truths. There is also no connection with the canon in this case, since the term *kṣāntiḥ* in this sense is clearly a neologism. However, the following may perhaps serve as an explanation. According to the new doctrine, the disappearance of the *anuśayāḥ* takes place together with the cognition of the Noble Truths; indeed, this is given special emphasis. Now, the canonical path of liberation distinguishes between two moments in the disappearance of the *āsravāḥ*: they disappear and one becomes conscious that one has been liberated from them. It would therefore be logical to trace the distinction between *kṣāntiḥ* and *jñānam* back to this as well. This is supported by the fact that *kṣāntiḥ* and *jñānam* are also characterized as *ānantarya-* and *vimuktimārgaḥ*. The *ānantaryamārgaḥ*, which is also called "*prahāṇamārgaḥ*," means the disappearance of the *anuśayāḥ*, and the *jñānam*, termed the *vimuktimārgaḥ*, would thus be the knowledge of their disappearance.

So much for the *darśanamārgaḥ*. It seems complicated at first glance, yet is nonetheless simple. The 4 Noble Truths were the given factors, and apart from the purely external classification according to spheres which is determined by the doctrine of the *anuśayāḥ*, the only innovation affecting the essence of the process of cognition is the division of every cognition into *kṣāntiḥ* and *jñānam*. However, what is particularly striking and characteristic here is the conspicuous attempt to achieve a precise and clear demarcation between the various processes of cognition. The individual moments of cognition and their order are precisely determined and their order numerically established. And it is entirely characteristic that just as with the distinction between *kṣāntiḥ* and *jñānam*, the non-specific formulations of the canon are replaced with the assumption of definite processes of cognition.

Turning now to the *bhāvanāmārgaḥ*, one is struck by the breadth of treatment accorded to the path of contemplation and by the number of individual details it is furnished with. This cannot be attributed to the doctrine of the *anuśayāḥ*. For the four *anuśayāḥ* which are to be eliminated through contemplation are all directed towards the object of the 4 Noble Truths and are therefore to be eliminated without distinction through the repeated contemplation of these Truths. However, closer examination soon reveals the reason for this breadth of treatment. The distinction between 9 kinds of *bhāvanāprahātavyā anuśayāḥ* according to their respective strengths and also taking into account the spheres they are distributed among, results in a broad frame which is then filled in with material from the old canon. An additional factor is that the elimination of these *anuśayāḥ* can also occur in the state of the *pṛthagjanaḥ* before entering the *darśanamārgaḥ*, which again necessitated further distinctions.

We shall first examine the material that has been taken from the old canon. Besides the actual doctrine as such, which is limited to the fundamental ideas and systematically elaborated, the canon contains a wealth of instructions, directions and advice, such as the

Buddha had given his disciples during the course of a long life of teaching, in order to advise and support them in their spiritual endeavors. Some of this pertains to the moment, but much recurs again and again because it proved again and again to be necessary and thus acquired fundamental significance. The concomitant to this was that the disciple was shown how far he had progressed, what he had achieved and what he could thus expect and hope for. One of these instructions which recurs frequently reads as follows:[27]

> *idha bhikkhu tiṇṇaṃ saṃyojanānaṃ parikkhayā sotāpanno hoti avinipātadhammo niyato sambodhiparāyano ...*
> *puna ca paraṃ bhikkhu tiṇṇaṃ saṃyojanānaṃ parikkhayā rāgadosamohānaṃ tanuttā sakadāgāmī hoti, sakid eva imaṃ lokaṃ āgantvā dukkhass' antaṃ karoti ...*
> *puna ca paraṃ bhikkhu pañcannaṃ orambhāgiyānaṃ saṃyojanānaṃ parikkhayā opapātiko hoti tattha parinibbāyī anāvattidhammo tasmā lokā ...*
> *puna ca paraṃ bhikkhu āsavānaṃ khayā anāsavaṃ cetovimuttiṃ paññāvimuttiṃ diṭṭhe va dhamme sayaṃ abhiññā sacchikatvā upasampajja viharati ...*

Four levels are distinguished here. The disciple becomes *srotaāpannaḥ* with the disappearance of the 3 *saṃyojanāni*. If, in addition to this, *rāgaḥ, dveṣaḥ,* and *mohaḥ* have become weakened, he becomes *sakṛdāgāmī*. If the 5 *avarabhāgīyāni saṃyojanāni* disappear, he becomes *anāgāmī* (*opapātiko*). Finally, he attains liberation with the disappearance of the *āsravāḥ* and becomes an *arhan*, as is expressly stated at some points in the text. Another passage, which occurs only rarely, presents a further division as follows:[28]

> *idha bhikkhu sīlesu paripūrakārī hoti samādhismiṃ mattaso kārī paññāya mattaso kārī. so tiṇṇaṃ saṃyojanānaṃ parikkhayā sattakkhattuparamo hoti, sattakkhattuparamaṃ deve ca manusse ca sandhāvitvā saṃsaritvā dukkhass' antaṃ karoti. so tiṇṇaṃ saṃyojanānaṃ parikkhayā kolaṃkolo hoti, dve vā tīṇi vā kulāni sandhāvitvā saṃsaritvā dukkhass' antaṃ karoti. so tiṇṇaṃ saṃyojanānaṃ parikkhayā ekabījī hoti, ekaṃ yeva mānusakaṃ bhavaṃ nibbattetvā dukkhass' antaṃ*

karoti. so tiṇṇaṃ saṃyojanānaṃ parikkhayā rāgadosamohānaṃ tanuttā sakadāgāmī hoti, sakid eva imaṃ lokaṃ āgantvā dukkhass' antaṃ karoti.

idha pana bhikkhu sīlesu paripūrakārī hoti samādhismiṃ paripūrakārī paññāya mattaso kārī. so pañcannaṃ orambhāgiyānaṃ saṃyojanānaṃ parikkhayā uddhaṃsoto hoti akaniṭṭhagāmī. so pañcannaṃ orambhāgiyānaṃ saṃyojanānaṃ parikkhayā sasaṅkhāraparinibbāyī hoti. so pañcannaṃ orambhāgiyānaṃ saṃyojanānaṃ parikkhayā asaṅkhāraparinibbāyī hoti. so pañcannaṃ orambhāgiyānaṃ saṃyojanānaṃ parikkhayā upahaccaparinibbāyī hoti. so pañcannaṃ orambhāgiyānaṃ saṃyojanānaṃ parikkhayā antarāparinibbāyī hoti.

idha pana bhikkhu sīlesu paripūrakārī hoti samādhismiṃ paripūrakārī paññāya paripūrakārī. so āsavānaṃ khayā anāsavaṃ cetovimuttiṃ paññāvimuttiṃ diṭṭhe va dhamme sayaṃ abhiññā sacchikatvā upasampajja viharati.

Here, too, the distinction between the various levels according to the disappearance of the *saṃyojanāni* forms the point of departure. However, a number of intermediate levels have been introduced, some new levels added and everything accommodated within a much larger framework. This is provided by the doctrine of the threefold *śikṣā*, the *adhiśīlam, adhicittam,* and *adhiprajñaṃ śikṣā,* in that a distinction is made as to whether the disciple has practised to perfection only the first, the first two, or all three.

The new doctrine has taken over from these two texts the most important levels that the disciple has to pass through, adding the three levels taught in the first text, the *srotaāpannaḥ, sakṛdāgāmī,* and *anāgāmī*, to the *bhāvanāmārgaḥ*, in as much as this is practised before the *darśanamārgaḥ*. It adds the levels taught in the first part of the second text to the *bhāvanāmārgaḥ* which is practised after the *darśanamārgaḥ*. However, it has only taken these concepts themselves from the canonical texts. Their derivation from the disappearance of the various *saṃyojanāni* has been dropped. On the other hand, they are associated with the elimination of the various groups of *bhāvanāprahātavyā anuśayāḥ*. We thus have here yet another example of the new doctrine incorporating old canonical concepts, recasting and reusing them, however, for its own purposes.

Apart from these levels that the disciple has to pass through, the new doctrine also took over other doctrinal concepts from the old canon, in particular the determination of the disciples as *śraddhānusārī* or *dharmānusārī, śraddhādhimuktaḥ* or *dṛṣṭiprāptaḥ*. The designations of *śraddhānusārī* and *dharmānusārī* are also often found alone:[29] the disciple is termed *śraddhānusārī* who grasps the subjects presented by the Buddha in faith (*yo ime dhamme evaṃ saddahati adhimuccati*). The disciple is *dharmānusārī* when the things reveal themselves to him to a certain degree (*yassa ime dhammā evaṃ paññāya mattaso nijjhānaṃ khamanti*). Normally, however, all four designations appear together in the frequently recurring enumeration of the seven types of *pudgalāḥ*; the *ubhayatobhāgavimuktaḥ, prajñāvimuktaḥ, kāyasākṣī, dṛṣṭiprāptaḥ, śraddhādhimuktaḥ, dharmānusārī,* and *śraddhānusārī*. We may here disregard the first three, which form a group in themselves.[30] The rest are explained in this context as follows:[31]

> *idha ekacco puggalo ye te santā vimokkhā atikkamma rūpe āruppā te na kāyena phassitvā viharati, paññāya c' assa disvā ekacce āsavā parikkhīṇā honti, tathāgatappaveditā c' assa dhammā paññāya vodiṭṭhā honti vocaritā. ayaṃ vuccati puggalo diṭṭhippatto...*
>
> *idha ekacco puggalo ye te santā vimokkhā atikkamma rupe āruppā te na kāyena phassitvā viharati, paññāya c' assa disvā ekacce āsavā parikkhīṇā honti, tathāgate c' assa saddhā niviṭṭhā hoti mūlajātā patiṭṭhitā, ayaṃ vuccati puggalo saddhāvimutto ...*
>
> *idha ekacco puggalo ye te santā vimokkhā atikkamma rūpe āruppā te na kāyena phassitvā viharati, paññāya c' assa disvā āsavā aparikkhīṇā honti, tathāgatappaveditā c' assa dhammā paññāya mattaso nijjhānaṃ khamanti, api c' assa ime dhammā honti seyyathīdaṃ saddhindriyaṃ viriyindriyaṃ satindriyaṃ samādhindriyaṃ paññindriyaṃ. ayaṃ vuccati puggalo dhammānusārī ...*
>
> *idha ekacco puggalo ye te santā vimokkhā atikkamma rūpe āruppā te na kāyena phassitvā viharati, paññāya c' assa disvā āsavā aparikkhīṇā honti, tathāgate c' assa saddhāmattaṃ hoti pemamattaṃ, api c' assa ime dhammā honti seyyathīdaṃ*

saddhindriyaṃ viriyindriyaṃ satindriyaṃ samādhindriyaṃ paññindriyaṃ. ayaṃ vuccati puggalo saddhānusārī ...

Leaving aside the introductory words, which merely serve as a link to the previous paragraph, a basic distinction is being made here, according to whether the disciple bases himself on cognition or faith. The *dṛṣṭiprāptaḥ* and *dharmānusārī* base themselves on cognition, the *śraddhādhimuktaḥ* and *śraddhānusārī* on faith, *dṛṣṭiprāptaḥ* and *śraddhādhimuktaḥ* to a much greater extent. This is why some of the *āsravāḥ* have already disappeared in the case of the latter, while this is not yet so with the *dharmānusārī* and the *sraddhānusārī*. Finally, the 5 capacities of faith and so forth which belong to these two are enumerated.

If we compare this with the new doctrine, it is particularly striking that the latter has dropped the distinction between cognition and faith. This is understandable, however, taking into account the fact that it bases the elimination of the *anuśayāḥ* exclusively on *darśanam* and *bhāvanā*; that is, the new doctrine has no place for faith. In order to preserve the distinction between *dharmānusārī* and *śraddhānusārī* nevertheless, it assigns the 5 capacities of faith and so forth mentioned above to the former to a greater and to the latter to a lesser degree. This idea suggested itself since it provided a link with canonical texts where the various stages of the disciples are also derived from the strength or weakness of these capacities.[32] The distinction between *dharmānusārī* and *śraddhānusārī* on the one hand and *dṛṣṭiprāptaḥ* and *śraddhādhimuktaḥ* on the other is based in the new doctrine on the latter's having completed the *darśanamārgaḥ*, while the former have not. In addition, the doctrine teaches that *dharmānusārī* and *śraddhānusārī* who have through contemplation eliminated a number of *bhāvanāprahātavyā anuśayāḥ* before entering the *darśanamārgaḥ*, are on the way to the corresponding fruit of asceticism (*pratipannakaḥ*), while as *dṛṣṭiprāptaḥ* and *śraddhādhimuktaḥ* after the completion of the *darśanamārgaḥ*, they are in possession of that fruit (*phalasthaḥ*). Here the doctrine again makes use of canonical concepts and terms. For the canon also describes the disciple as being on the way to arhanhood (*arahattāya paṭipanno*) or on the way to the realization of this or that fruit (*anāgāmiphalasacchikiriyāya paṭipanno* etc.).[33]

With this, we have discussed the most important canonical concepts that the new doctrine took over and incorporated into the *bhāvanāmārgaḥ*. The question of what this had achieved is easily answered: the Buddhist schools were always concerned to preserve continuity with the doctrines of the old canon, since it was the teachings of the Buddha that they wanted to promulgate. Thus, right up into later ages, up to the time of Vasubandhu and Saṃghabhadra, we repeatedly encounter efforts to create a place for canonical concepts in the system, even if these had become obsolete and meaningless. The need to create a link with the old canon was of particular importance here, since the doctrine of the *bhāvanāprahātavyā anuśayāḥ* and the *bhāvanāmārgaḥ* which serves their elimination was completely new. In addition to this, as I stated at the outset, only an empty scheme of the *bhāvanāmārgaḥ* could have been derived from the doctrine of the *anuśayāḥ*. The addition of the canonical material resulted in a vivid picture of a disciple's career, whereby old, familiar ideas are encountered at every turn.

This, then, represented a significant gain. However, it would be quite wrong to see the essential achievement of the new doctrine in the adoption of the canonical material. What is far more important and characteristic is the way that the new doctrine made use of it and in particular the new ideas that it gave rise to.

As far as the disciple's career in general is concerned, the new doctrine presents a complete and uniform conception instead of the separate, disconnected approaches in the old canon. This was achieved by making everything dependent on the elimination of the *anuśayāḥ*. The sequence of their elimination determines the sequence of the stages that the disciple must pass through. Each stage thus receives its fixed place in the path to liberation. The causal substantiation is given here in that it is the elimination of the *anuśayāḥ* that leads to liberation. As we have already repeatedly seen, the new doctrine thus also here combines strict systematics with the endeavor to demonstrate the causal connections.

Nonetheless, up to this point everything is relatively simple. However, the adoption of the concepts of the *śraddhānusārī* and *dharmānusārī*, *śraddhāddhihimuktaḥ*, and *dṛṣṭiprāptaḥ*, which is connected with the distinguishing of a *bhāvanāmārgaḥ* before and after the *darśanamārgaḥ*, touches on problems of decisive importance. Let us first clarify what this concerns. The old path of liberation merely involves a single liberating process, through which the 4 Noble Truths are cognized and the *āsravāḥ* eliminated. This was no longer adequate when in addition to the *anuśayāḥ* which are eliminated through cognition, others eliminated through contemplation were also included. This resulted in the distinction between a path of seeing and a path of contemplation, the *darśanamārgaḥ* and the *bhāvanāmārgaḥ*. However, this gave rise to the difficult question of the relationship between the two paths: how does the one follow on the other? Which one comes first? The idea that had given rise to the concept of the *bhāvanāprahātavyā anuśayāḥ*, namely, that certain *anuśayāḥ* require repeated contemplation of the cognized Truths to be eliminated, logically led to the *bhāvanāmārgaḥ* being put before the *darśanamārgaḥ*. On the other hand, it had to be admitted that someone who has not followed the path of the disciple, or disciples who have not yet achieved the liberating cognition are also able to overcome passions. Because in their case this does not happen on the path of *darśanamārgaḥ*, it must therefore happen on the *bhāvanāmārgaḥ*. Thus, the distinction between the *bhāvanāmārgaḥ* before and after the liberating process of cognition was established. Now, however, other questions arose. Should not the contemplation which eliminates the same *anuśayāḥ* before and after the *darśanamārgaḥ* also have the same result? Why is a certain fruit achieved afterwards and not before? Why does the *pṛthagjanaḥ* not also become *srotaāpannaḥ* etc., if he has eliminated the respective *anuśayāḥ*? There was one thing above all which militated against the inclusion of the double *bhāvanāmārgaḥ*: the liberating process of cognition would lose its decisive importance if yet another path of contemplation were necessary after it. It would no longer be the conclusion of the path that the disciple had to follow, as in the old canon, and would not bring ultimate liberation.

In order to eliminate these difficulties, the new doctrine now employed the concepts of *śraddhānusārī* and *dharmānusārī*, *śraddhādhimuktaḥ* and *dṛṣṭiprāptaḥ*, using them in the sense that it had conferred upon them. It taught that the disciple becomes *śraddhānusārī* or *dharmānusārī* when he enters the *darśanamārgaḥ*, meaning that he becomes *pratipannakaḥ*; that is, he has entered on the path to that fruit of asceticism which corresponds to the *anuśayāḥ* he has thus far eliminated through contemplation. The new doctrine also taught that the disciple becomes *śraddhādhimuktaḥ* or *dṛṣṭiprāptaḥ* with the conclusion of the *darśanamārgaḥ*, and connected this to the idea that he has then become *phalasthaḥ*, that is, he has acquired the corresponding fruit. However, this means that the *bhāvanāmārgaḥ* is only effective through the *darśanamārgaḥ*. If it has been practised before the *darśanamārgaḥ*, the fruit this has brought about merely makes itself ready when the *darśanamārgaḥ* has been entered upon, and it is only acquired when the *darśanamārgaḥ* is concluded. The only *bhāvanāmārgaḥ* to bring forth its fruit immediately is that which is practised after the *darśanamārgaḥ*. In this way the difficulties mentioned above are obviated. The difference between the *bhāvanāmārgaḥ* before and after the *darśanamārgaḥ* is explained. At the same time, the latter gains new significance. It is true that it is now not the only path to liberation; this would no longer be reconcilable with the conceptions of the new doctrine. But because the *bhāvanāmārgaḥ* only becomes effective through it, it acquires in a way a key position and its decisive importance is assured. However, this meant that the old canonical doctrine had been fundamentally changed. Perhaps the use of old canonical concepts and terms, which originally had quite different meanings, was here particularly intended to obscure just how drastic this change actually was.

We have now discussed the aspects that are essential for an understanding of the *bhāvanāmārgaḥ* in Dharmaśrī's work. The last section of his work, which describes the ultimate moments of the path of liberation and thus the actual process of liberation itself, now also presents no difficulties, since it can be easily explained in terms of the material we have just clarified.

From what has been said about the relationship between *darśanamārgaḥ* and *bhāvanāmārgaḥ* in the new doctrine, it follows that it is only the *bhāvanāmārgaḥ* that can bring liberation, and this can only be the *bhāvanāmārgaḥ* that follows the *darśanamārgaḥ*. Again, it is only the former that can contain the final moments which bring ultimate liberation. Accordingly Dharmaśrī begins this part of his work by naming the two forms of the *bhāvanāmārgaḥ*, which he here calls "*laukikaḥ*" and "*anāsravo mārgaḥ*." He adds that the worldly path can only eliminate the *anuśayāḥ* of the 8 lower levels of the spheres. The *bhāvanāprahātavyā anuśayāḥ* of the ninth level, the *naivasaṃjñānāsaṃjñāyatanam*, are only accessible to the undefiled, supramundane path. Like all *bhāvanāprahātavyā anuśayāḥ*, they comprise 9 kinds according to their strength, which can be eliminated by an *ānantaryamārgaḥ* and a *vimuktimārgaḥ* respectively. With the ninth *ānantaryamārgaḥ*, the last *anuśayāḥ* disappear, and accordingly it is this which brings actual liberation.

All this is derived consistently from the new doctrine's conception of *darśanamārgaḥ* and *bhāvanāmārgaḥ* and their relationship to each other and is in this respect without flaw. However, it was completely novel to the old canonical tradition and to a certain degree divided from it by a gulf which needed to be bridged. The process of liberation as conceived by the new doctrine needed to be presented in a striking form which would make clear the role that had been ascribed to it. It was also necessary to establish a link with some canonical concepts.

This was achieved in the following manner. First, the ninth *ānantaryamārgaḥ*, which eliminates the last *anuśayāḥ* and thus brings about liberation, was given the name *vajropamasamādhiḥ*. In this way, it is elevated above all the previous similar processes. Links with the canon are also not lacking. While there is no *vajropamasamādhiḥ* in the canon, it does contain a *vajropamaṃ cittam*. For occasional mention is made in the canon of three types of human being: the *arukūpamacitto puggala*, the *vijjūpamacitto puggalo*, and the *vajirūpamacitto puggalo*.[34] The latter two are described as follows:

> *idha ekacco puggalo idaṃ dukkhaṃ ti yathābhūtaṃ pajānāti, ayaṃ dukkhasamudayo ti yathābhūtaṃ pajānāti, ayaṃ dukkhanirodho ti yathābhūtaṃ pajānāti, ayaṃ dukkhanirodhagāminī paṭipadā ti yathābhūtaṃ pajānāti. seyyathāpi cakkhumā puriso rattandhakāratimisāyaṃ vijjantarikāya rūpāni passeyya, evam eva kho idhekacco puggalo idaṃ dukkhaṃ ti yathābhūtaṃ pajānāti, ayaṃ dukkhasamudayo ti yathābhūtaṃ pajānāti, ayaṃ dukkhanirodho ti yathābhūtaṃ pajānāti, ayaṃ dukkhanirodhagāminī paṭipadā ti yathābhūtaṃ pajānāti ...*

> *idha ekacco puggalo āsavānaṃ khayā anāsavaṃ cetovimuttiṃ paññāvimuttiṃ diṭṭheva dhamme sayaṃ abhiññā sacchikatvā upasampajja viharati. seyyathāpi vajirassa natthi kiñci abhejjaṃ maṇi vā pāsāṇo vā, evam eva kho idhekacco puggalo āsavānaṃ khayā anāsavaṃ cetovimuttiṃ paññāvimuttiṃ diṭṭheva dhamme sayaṃ abhiññā sacchikatvā upasampajja viharati ...*

Here, the cognition during the process of liberation is compared to a bolt of lightning and a diamond. It was thus natural to give the last *ānantaryamārgaḥ* the name *vajropamasamādhiḥ*. This was a felicitous invention, since it was new, like the process of cognition that it denoted, yet also invoked canonical associations.

Giving the name *kṣayajñānam* to the last cognition provided a further association with the canon. The old path of liberation already speaks of a *kṣayajñānam* in the following passage: *so evam samāhite citte parisuddhe pariyodāte anaṅgaṇe vigatūpakkilese mudubhūte kammaniye ṭhite āneñjappatte āsavānaṃ khayañāṇāya cittaṃ abhininnāmeti.*[35] In addition, the old canon mentions a *kṣayajñānaṃ* together with an *anutpādajñānam*, which are both mentioned alone and also enumerated within a larger group of *jñānāni.*[36] Both are derived from the ultimate words of the old path of liberation, where it says: *khīṇā jāti, vusitaṃ brahmacariyaṃ, kataṃ karaṇīyaṃ, nāparaṃ itthattāyāti pajānāti,* a derivation that remained as a memory until a relatively late period.[37]

In Dharmaśrī's description, *kṣayajñānam* is used in the first sense, as the cognition of the elimination of the *anuśayāḥ*. And since, as we have seen,[38] according to the new doctrine, every *ānantaryamārgaḥ* as *kṣāntiḥ*, that is, as the elimination of the relevant *anuśayāḥ*, is followed by a *vimuktimārgaḥ* as *jñānam,* that is, as the consciousness of their elimination, so here the *kṣayajñānam* is the ninth *vimuktimārgaḥ* that follows the ninth *ānantaryamārgaḥ* and concludes the whole process of liberation.

The designation of the last *vimuktimārgaḥ* as *kṣayajñānam* demonstrates the intention of forming a link with the old canonical doctrine. However, this is not all. Immediately afterwards Dharmaśrī has the cognition that from now on all rebirths are eliminated. Thus, here and in the old canon, *kṣayajñānam* and *anutpādajñānam* are side by side at the end of the path of liberation. Involuntarily the memory of the old, familiar doctrine is evoked, creating the impression that it is being described in both cases.

Finally, this section displays yet another point of contact with the old canon. Before the last *ānantaryamārgaḥ* it is mentioned that the disciple who has come thus far in attaining the *nirodhasamāpattiḥ* becomes a *kāyasākṣī*. I have disregarded this so far because it does not necessarily belong to the path of liberation as developed in the new doctrine. This is, rather, an ancient canonical view which is evidently based on meditational experiences, namely, that the disciple can attain a state where he touches the nirvana with his body.[39] This idea seems to have made a particular impression from ancient times onwards and thus had to be included in the new doctrine in spite of the fact that it could not be derived from the latter's basic tenets. And its inclusion here at the end of the path of liberation is not inappropriate. With this, yet another link with the old canon had been achieved, and this diminished the impression of unfamiliar novelty which the new doctrine would otherwise inevitably have invoked.

What remains is to discuss the preparation of the *darśanamārgaḥ* in Dharmaśrī's description. (§ 1) This is divided into two parts, the 4 *smṛtyupasthānāni* (v. 3–4) and the 4 *kuśalamūlāni, ūṣmāṇaḥ* and so forth (v. 5–7). The former are taken from the old canon. The latter have no canonical correspondence.

Let us first examine the *smṛtyupasthānāni*. In the old canon, these belong to the most common preparatory exercises. Generally they are only discussed briefly.[40] Occasionally, however, one comes across detailed descriptions.[41] If we now compare these with Dharmaśrī's description, it is striking that even taking the concision of the latter into account, there are no individual correspondences. The contemplation of the body as impure, impermanent, suffering, and non-self is important in Dharmaśrī's version as preparation for what follows, but it has no counterpart in the Satipaṭṭhānasutta. The treatment of the *dharmasmṛtyupasthānam* is also completely different. According to the Satipaṭṭhānasutta, the disciple, in the case of the *dharmasmṛtyupasthānam*, contemplates one after the other the 5 *nīvaraṇāni*, the 5 *upadānaskandhāḥ*, the 12 *āyatanāni*, the 7 *bo-*

dhyaṅgāni, and the 4 Noble Truths. There is no question of uniting the objects of all the *smṛtyupasthānāni* and their contemplation as impermanent, empty, non-self, and suffering as in Dharmaśrī's work. It is, however, important in the latter as preparation for what is to follow. Under these circumstances it would seem justified to regard the use of the *smṛtyupasthānāni* in the new doctrine merely as a means of gaining a canonical starting point with which the new doctrine can be linked and from which it can as far as possible be derived.

The situation in the case of the *kuśalamūlāni* is quite different. Even their rigorous systematic structure is striking. Four levels follow one another. On each level the 4 Noble Truths are contemplated, each in fourfold form. This intensifies from level to level until the final level leads into the *darśanamārgaḥ.* The systematic structure indicates that this is a creation of the new doctrine. And in fact it has no canonical correspondence. On the old path of liberation, the elimination of the 5 *nīvaraṇāni* and the entering upon the various levels of meditation are immediately followed by the attaining of the cognition. There are no further preparatory levels.

Neither are there any individual correspondences. The names of the *kuśalamūlāni* are new. And although there are occasional linguistic associations,[42] these nonetheless turn out to be new concepts. In terms of content, too, there are only superficial similarities. Essentially, they are different. Let us take for example the Jhānasutta of the Aṅguttaranikāya, which is particularly instructive in this respect.[43] Here it is discussed with reference to which levels of meditation the elimination of the *āsravāḥ* takes place on. It then reads:

> *idha bhikkhu vivicc' eva kāmehi vivicca akusalehi dhammehi savitakkaṃ savicāraṃ vivekajaṃ pītisukhaṃ paṭhamaṃ jhānaṃ upasampajja viharati. so yad eva tattha hoti rūpagataṃ vedanāgataṃ saññāgataṃ saṅkhāragataṃ viññāṇagataṃ, te dhamme aniccato dukkhato rogato gaṇḍato sallato aghato ābādhato parato palokato suññato anattato samanupassati. so tehi dhammehi cittaṃ paṭivāpeti. so tehi dhammehi cittaṃ paṭivāpetvā amatāya dhātuyā cittaṃ upasaṃharati, etaṃ santaṃ etaṃ paṇītaṃ yad idam sabbasaṅkhārasamatho sabbūpa-*

dhipaṭinisaggo taṇhākkhayo virāgo nirodho nibbānaṃ ti. so tattha ṭhito āsavānaṃ khayaṃ pāpuṇāti. no ce āsavānaṃ khayaṃ pāpuṇāti, teneva dhammarāgena tāya dhammanandiyā pañcannaṃ orambhāgiyānaṃ saṃyojanānaṃ parikkhayā opapātiko hoti tattha parinibbāyī anāvattidhammo tasmā lokā.

The same is said of the other levels of meditation. The difference to the new doctrine is immediately obvious. It is true that the text speaks of things being contemplated as impermanent, suffering etc., but this contemplation is not directed towards the 4 Noble Truths and the elimination of the *āsravāḥ* does not follow on the cognition of these Truths. There is no scale of progression or established enumeration. The difference between the canonical tradition and the new doctrine is especially marked here.

However, if the *kuśalamūlāni* are in fact a creation of the new doctrine, what is then the reason for this innovation and what led to its creation?

To achieve clarity on this point it would seem above all imperative to take the following into account: in the canon, the attainment of the liberating cognition and thus of the elimination of the *āsravāḥ* is premised by entry into the state of meditation. On the path of liberation followed by the disciple according to the Buddha's example, it is described how the former ascends from the first to the fourth level of meditation. After this, enlightenment occurs. He cognizes his previous existences, the general destiny of beings in the cycle of existences and ultimately the 4 Noble Truths and the *āsravāḥ* and thereby attains liberation.

In Dharmaśrī's version of the new doctrine there is no mention of this. Without interruption the *smṛtyupasthānāni, kuśalamūlāni,* and the *darśanamārgaḥ* follow one another without any mention being made of entry into meditation. It is merely noted in passing (v. 7) that *kṣāntiḥ* and *laukikāgradharmāḥ* belong to the *anāgamyam, dhyānāntaram,* and the 4 *mauladhyānāni,* and that the *ūṣmāṇaḥ* and *mūrdhānaḥ* also belong to the *kāmadhātuḥ*. That is not all. Not only is there no express mention of entry into meditation; the naming of the *anāgamyam* at the point mentioned demonstrates quite clearly that the path of liberation can be followed without entering into meditation.

This is a radical innovation. However, it can perhaps be explained in the following manner. According to common conceptions, entry into meditation is accompanied by supranatural cognitions and experiences: either a clairvoyant seeing of things which are inaccessible to ordinary cognition or a cognition which goes beyond the ordinary forms of human cognition.

According to the canonical path of liberation, during enlightenment, the Buddha, and also the disciple, do in fact experience a clairvoyant seeing of their previous existences and the destiny of beings in the cycle of existences. However, the situation regarding the cognition of the 4 Noble Truths is quite different. Even if the Buddha has arrived at it in the state of meditation, this is a rational cognition which operates in ordinary forms of thought, which can be imparted to the disciple and which he can follow. This seems to have been the reason why the new doctrine detached the cognition of the 4 Noble Truths from its close association with meditation and declared that it was also possible without meditation.

This procedure would correspond wholly to the manner of the author of the new doctrine as we have become familiar with it thus far. The man who distinguished between the *anuśayāḥ* which are to be eliminated by cognition and those which are eliminated through contemplation, who accordingly taught the *bhāvanāmārgaḥ* besides the *darśanamārgaḥ*, this man would have been capable of understanding the cognition of the Noble Truths in all its particularity and to separate it from the meditational experiences as they were commonly understood.

However, the question remains of how the new doctrine conceived this cognition. For a cognition that the Buddha came upon during enlightenment cannot be a cognition of the ordinary, everyday kind. This question can be answered by calling to mind the path of liberation described by Dharmaśrī. There, the Noble Truths are contemplated step by step, in an increasing degree of intensity, until finally the *darśanamārgaḥ* develops in the course of a few moments to *darśanam*, to seeing, and thus to the certainty of their rightness. It is thus an intuitive cognition, which, after intense preparation, occurs as a sudden flash of conviction, which, as an intense experience, goes beyond ordinary cognition and yet is different from the characteristic meditational experiences.

This also explains the structure of the path of liberation according to the new doctrine. It focuses solely on the cognition of the 4 Noble Truths, since only they lead to the elimination of the *anuśayāḥ*. Since this cognition is of an intuitive nature, meditation, as unnecessary, fades into the background. Tradition did not permit it to be omitted entirely. Instead, the clairvoyant seeing of previous existences and the laws of the cycle of existences have been omitted from the actual path of liberation. On the other hand, the occasioning of the intuition demanded separate preparation. And this end was served by the *smṛtyupasthānāni* and the *kuśalamūlāni* introduced by the new doctrine.

This explanation of the path of liberation has at the same time given us an insight into one of the most idiosyncratic features of the new doctrine, namely, its conception of liberating cognition. That it is a consciously new interpretation of the liberating process of cognition is obvious from the fact that a new name was chosen for it. This was the term *abhisamayaḥ*, which I translate by *Erschauen* ("beholding"). The word is not as such new; it also appears in the old canon. However, there it is not used terminologically. *Abhisamayaḥ* is used interchangeably with *abhisambodhaḥ*, *abhisameti* with *pajānāti*.[44] In the new doctrine, by contrast, *abhisamayaḥ* became and remained an established term. Since the word was later used for names[45] and moreover serves to denote one of the most characteristic concepts of the new doctrine, I have named it Abhisamayavāda.

This concludes our discussion of the principal features of the new doctrine. As we have seen, it represents a self-contained system of thought, in which one part conditions the other. The doctrine of the path of liberation premises the doctrine of the *anuśayāḥ* and vice versa. In this, the same characteristic features are displayed throughout, an acute perception of the particular nature of things and systematic thought that seeks to establish causal connections everywhere. I therefore feel justified in seeing the new doctrine in all its essential features as the unique creation of a remarkable man. It surely represents the most important step on the way to the creation of the philosophical system of the

Sarvāstivāda. Here the archaic way of thinking of the old canon has given way to consistent philosophical thought.

Nonetheless, what has been discussed up to this point are merely the principal features of the new doctrine. These in turn give rise to a considerable number of individual problems. But before we concern ourselves with these we must turn to another task. In order to evaluate matters correctly, it is imperative to ascertain their proper place in the general course of development. We will thus be constantly obliged to take the doctrines of other Buddhist schools into account. In order to facilitate this we will first take a look at the canonical Abhidharma works of other schools. [Cf. chapters III and IV.]

VIII

The Sarvāstivāda

A Study of its Historical Development

The investigations we have undertaken so far have attempted to trace the origin of the oldest Abhidharma, which was first concluded with the comprehensive redaction of the Abhidharmapiṭaka of the various schools. In a recapitulating lecture,[1] I then tried to establish a link with the later systems. However, all of this only concerned the development in general. It provides only a broad framework, which has then to a great extent to be filled in. It is this purpose that the following studies are intended to serve.

The present investigation will examine the development of one of the most interesting philosophical questions, tracing its origin and the gradual evolution of its ideas. It is the problem of the Sarvāstivāda, which had long been a subject of intense debate, the doctrine of the real existence of past and future, behind which, in the wider context, stands the whole problem of time.

It is best to begin our investigation in a later period, from which enough sources have been preserved to provide firm ground under our feet. The sources which should be considered include above all the Abhidharmakośa of Vasubandhu the Younger, whom I believe to have lived from A.D. c. 400 to 480.[2] A number of commentaries on this work have survived, most of which, however, provide very little illumination. Second, the Nyāyānusāra by Saṃghabhadra, a younger contemporary of Vasubandhu's, a work which is approximately three times as long as the Abhidharmakośa, and which is particularly comprehensive.[3] In addition there is the Abhidarmadīpa by an anonymous author belonging to a branch of the same school as Saṃghabhadra, which has only partially survived.[4]

Prior to this group of works, at an interval of time which cannot be precisely determined at present, is the account of the Vibhāṣā, the great commentary on the Jñānaprasthāna. It has survived in three different versions:[5] in Hiuan-tsang's translation,[6] in the translation of Buddhavarman,[7] and in the Vibhāṣā of Che-t'o-p'an-ni.[8] The description in the Tattvasaṃgraha of Śāntarakṣita, who lived from A.D. c. 725 to 788,[9] may be seen as a late echo of a once lively intellectual debate.

In view of these circumstances, it will be best to start with Vasubandhu's treatment of this subject, which remained definitive throughout the following period. It is to be found as a lengthy digression in the fifth book of the Abhidharmakośa, which deals with the *anuśayāḥ*. Since Vasubandhu did not himself belong to the school of the Sarvāstivādin, but to that of the Sautrāntika, he first presents the doctrine and then attempts to refute it from his standpoint. His presentation is divided roughly as follows:

1. First the doctrine of the Sarvāstivāda is briefly formulated and proven from the scriptures (*āgamataḥ*) and by logical reasons (*yuktitaḥ*) (p. 295,2–296,1).
2. Then four different conceptions of the Sarvāstivāda are presented and attributed to four notable teachers of the school. The first two and the last are rejected and the third declared to be correct (p. 296,1–297,13).
3. Now Vasubandhu's polemic commences, starting with the third doctrine (p. 297,13–298,22).
4. Then he turns to the reasons set out in the first section and attempts to refute them in succession (p. 299,1–301,16).

It is clear at a glance that it is the second part of the presentation, which contains the different doctrines, that is of importance for the history of the Sarvāstivāda. This passage in Vasubandhu's work reads as follows:

> *bhāvānyathiko bhadanta-Dharmatrātaṃ. sa kilāha: dharmasyādhvasu pravartamānasya bhāvānyathātvaṃ bhavati, na dravyānyathātvam. yathā suvarṇabhājanasya bhittvā 'nyathā kriyamāṇasya saṃsthānānyathātvaṃ bhavati, na varṇānyathātvam. yathā ca kṣīraṃ dadhitvena pariṇamad rasavīryavipākān parityajati, na varṇam. evaṃ dharmo 'py anāgatād*

adhvanaḥ pratyutpannam adhvānam āgacchan anāgatabhāvaṃ jahāti, na dravyabhāvam. evaṃ pratyutpannād atītam adhvānaṃ gacchan pratyutpannabhāvaṃ jahāti, na dravyabhāvam iti.

lakṣaṇānyathiko bhadanta-Ghoṣakaḥ. sa kilāha: dharmo 'dhvasu pravartamāno 'tīto 'tītalakṣaṇayukto 'nāgatapratyutpannābhyāṃ lakṣaṇābhyām aviyuktaḥ. anāgato 'nāgatalakṣaṇayukto 'tītapratyutpannābhyām aviyuktaḥ. evaṃ pratyutpanno 'py atītānāgatābhyām aviyuktaḥ. tad yathā puruṣa ekasyāṃ striyāṃ raktaḥ śeṣāsv avirakta iti.

avasthānyathiko bhadanta-Vasumitraḥ. sa kilāha: dharmo 'dhvasu pravartamāno 'vasthām avasthāṃ prāpyānyo 'nyo nirdiśyate, avasthāntarato na dravyāntarataḥ. yathaikā vartikā ekāṅke nikṣiptā ekam ity ucyate, śatāṅke śataṃ, sahasrāṅke sahasram iti.

anyathānyathiko bhadanta-Buddhadevaḥ. sa kilāha: dharmo 'dhvasu pravartamānaḥ pūrvāparam apekṣyānyo 'nya ucyate, nāvasthāntarato na dravyāntarataḥ.[10] *yathaikā strī mātā cocyate duhitā ceti.*

This passage recurs with minor alterations and often verbatim in the various texts; in Saṃghabhadra (p. 631a13–b5), in the Abhidharmadīpa (p. 259,10–260,13) and in Kamalaśīla's commentary on the Tattvasaṃgraha (p. 504,7–23 = p. 614,7–615,7).[11] This is not in itself remarkable, for it was influenced by Vasubandhu's example. However, it is important that the same text is also to be found in the Vibhāṣā, and in all three versions (A p. 396a10–b23; B p. 295c6–296a2; C p. 466b7–28). In addition, it is also remarkable that this text comes at the end of the Vibhāṣā, as a kind of appendix. And as we shall see, the main part in the presentation of the Vibhāṣā represents a stage of doctrinal development which is already in advance of this text. However, this means that this text belongs in terms of content to an earlier period and that it has been included in the Vibhāṣā merely as a kind of doxographical appendix. Vasubandhu then placed it to skillful literary effect at the beginning of his presentation of the doctrine, thereby evoking the impression of a comprehensive description. And his example led to later scholars endowing this text with an importance which was no longer appropriate to that period.

What is the meaning of this text, which dates from the beginning of the period we are looking at? What is the problem that these authors were attempting to solve in such different ways? It is not the real existence of things in all three times, that is, present, past, and future. For that was part of the established doctrine of the school and is already presupposed by all the attempts at solution given here. It is also presupposed that things then occur in different stages of time (*adhvānaḥ*). What they were here trying to determine was rather their nature in the different stages of time. Thus, the question they were trying to answer was: if things are really existent in all three stages of time in the same way, what makes them different when one refers to them at one time as future, and at another as past or present?[12]

However, before we take a closer look at the various attempts to answer this question, we must ask a preliminary question: What prompted this sudden interest in this problem and these very different attempts at its solution, given the fact that the doctrine of the Sarvāstivāda had already been in existence for such a long time? I believe this can be explained by the general course of development. In the first centuries A.D., under the influence of the philosophical systems that had achieved significance, new and energetic endeavors grew in Buddhism to develop the doctrine. Whereas up until this time the experts had worked with the traditional concepts, ordering, classifying them and trying out all the different possibilities of application, now they were aiming at a deeper understanding and they thus attempted to interpret and justify these concepts. This is what happened here, too. It had already long been taught that the past and the future are really existent. Now justification was being sought for the nature of and reason for this; many different theories were posited and examined for their validity.

The first and apparently oldest of these theories, the doctrine of Dharmatrāta, which posited a difference in the state (*bhāvaḥ*) of things in the different stages of time, seems to have been quickly rejected. The reason given in the Mahāvibhāṣā (p. 396b18–22)[13] is that no such state can exist side by side with the essence (*svabhāvaḥ*) of things. Furthermore, this state would have to arise and disappear during the transition from one stage of time to another, which is impossible. Vasubandhu raises the objection that this doctrine is identical to the Sāṃkhya *pariṇāmavādaḥ* and the later authors took this over from him. However, the main reason for the rejection of this doctrine was in any case that the Buddhism of that period shrank from assuming a plurality or change in the essence of things. This is clearly demonstrated by the following three doctrines, which uniformly assume an unchanging essence of things and derive the difference of things in the three stages of time from external conditions.

The first of the three doctrines, that of Ghoṣaka, used, as would seem obvious, the characteristics of the conditioned elements (*saṃskṛtalakṣaṇāni*) as the reason for this difference. This way the essence of things itself remained untouched. Moreover, Ghoṣaka taught that things are always connected with one attribute, but are not unconnected with the other two, so that neither in this respect did any change ensue from the change in the stages of time. This doctrine, too, seems to have been quickly rejected. As already stated in the Mahāvibhāṣā (p. 396b17f.),[14] this would mean that the different stages of time would coincide, since all three characteristics occur on each level. And the scholars of later ages found this argument sufficient.[15]

Finally, the last two teachers, Vasumitra and Buddhadeva, avoided not only anything that touched on the essence of things itself, but moreover derived the difference of things in the different stages of time exclusively from external connections: Vasumitra deriving it from the place they take up within time, rather like counting blocks which are placed in different compartments, Buddhadeva deriving it from their relation to earlier and later things. Buddhadeva's doctrine was rejected immediately.[16] For according to the doctrine which was already held by the Sarvāstivāda at that time, which sees in all things a chain of consecutive moments, there is also successiveness in the past and in the future, and thus there must also be a present and a future in the past, as well as a past and a present in the future. Thus, it was Vasumitra's doctrine which eventually prevailed.

Thus far everything is clear and the appearance of ever new doctrines that attempted to avoid the mistakes of earlier doctrines is understandable. Now, however, we are confronted with something rather odd.

In the Vibhāṣā, the description of Vasumitra's doctrine is followed by the following paragraph (A p. 396b5–8; B p. 295c20–22; C p. 466b21–24): "The manner in which this teacher determines the stages of time is free of error. Namely, he determines the difference in the stages of time on the ground of efficacy (*kāritram*). If the conditioned elements (*saṃskṛtadharmāḥ*) do not yet possess efficacy, this is called the "future stage of time." If they possess efficacy, this is called the "present stage of time." And if this efficacy has disappeared, this is called the "past stage of time." In the texts of Vasubandhu and Saṃghabhadra, and in the Abhidharmadīpa, this addition is missing.[17] But subsequently the doctrine that this addition contains is always presupposed and expressly attributed to Vasumitra.[18]

A moment's consideration will lead to the realization that here two different, even contradictory doctrines have been conflated. Vasumitra's doctrine avoids assuming any change in the essence of things. The doctrine of efficacy (*kāritram*) takes a changing nature into account. The intention of Vasumitra's doctrine is clearly demonstrated by the comparison with the counting blocks, which excludes the idea of efficacy. The doctrine of efficacy, however, is on its own a wholly sufficient explanation of the difference in the stages of time. The place occupied by things in time loses in importance. What is the explanation for all this?

In order to answer this question, we must look at the wider context. For this purpose it would be best to look at the beginning of the discussion of the Sarvāstivāda in the Vibhāṣā.[19]

This discussion begins (1) with the presentation of a doctrine attributed to the Dārṣṭāntika and Vibhajyavādin. According to this, time (*kālaḥ*) is eternal, the conditioned factors (*saṃskārāḥ*) are not eternal. The conditioned factors move through the stages of time (*adhvānaḥ*). Like fruits taken out of one basket and placed in another, like human beings leaving one house and entering another, so the conditioned factors migrate from the temporal stage of the future to the temporal stage of the present, and from the present into the temporal stage of the past.[20]

Next (2) brief mention is made of a doctrine which denies the existence of what is past and future and sees unconditioned elements (*asaṃskṛtadharmāḥ*) in the present. It is immediately refuted in relatively close detail.[21]

Then follows (3) the refutation of the first doctrine. It reads as follows: first it is established that the past, future, and present elements only form one part respectively of the 5 *skandhāḥ*, the 12 *āyatanāni*, and the 18 *dhātavaḥ*. The three stages of time are thus according to their essence nothing more or less than these elements.[22] However, if they are these elements, then why are they called paths (*adhvānaḥ*)? For arriving and departing is not possible under these circumstances.[23] This is confirmed by a verse by Vasumitra, which is attached as a proof. So what is the differentiation between the three paths, the three stages of time based on? The answer given is: on the efficacy (*kāritram*) of the elements. If this efficacy has not yet occurred, then they are future. If it is in operation, then they are present. And if it has disappeared, then they are past.[24] Subsequently it is explained how efficacy is to be imagined in the individual cases of the *skandhāḥ*,[25] the *āyatanāni*,[26] the *saṃskṛtalakṣaṇāni*,[27] the conditions (*pratyayāḥ*) and causes (*hetavaḥ*),[28] in respect of the various effects (*phalāni*)[29] and in respect of the various causes (*hetavaḥ*).[30]

Of these three sections, we can discard the second for the present. The first and the third sections are all the more important for the answer to the above question. Moreover, there is also a parallel to the first of these sections, which confirms and completes its description. In the Vibhāṣā to the 5th Skandhaka of the Jñānaprasthāna, the same question concerning the essence of time occurs and there it says:[31] "The Dārṣṭāntika and Vibhajyavādin assume that time (*kālaḥ*) is different from the essence of the *saṃskārāḥ*. The essence of the *saṃskārāḥ* is not eternal, the essence of time is eternal. The non-eternal *saṃskārāḥ* migrate through eternal time as fruits change in baskets or as human beings leave one house and enter another. To reject this view and to show that the essence of the three stages of time (*adhvānaḥ*) are the *saṃskārāḥ*, and that because the *saṃskārāḥ* are not eternal, time is also not eternal, was the reason that this text was composed."

The essence of this discussion is as follows. The Dārṣṭāntika and Vibhajyavādin taught, as did the Sarvāstivādin, that things migrate through the different stages of time. At first their doctrine comes closest to that of Vasumitra. For taking fruit from one basket and putting it in another is the same as moving counting blocks from one compartment to another. The only difference is that they taught that time (*kālaḥ*) through which things migrate is eternal. This is rejected by the Sarvāstivādin. In addition to this they explain that the stages of time (*adhvānaḥ*), too, are nothing but the past, present, and future things themselves. Thus, there is no migration through the stages of time. The difference between the times is, rather, based solely on the efficacy (*kāritram*) of things.

If we now ask what this all means, I believe that we can say that an awareness of the problem of time had arisen. The history of philosophy mainly consists, after all, of a growing awareness of various problems. The earliest teachers, from Dharmatrāta onwards, had spoken in an unsophisticated, popular manner of migration through the stages of time. Now the question had arisen of how this was possible, of what time was. And thus the eternity of time came to be assumed perhaps under the influence of foreign doctrines such as the Vaiśeṣika. But with this, a new, foreign concept had been taken into the system and the orthodox branch of the school retaliated. It rejected the concept of time *(kālaḥ)*. But that was not enough. As a consequence, one also had to reject the ideas that had led to the positing of the concept of time, above all that of migration through time. However, this meant that the old doctrines, too, had become untenable in their original form. And a new reasoning for the explanation of the difference of things in present, past, and future had to be found. And this was discovered in the doctrine of efficacy.

Returning to the question we started from, we can say that our opinion that Vasumitra's doctrine and the doctrine of efficacy contradict each other is confirmed. Vasumitra's doctrine, which assumes the migration of things through the stages of time, is, even if it does not have a concept of time, closely related to the doctrine of the Dārṣṭāntika and Vibhajyavādin, whereas the doctrine of efficacy, which does not recognize stages of time and denies migration through them, is no less opposed to it than to the doctrine of the Dārṣṭāntika. Indeed, the relationship between them is almost that of thesis and antithesis. This, however, compels the conclusion that the equating of Vasumitra's doctrine with the doctrine of efficacy must be wrong.

But then what led to this equation? I believe that it was because they both bore the same name. The passage we have quoted from the Vibhāṣā names one Vasumitra as the representative of the doctrine of efficacy. This is not particularly remarkable, since Vasumitra was a name that frequently recurred at this period of Buddhism.[32] But just as in early Christendom, when the various different bearers of the name John were subsumed under one name and the works of different authors ascribed to one and the same author, so the same situation must have prevailed here and led to the older Vasumitra and the originator of the doctrine of efficacy being seen as the same person. That Vasubandhu's time did not take exception to this or to the associated contradictions is understandable. For the old doctrines were already remote and only transmitted out of doxographical interest.

Furthermore, a faint memory of the fact that several authors were involved here could have been preserved in the fact that the Abhidharmadīpa, after giving an account of the doctrines of the four early teachers and naming the bhadanta-Vasumitra (p. 260,3–6), then, designating the third doctrine as correct (p. 260,14–16), speaks of a sthavira-Vasumitra and characterizes him as an opponent of the Sāṃkhya and Vaiśeṣika (*pañcaviṃśati-tattvanirāsī paramāṇusaṃcayavādonmāthī ca*).

With this, we have now established a part of the historical development of the Sarvāstivāda. It begins with the question of on what grounds past and future things differ from present ones, if all are really existent. Various attempts at answering this question were made, starting with Dharmatrāta. Then the time problem cropped up. In the ensuing debate, the doctrine underwent a radical transformation and the concept of efficacy was established. This marked the end of the first phase of development. For, as a glance at Śāntarakṣita's Tattvasaṃgraha shows, this concept was retained right to the last. Everything else was limited to a thorough consideration and determination of this concept and defending it against opponents' attacks.

Next we shall proceed to trace the development of this concept of efficacy in detail. We shall again take Vasubandhu's account as our starting point.

As we have already established, it is the 3rd section in Vasubandhu's description which deals with efficacy (*kāritram*). He begins with a discussion of the various attempts to define this concept more precisely. It reads as follows (p. 297,13–17):

> *parigatam etat sarvam. idaṃ tu vaktavyam: yady atītam api dravyato 'sty anāgatam api, kasmāt tad atītam ity ucyate*

'nāgatam iti vā.—nanu coktam: adhvānaḥ kāritreṇa vyavasthitā iti.—yady evaṃ, pratyutpannasya tatsabhāgasya cakṣuṣaḥ kiṃ kāritram?—phaladānapratigrahaṇam.—atītānām api tarhi sabhāgahetvādṣnāṃ phaladānāt kāritraprasaṅgo 'rdhakāritrasya veti lakṣaṇasaṃkaraḥ.

As is usually the case with Vasubandhu, everything here is given in an extremely compressed form and limited almost exclusively to brief references. Fortunately, however, Vasubandhu's account has a counterpart in Kamalaśīla's Tattvasaṃgrahapañjikā. This source is admittedly late, but since its particulars are confirmed by Sthiramati in his Ṭīkā to the Abhidharmakośa and are thus proved to be ancient material,[33] we are justified in seeing in it a reliable transmission. The relevant passage reads as follows (p. 506,12–25 = p. 617,8–23):

kiṃ punar atra kāritram abhipretam? yadi darśanādilakṣaṇo vyāpāraḥ, yathā pañcānāṃ cakṣurādīnāṃ darśanādikam, yataś cakṣuḥ paśyati śrotaṃ śṛṇoti ghrāṇaṃ jighrati jihvāsvādayatītyādi, vijñānasyāpi vijñātṛtvaṃ vijānātīti kṛtvā, rūpādīnām indriyagocaratvam, evaṃ sati pratyutpannasya tatsabhāgasya cakṣuṣo nidrādyavasthāyāṃ karitrābhāvād vartamānatā na syāt.

atha phaladānagrahaṇalakṣaṇaṃ kāritram, yathā cakṣuṣā sahabhuvo dharmā jātyādayaḥ puruṣakāraphalam anantarotpannaṃ cakṣurindriyaṃ puruṣakāraphalam adhipatiphalaṃ[34] *niṣyandaphalaṃ ca, etat phalaṃ jananāt prayaccha ddhetubhāvāvasthānād gṛhṇac cakṣur vartamānam ucyata iti, evaṃ tarhy atītānām api sabhāgasarvatragavipākahetūnāṃ phaladānābhyupagamād vartamānatvaprasaṅgaḥ.*

atha samastam eva phaladānagrahaṇalakṣaṇaṃ kāritram iṣyate, evam atītasya sabhāgahetvāder ardhavartamānatvaprasaṅga iti.

etaddoṣabhayād ācārya-Saṃghabhadra āha: dharmāṇāṃ kāritram ucyate phalākṣepaśaktiḥ, na tu phalajananam. na cātītānāṃ sabhāgahetvādīnāṃ phalākṣepo 'sti, vartamānāvasthāyām evākṣiptatvāt. na cākṣiptasyākṣepo yukto, anavasthāprasaṅgāt. tasmād atītānāṃ na kāritrasambhava iti nāsti lakṣaṇasaṃkara iti.

Here everything that is merely alluded to in Vasubandhu's text is set out clearly and lucidly, and the gradual development of the concept of efficacy (*kāritram*) can be perceived without difficulty.

Originally, efficacy was understood merely as activity (*vyāpāraḥ*) on the analogy of the process of cognition, in the case of which, according to the old canonical doctrine, object, organ, and the cognition itself are active or efficacious. The first doubts concerning this view resulted from the realization that the organ, for example, the eye, is not always active, for instance, during sleep, and that, in this case, it thus cannot be present, if the presence of things is founded on their efficacy or activity.

This objection was countered by substituting simple activity by all the causal processes connected with it, which accorded with the doctrine of the causes (*hetavaḥ*), conditions (*pratyayāḥ*), and effects (*phalāni*) that had already been fully developed by the Vibhāṣika school by that time. According to this, the organ, in this case the eye, not only results in the cognition but also contributes to the origination of its own characteristics (*lakṣaṇāni*), namely birth (*jātiḥ*), old age (*jarā*), duration (*sthitiḥ*), and transitoriness (*anityatā*), and according to the doctrine of the momentariness of things, it also causes its own ensuing moment. In this it is not only *sabhāga*- but also *sarvatraga*-, and *vipākahetuḥ*, and its effects are partly *puruṣakāraphalam*, partly *puruṣakāra*-, *adhipati*-, and *niṣyandaphalam*. Now these effects are also caused when the eye does not bring about a cognition. Thus, if one were to determine the efficacy in the sense of this whole causal activity, the objection raised could be refuted, since the eye, according to this view, is also efficacious when it does not see, that is, it is present even then.

However, the following must also be taken into account. The doctrine of the causal processes differentiates two kinds of activity: the grasping of the effect (*pratigrahaṇam*), when the cause establishes the connection to the later effect, that is, gives rise to it (*ākṣipati*); and the giving of the effect (*dānam*), when it produces the effect. And in order to express both, efficacy was defined as the giving and grasping of the effect (*phaladānapratigrahaṇam*).

At this point the opponent cuts in with an objection. According to this doctrine, the activity of the causes does not only take place in the present. It is true that the grasping, that is, the giving rise to the effect only occurs while they are present.

However, the giving, the producing of the effects takes place only partly in the present and partly when the causes are already past. This means, however, that the new definition of efficacy applies not only to what is present but also to what is past. Thus, the opponent could rightly assert that according to this view of things, efficacy is unsuited to serve as a characteristic of the present.

A final attempt to salvage this definition claims that efficacy only exists when both the giving and the grasping of the effects are given. However, Vasubandhu quickly dismisses this attempt with the remark that those of the causes which are past would then be apportioned half an efficacy (*ardhakāritram*) and thus half a present (*ardhavartamānatvam*).

Such are the attempts to determine efficacy as far as they were available to Vasubandhu and were opposed by him. To this Kamalaśīla adds the definition given by Saṃghabhadra, a younger contemporary and adversary of Vasubandhu's. The former defines efficacy as *phalākṣepaśaktiḥ*. He has thus taken over from the two forms of causal activity only the *pratigrahaṇam*, that is, the *phalākṣepaḥ*. And since even according to the traditional doctrine this is only given in the case of present causes, the objection that the definition also applies to past causes is void. It is furthermore of importance that Saṃghabhadra defines efficacy by nature as a power (*śaktiḥ*). However, all of this is connected to the extensive transformation of the doctrine which Saṃghabhadra had undertaken and it would thus be better to return to this at a later point. For the present, we shall see what else Vasubandhu had to say on the doctrine of efficacy.

This is admittedly not very much. Whereas he has been concerned up to this point to refute the various explanations of efficacy, he now proceeds to oppose the assumption of efficacy as an entity in its own right (p. 297,18ff.). He proceeds basically as follows: first he asks why efficacy is not always efficacious, although according to the Sarvāstivāda it is supposed to be always existent. To the answer of the adversary, that this is based on the absence of the necessary causes, he opposes the Sarvāstivāda in all its complexity. Finally, prompted by an objection from the adversary, he answers the question of how matters stand if the efficacy is not different from the things themselves. He goes about this in a consistently hard, incisive dialectical manner which is reminiscent of

Nāgārjuna. Basically, however, the argument remains on a superficial level and little is said about the nature of things.

It is therefore all the more surprising when one compares this with the corresponding passages in Saṃghabhadra's work (p. 631b19ff.). Here we find a comprehensively developed doctrine which differentiates between efficacy as a state of being (*bhāvaḥ*) and the essence of things (*svabhāvaḥ*), from which it is neither different nor not different, and which attempts to solve the problems raised on this basis. However, this doctrine is not entirely a new creation of Saṃghabhadra. Rather, Vasubandhu has passed it over in favor of his dialectic. This can be seen from the fact that at the end of his discourse he himself quotes a verse (p. 298, 21f.) which is obviously not one of his and in which the differentiation between state of being (*bhāvaḥ*) and essence (*svabhāvaḥ*) is presupposed. Thus, there were important doctrines in the Sarvāstivāda of which we learn nothing from Vasubandhu's formal dialectics.

However, in the present case we fortunately have recourse to a passage of the Vibhāṣā which contains a preliminary stage of the doctrine as represented by Saṃghabhadra and which reveals its development.[35] Nevertheless, we must pay careful attention to the nature of the transmission so that there is no danger of us arriving at a false conclusion. This passage consists of several paragraphs, one of which reproduces almost the same doctrine that we found in Saṃghabhadra's work. This might tempt one into assigning this doctrine a very early date. A comparison of the various versions shows, however, that this paragraph is only contained in the Mahāvibhāṣā (p. 394b27-c9), that is, it obviously represents a later addition.[36] We would thus be well advised to disregard it for the present.

For the rest, the passage mentioned consists of four paragraphs which have the following structure. Each of these paragraphs begins with a question. Then two alternatives are posited and the difficulties resulting from each case are pointed out.[37] Finally a solution is attempted. The questions read as follows:

1. Do the elements arise as already arisen, or do they arise as unarisen? (A p. 394b19-27); B p. 295a6–11; C p. 465c11–17)
2. Are these the same elements which arise and disappear, or are those which arise and those which disappear different? (A p. 394c9–16; B p. 295a17–24; C p. 465c17–25)

3. Does the arising of the stage of time (*adhvā*) result, or does the arising result from the stage of time (*adhvānaḥ*)? (A p. 394c16–24; B p. 295a11–17; C p. 465c25–466a1)
4. Is it the own-essence (*svabhāvaḥ*)[38] that arises, or is it an other-essence (*parabhāvaḥ*) that arises? (A p. 394c24– 395a1; B p. 295a24–28; C p. 466a1–6)

A solution is attempted in the first three cases by referring to the influence of conditions (*kāraṇāni*?).[39] In the fourth case, it is said that it is neither an own-essence nor an other-essence that arises but rather the relevant (*yathāsvāḥ*) properties (*dharmāḥ*) of the essence.[40]

In this text, the problems of the Sarvāstivāda are considered for once from another point of view. It is not the question of how things differ from each other in the three stages of time which is asked but rather of what happens to them when they migrate from one stage of time to another, in particular when they enter the present from the future, that is, when they arise. The answers given are also new. The varying course of things when they enter the present from the future is explained by the impact of the causes. In addition a change in the properties of the things is assumed.

However, this is fairly limited and much still remains open. Mention is only made of causes in general and not of particular causes (*hetavaḥ*) and conditions (*pratyayāḥ*), as would correspond to the fully developed causality doctrine of the school. The relation of the essence of things to their changing nature remains unexplained. In general everything makes a very awkward and deficient impression, as if the new ideas could be grasped but not yet adequately dealt with. However, these new ideas continued to have influence. How this happened is demonstrated by the later addition to our text mentioned above. There the question of why the elements that have already arisen arise is explained in the following manner (A p. 394c4–8):

"The essence (*svabhāvaḥ*) (of things) was present, but not its efficacy (*kāritram*). Now if the causes and conditions coincide, then efficacy arises.—(Question:) Is efficacy the same as the essence (of things) or is it different?—(Answer:) It cannot be said with any certainty whether it is the same or different. It is the same here as in the case of each of the individual impure (*sāsravāḥ*) elements, where several characteristics (*lakṣaṇāni*) adhere to their essence, such as transitoriness (*anityatā*) etc., without one being able to say with any certainty that they are the same or different."

Here the new ideas are linked with the concept of efficacy. It says: If things enter the present from the future, efficacy is produced by the concurrence of the causes. Here the essence of things (*svabhāvaḥ*) already exists; what arises is simply a new attribute (*lakṣaṇam*), a new property (*bhāvaḥ*), that is, efficacy. In addition, the relation between efficacy and the essence of things is determined. They are neither different nor not different, just like the familiar characteristics of earthly things such as transitoriness and so forth.

This doctrine represents an important step in the development of the Sarvāstivāda. And it is older than Vasubandhu. This is evident from the verse (p. 298, 20–22) referred to above which he quotes, even if he does not then deal with it in detail.

It was this doctrine that Saṃghabhadra took over and added to and developed in his fashion. There are two things in particular worth remarking on here. He defined the new property (*bhāvaḥ*) which arises when things enter the present from the future, that is, efficacy (*kāritram*), according to his interpretation, as a power which gives rise to the effect (*phalākṣepaśaktiḥ*). And he treats in detail the question of the relation of this property to the essence of things (*svabhāvaḥ*) and endeavors in every way possible to defend the doctrine he has taken over from the attacks made on it by adversaries.

As regards his definition of efficacy, he bases his argument, as we have already seen, on the traditional distinction between the giving and the grasping of the effect (*phaladānapratigrahaṇam*). However, he developed this distinction broadly in his own manner within the framework of the doctrine of causality as a whole. And since the manner in which he developed it is interesting and characteristic for his work, we shall examine it briefly.

According to Saṃghabhadra, causal activity can occur in two ways among the transitory things (*saṃskṛtadharmāḥ*) within which causal processes occur: as cause (*hetuḥ*) and as condition (*pratyayaḥ*). A cause brings about the arising of an effect, while conditions contribute to the process. This is valid for internal as well as external causal processes.[41]

With the arising of the human embryo, for example, the first stage of development, the *kalalam*, is the cause for the arising of the second, the *arbudaḥ*. The cognition, which according to the law of dependent co-arising, the *pratītyasamutpādaḥ*, brings about rebirth as *pratisandhicittam*, contributes as a condition in the process. Although the *arbudaḥ* does not arise independently from the cognition, it does not arise from the cognition as cause, because they each belong to different causal chains (*saṃtānāḥ*). However, neither can it be said that the cognition at the arising of the *arbudaḥ* does not act as a condition, because its presence and non-presence are based on the latter's presence and non-presence. Nor can it be said that the cognition, together with the *kalalam*, brings about the *arbudaḥ* as a cooperating condition. For then, together with a seed, it would also give rise to the sprout as a cooperating condition.

Similarly, in the external causal processes, the seed (*bījam*) is the cause of the arising of the sprout (*aṅkuraḥ*). The earth and so forth contributes as a condition. Although the sprout does not arise independently of the earth and so forth, it does not arise from the earth as cause, because the sprout arises in immediate sequence (*anantaram*) to the seed. Neither can it be said, however, that the earth and so forth does not act as a condition in the case of the seed, because the presence and non-presence of the seed depends on the earth and so forth. And neither can it be said that the earth and so forth, together with the seed, brings forth the sprout as a cooperating condition. For then it would also, together with the *kalalam*, bring about the *arbudaḥ* as a cooperating condition.

This distinction between cause and condition is explained in yet another way. It is stated, for example,[42] that the cause brings about, the condition furthers, like the mother who bears the child and the foster-mother who brings it up. The condition fosters what the cause has brought forth; when the causal chain (*saṃtānaḥ*) has been brought forth, the conditions further its development. Thus it is said that the cause is singular and that the conditions on the other hand are plural, like the seed and the manure and so forth. The cause is not shared (by several things), the conditions are shared, as with the eye and the forms (with the arising of the visual cognition). And so on and so forth.

Further determinations are added. Each, cause and condition, is a capacity (*che-li, sāmarthyam?*) or a power (*kong-neng, śaktiḥ*).[43] If this acts as a cause, it produces its effect. If it acts as a condition, it fosters a difference of property (*bhāvaḥ*).[44] Or it can also be said in this case that it is the cause for the arising of another property (*anyabhāvajanane hetutā*).[45] In this case the cause precedes (*pūrvajaḥ*) the effect; the conditions are simultaneous (*sahajaḥ*).[46] The cause is exclusively present; the conditions can be present and past.[47] Their behavior in the case of impediments also differs. Thus, in the dark, the power of the eye, which—as condition—brings forth visual cognition (*cakṣurvijñānam*), is immobilized; the power which—as cause—brings forth the future eye, that is, the next moment in the causal chain, remains unimpaired.[48]

Saṃghabhadra now uses this doctrine and its distinction between cause and condition to define efficacy (*kāritram*), by limiting the concept of efficacy to the cause that is exclusively present, thus invalidating the objections from opponents. He says:[49] The capacity (*sāmarthyam?*) of the elements is twofold in all. One is called "efficacy" (*kāritram*). The second is "power" (*śaktiḥ*). Efficacy is the name given to the power which gives rise to the effect (*phalākṣepaśaktiḥ*). But efficacy on its own does not include all (kinds of) power. There is also power which is different from efficacy. Thus, in the dark, it is only the power of the eye to see forms which is impeded. Efficacy is not impeded. That is, the obstacle of darkness impedes the power of sight (*darśanaśaktiḥ*). Therefore the eye is not able to see forms in the dark. The efficacy which causes the effect is not impeded by darkness. Therefore the eye is able to give rise to the effect even in the dark. Thus, efficacy is not absent in the present state because the present is based solely on efficacy. If all efficacy has disappeared, something becomes unconditioned (*asaṃskṛtam*).[50] Being the cause for the arising of another property (*anyabhāvajanane hetutā*) is not efficacy but power alone, because only what is present causes its effect, because the unconditioned (*asaṃskṛtam*) does not cause an effect, and because only that which causes its effect is called "efficacy."

This should suffice to demonstrate how Saṃghabhadra justifies the concept of efficacy and derives it from the doctrine of causality. We shall now go on to look at how he saw the relation between the changing property (*bhāvaḥ*) and the essence of things (*svabhāvaḥ*) in the doctrine he took over and how he attempted to refute the attacks made by adversaries against this doctrine. The situation he faced here was as follows.

The old school from the time of Ghoṣaka onwards had strictly avoided assuming a change in the essence of things when they migrate through the stages of time. Neither did the doctrine of efficacy at first represent a break in respect of this, as long as this was defined merely as activity (*vyāpāraḥ*), which was apparently not seen as an entity in its own right. This changed when the school's doctrine of causality was enlisted to interpret efficacy. For when considering the function of the causes and conditions taught by the school, there was a tendency to think of it as being a property in its own right. And so it was understandable that it was combined with the doctrine that had appeared in the meantime, which distinguished a changing property (*bhāvaḥ*) in addition to an unchanging essence (*svabhāvaḥ*) at the transition of things from the future into the present.

Virulent attacks were immediately launched against the supposition of efficacy as a property in its own right by opponents who saw a wide variety of problems resulting from this supposition. An idea of this can be gained from Vasubandhu's polemics, many arguments of which derive from earlier times, probably from Śrīlāta.[51] The Sarvāstivādin attempted to defend themselves by emphasizing the idiosyncratic character of this property, which is neither different nor not different from the essence of things. However, this only provoked derisive rejoinders such as the verse quoted by Vasubandhu (p. 298,21f.):

> *svabhāvaḥ sarvadā cāsti bhāvo nityaś ca neṣyate /*
> *na ca svabhāvād bhāvo 'nyo vyaktam īśvaraceṣṭitam //*

Ultimately there was no choice but to refer to the profound nature of things, which is beyond human logic (*yan na netuṃ śakyate, tatrātmakāmenaivaṃ veditavyam: gambhīrā khalu dharmatā, nāvaśyaṃ tarkasādhyā bhavatīti*).[52]

This is the state of affairs as recounted by Vasubandhu. Saṃghabhadra starts from this point and attempts to defend the doctrine of his school. He had a perfectly clear view of the situation. Thus, he is also conscious of the fact that the doctrine of the changing property (*bhāvaḥ*) of things took up a doctrine which had earlier been discarded by the school, namely the doctrine of Dharmatrāta, the *bhāvānyathāvādī*. And in his account of the earlier representatives of the Sarvāstivāda he therefore defends this doctrine (p. 631b5–10).

His refutation of his opponents' attacks proceeds in the following manner.

He rejects the reproaches which his opponents derived from the enduring essence of things established in the Sarvāstivāda with reference to the fact that the changing property of things *(bhāvaḥ)* exists beside this enduring essence *(svabhāvaḥ)*, and that efficacy is a property of this kind. The adversary, who does not take this into account, as Saṃghabhadra repeatedly and quite correctly emphasizes, therefore misunderstands the doctrine he is opposing, that is, he has started from false premises.

Saṃghabhadra counters the attacks directed by the opponents against the doctrine of the changing property by going on the counter-attack as it were, and showing how his opponent's criticisms in fact apply to the latter's own doctrine.

According to his opponent's doctrine, all things consist of a chain of moments (*saṃtānaḥ*), which gradually changes as a consequence of the addition of the various conditions. Nevertheless, it cannot be denied that the particular character of things remains unchanged. Thus, one sees in the case of fire that in spite of the variety of fuels such as straw, and so forth, that is despite the difference of the conditions, the character of burning remains unchanged. Similarly, with the sensations (*vedanāḥ*), despite the difference of the conditions, the character of the wholesome (*hitaḥ*) and the harmful remain unchanged. And the same is valid for the other mental elements.[53] On the other hand, according to ancient doctrine, all things possess various properties in addition to their essence. The element earth (*pṛthivīdhātuḥ*) can be internal and external. The sensation can be one's own and alien, pleasant and unpleasant and so forth.[54] That these properties are not different from the essence of things and yet despite this modify their character, can be justified by parallels in the doctrine of the opponent. According to this, a good mental moment can contain seeds (*bījāni*) which are produced by evil elements. These seeds are not different from the good mental moment, but despite this they modify it.[55] He even cites parallels from the opponent's doctrine for the fact that although the conditions which are efficacious in all of this are continually present, they do not always operate. For the opponent does not say that the conditions disappear and that following an interim period the effects arise out of this. He assumes that the conditions produce various seeds (*bījāni*) which continue to exist during the interim period[56] in the chain of moments. The effects then arise out of this, but not always and not simultaneously. It can even happen that a seed produced by the conditions does not bring forth its effect for generations.[57]

The similarities which exist between the two doctrines in spite of all the differences, become especially clear through the comparative confrontation that Saṃghabhadra engages in in response to an objection made by his opponent.[58]

The opponent says: We assume that during the momentary chain of elements, the own characteristic (*svalakṣaṇam*) changes from moment to moment; it was originally not present, now it is present, and after it has been present it disappears again. You assume that the conditioned (*saṃskṛtam*) own characteristic always exists; it is only the particularities (*viśeṣaṇāni*) which were not originally present, are now present and after they have been present, disappear again. How can this be compared?

Saṃghabhadra replies: If I assumed that the own characteristic (*svalakṣaṇam*) was not originally present, or equally if you were to say that the own characteristic was originally present, this would mean the same thing. How then would a comparison be possible? A comparison implies that this and that thing are partially different and partially similar. Now in the present case the alleged comparison put forward implies the following. ... We assume that the momentary chain of the own characteristic exists continuously. We do not teach that the essence of the elements exists and does not exist. But there are particularities (*viśeṣaṇāni*), the presence of which is dependent on conditions. Therefore we do not assume that these particularities are present at all times. You assume that the elements are not originally present and then arise. But you do not assume that different characteristics arise from one moment to the next. Why should these similar elements not be compared? Thus, you assume in the case of the elements in the earlier and the later moment that the own characteristic, as it were, must be the same, but that differences exist. I also assume in the case of the elements in an earlier and a later state of being that the own characteristic must be the same, but that differences exist. Therefore the justification for the comparison of similarity is proven.

In this manner, Saṃghabhadra defends his doctrine against the attacks of his opponents. The resulting comparison of his own doctrine and that of his opponents and the demonstration of their similarity also now enables us to explain an innovation introduced by Saṃghabhadra. We have already pointed out that in his definition of efficacy as a power which gives rise to the effect (*phalākṣepaśaktiḥ*), the definition of efficacy as a power (*śaktiḥ*) represents something new. We have moreover seen that in the form of the doctrine of causality which he represents, the concept of power plays an important role. This also represented an innovation in the traditional doctrine of the school. Now it has been shown that Saṃghabhadra, in his justification of the doctrine that the conditions do not operate at all times, but only at a particular time, refers to the opposing doctrine of the seeds (*bījāni*), which are also only efficacious at a particular time. These seeds—just like efficacy, which also only represents a temporary property of things—are neither different from nor not different from things. In addition, they are also called "powers."[59] I believe that this model, together with these similarities, led Saṃghabhadra to define efficacy as a power as well.

Here I want to interrupt our discussion of the development of the Sarvāstivāda for the present. For to judge by Śāntarakṣita's account, nothing of importance was added in the later period. Nonetheless, the development, inasfar as we have examined it, spans a fairly long period of time. If we now try to summarize and put into context what we have covered up till now, the following picture emerges.

Dharmatrāta marks the beginning of this development. He explained the difference of things in the different stages of time by a difference in their state of being (*bhāvaḥ*). This was soon abandoned because no one wanted to accept a change of this type in the essence of things. There then followed various attempts to derive the difference of things from their relationship to one another. This was found satisfactory at first, particularly in the form taught by Vasumitra. Then, however, the problem of time cropped up. Up until this time the matter had not been given any particular thought and the migration of things through the stages of time had been spoken of. Now a divergent branch of the school, the Dārṣṭāntika, had deduced from this the presence of a time (*kālaḥ*) as an element in its own right, in which the migration takes place. However, the Vibhāṣika school, in their rigid adherence to the old transmitted doctrine, was unable to accept this assumption, which claimed an entity that was alien to the ancient doctrine of the school. It declared, rather, that an entity of this kind did not exist, that the stages of time (*adhvānaḥ*) were nothing but the things that occurred in these stages of time and it also gave a different interpretation to the migration through the stages of time. However, this again prompted the question of how the difference of things which belong to different stages of time can be explained. The answer given was that this difference is based on the efficacy (*kāritram*) of the things, which is not yet present in the future, appears in the present and has disappeared again in the past. This explanation sufficed for a time and was unproblematic as long as efficacy was defined simply as activity (*vyāpāraḥ*). This changed when more precise attempts were made to grasp its nature with the aid of the school's doctrine of causality, in itself an extremely complex creation, which gave rise to various problems. In the meantime, a doctrine had been created which assumed in the case of things in the different stages of time a changing property (*bhāvaḥ*) in addition to their unchanging essence (*svabhāvaḥ*), which was neither different nor not different from the essence of the things. Then efficacy was equated with this property. And it was in this form that Saṃghabhadra, the last great representative of this school, took this doctrine over, developed it, and defended it from the attacks of his opponents.

This the picture of the development of the Sarvāstivāda that has emerged from our investigation. This development covered a long period, which I believe lasted for approximately two hundred years. Yet there is still something else to consider.

As we have already seen and as will become apparent time after time, the Sarvāstivāda evolved in constant confrontation with divergent branches of the schools. A knowledge of these branches and their doctrines is therefore of paramount importance for an understanding of the development as a whole and above all for a deeper understanding of all the problems involved. For this reason, we will next turn to these different branches. Here, however, we are confronted with a task of especial difficulty, for hardly anything has been preserved of the works of even the most important representatives of these schools. Nevertheless, we must attempt to extract as much information as possible from the little that has survived.

For the first time, we have encountered divergent opinions at a relatively early stage, at the point where the time problem occurs. As we have seen, an account of this is given in the Vibhāṣā (see above, p. 189ff.), which reveals that the Dārṣṭāntika and the Vibhajyavādin taught that time (*kālaḥ*) was an entity in its own right. Of these it is the Dārṣṭāntika which are of particular importance for us and we will therefore concentrate on them first.

From the account in the Vibhāṣā concerning the assumption of time (*kālaḥ*) as an entity in its own right, it is apparent that the Dārṣṭāntika, in contrast to the rigidly conservative tendencies of the Vibhāṣika, constituted a branch of the school which was receptive to new developments in the doctrine. Of equal importance, however, is the fact that at that time they still took the Sarvāstivāda as their basis. For according to the way its doctrine is described in other aspects in the Vibhāṣā, it conforms fully with the orthodox doctrine, especially as represented by Vasumitra. Thus, in the question of the real existence of past and future, the Dārṣṭāntika originally represented the traditional doctrine of the Sarvāstivāda and only differed on one single question, that is, in the assumption of time as an entity in its own right.

Fortunately we find confirmation for this in the Abhidharmadīpa, where, in the course of the discussions, the opinion of bhadanta-Kumāralāta is quoted. Kumāralāta, the author of the Dārṣṭāntapaṅkti, was one of the oldest Dṛṣṭāntika, and we could perhaps regard him as the head of the school. It is said of him that (p. 277,21–23): *bhadanta-Kumāralātaḥ paśyati: vātāyana-praviṣṭasyāntaḥ (?) pārśvadvaye 'pi tuṭayaḥ*[60] *santi. raśmigatasya tu darśanam asya tuṭe, raśmipārśvagās tv anumeyāḥ. etena vyākhyātaṃ dharmāṇām adhvayor astitvam.* Thus Kumāralāta compared things on the three levels of time with motes of dust in the sun in front of a window. One can only see those which are in the light. The others on either side also exist, but one can only infer their existence. Thus, things, too, are immediately visible only in the present. But past and future are not any the less existent because of that. This is an acknowledgement of the Sarvāstivāda.

However, this also provides us with the starting point for further investigation. We can thus say that in the question of the past and future, the doctrine of the Dārṣṭāntika was initially wholly based on the Sarvāstivāda, and that at first, they only differed from the orthodox school in the assumption of time (*kālaḥ*) as an entity in its own right. It was only gradually that greater differences began to develop. But that this happened slowly and that an open break was avoided for a long time is evident from the fact that until quite a late date it was emphasized that the existence of past and future was not denied but that a simple claim was made for an existence in another form.[61] A detailed account of the course this development took and of how the break finally occurred will form the subject of the following investigation.[62]

Notes

Foreword

1. The first two volumes of this *Geschichte der indischen Philosophie* appeared 1953 and 1959 in Salzburg. A survey of the project is available from his literary estate (cf. appendix C in Erich Frauwallner, *Nachgelassene Werke I. Aufsätze, Beiträge, Skizzen,* ed. E. Steinkellner, Wien 1984, p. 137f.).

2. Cf. loc. cit., p. 63. This volume was to comprise §§ 9–12 of his survey in appendix C.

3. The results of these efforts were meant to cover § 9 of his survey.

4. These remaining texts will be edited at a later date.

I. The Earliest Abhidharma

1. Cf. Lamotte, *Histoire,* p. 197; Bareau, *Dhammasaṅgaṇi,* p. 8ff.

2. For further discussion of this sūtra see below p. 14f.

3. The advantage conferred by this numerical determination was that the groups of elements established in this fashion were protected from being arbitrarily extended or reduced.

4. SN XLV, 172–181 (Vol. 4, p. 57–60). I quote from the Pāli canon according to the Nālandā-Devanāgarī-Pāli-Series edition, since the edition of the Pāli Text Society is not presently available in its entirety.

5. T 1543, p. 784c9ff. = T 1544, p. 929b10ff.

6. It is also used in the introductory *mātṛkā* of the Dhammasaṅgaṇi (p. 7ff.).

7. Cf. below p. 16ff.

8. E.g. in the 3rd section of the Dharmaskandha or in the Jñānaprasthāna (T 1543, p. 802b9ff. = T 1544, p. 943b7ff.).

9. Cf. the essay "Pañcaskandhaka and Pañcavastuka", p. 135ff.

10. To cite only one example chosen at random: *tattha katamo moho? dukkhe aññāṇaṃ, dukkhasamudaye aññāṇaṃ, dukkhanirodhe aññāṇaṃ, dukkhanirodhagāminiyā paṭipadāya aññāṇaṃ, pubbante aññāṇaṃ, aparante aññāṇaṃ, pubbantāparante aññāṇaṃ, idappaccayatā paṭiccasamuppannesu dhammesu aññāṇaṃ, yaṃ evarūpaṃ aññāṇaṃ, adassanaṃ anabhisamayo ananubodho asambodho appaṭivedho asaṃgāhanā apariyogāhanā* . . . etc. etc. . . . *ayaṃ vuccati moho* (Dhammasaṅgaṇi, p. 271, 19–28).

11. Cf. p. 143ff.

12. This will be dealt with later. [Cf. p. 149ff.]

13. See below p. 16ff.

14. DN No. 34; Tch'ang A-han (T1) No. 10; surviving portions of the Sarvāstivādin version from the finds at Turfan have been published by K. Mittal and D. Schlingloff under the title *Dogmatische Begriffsreihen im älteren Buddhismus*, Berlin, 1957 and 1962. In the Tch'ang A-han there follow two additional sūtras in the same style.

15. Cf., for example, M. Winternitz, *Geschichte der indischen Litteratur*, vol. 2, Leipzig, 1920, p. 134ff.

16. *Geschichte der indischen Philosophie*, vol. 2, Salzburg, 1956, p. 158ff.

17. Abhidharmakośa, I v. 29c–30a (T 1558, p. 7b14–23; VP, p. 53f.), and II v. 28 (T 1558, p. 20a22–b7; VP, p. 165f.).

18. Cf., for example, how often the explanation of concepts such as *phasso, vedanā* and so forth are repeated with no variation in form.

19. See above p. 4.

20. Cf. the Dhātukathā in particular.

21. Even this kind of scholasticism has its apologists. One can of course argue that the working out of all these possibilities results in a clearer overall picture. Ultimately one could claim to understand the law of permutations more clearly if all possible cases are listed on the blackboard. However, for the ordinary mortal it is enough to explain the basic principles and establish the number of possibilities.

22. Cf. Bareau, *Dhammasaṅgaṇi,* p. 17.

23. I have not taken the Śāriputrābhidharma into account as it is as far removed from the Abhidharma of the other schools as the Vinaya of the Mahāsaṅghika is from the other Vinaya.

II. The Canonical [Abhidharma] Works [of the Sarvāstivāda School]

1. *Sphuṭārthā Abhidharmakośavyākhyā by Yaśomitra,* ed. U. Wogihara, Tokyo 1932–36, p. 11,25ff.

2. Cf. Lamotte, *Histoire,* p. 202ff. The relative unimportance of the sequence is indicated by the fact that Yaśomitra himself gives a different order shortly before this passage (p. 9,12ff.).

3. T 1821, p. 8b24f.

4. I have had to omit the Prajñaptiśāstra, as I do not have a Tanjur at my disposal in Vienna and the Tibetan translation is imperative for the treatment of this work.

1. Saṃgītiparyāya

5. The Saṃgītisūtra has been transmitted in several versions: Dīghanikāya No. 33; Tch'ang A-han (T1) No. 9, translated by S. Behrsing, *Asia Major* 7, 1931, p. 1-149 (the Dharmaguptaka version); the Sarvāstivādin version based on the Turfan finds [ed. V. Stache-Rosen, Dogmatische Begriffsreihen im älteren Buddhismus II, 2 parts, Berlin 1968]. That the Saṃgītisūtra should be regarded as a *mātṛkā* — although it is not expressly characterized as such — is obvious not only from the character of the text but also in that passages from it were incorporated into other *mātṛkāḥ*, cf. e.g. nos. 109-142 (p. 15-17) in the first *mātṛkā* of the Dhammasaṅgaṇi, which correspond, with insignificant alterations, to the dyad of the Saṅgītisūtra.

6. The framing narrative is contained in several sūtras. Cf. E. Waldschmidt, "Die Einleitung des Saṅgītisūtra", *ZDMG* 105, 1955, p. 300.

2. Dharmaskandha

7. VP, *Abhidharmakośa,* Introduction, p. XXXVII; Lamotte, *Histoire,* p. 206.

8. T 1541, p.663a5ff. = T 1542, p. 733a17ff. Cf. below p. 35.

9. The *srotaāpattyaṅgāni* are missing.

10. T 1537, p. 453c471; cf. T 1541, p.663a6 = T 1542, p. 733a181; in T 1541 the verse is mangled.

11. Abhidharmakośa V on v.46 (T 1558, p.109b13), cf. Sphuṭārthā p.493, 26ff.

12. The sūtra cited is reproduced in Yaśomitra's Sphuṭārthā Abhidharmakośavyākhyā (p. 90,25–91,5).

13. The sūtra to Ānanda adduced to which the Buddha gives the name Bahudhātuka at the end and which is reproduced in its entirety deals not only with the various groups of *dhātavaḥ*; however, the attached explanations are restricted to these. On the sūtra cf. also VP I, p. 49, notes.

14. Nyanatiloka was the first to point out the similarity of the two works, *Guide through the Abhidhamma-Pitaka,* Colombo, 1938, p. 1f.

15. E.g. at the end of the Vibhaṅga in the Dhammahadayavibhaṅga (p. 480, 1), where the *saccāni* also appear between the *dhātuyo* and the *indriyāni.*

16. It is characteristic that it is precisely this section in the Dhātukathā, in which a large part of the Vibhaṅga list is used as Abbhantaramātikā (p. 3), which is again distorted by additions, and that it is virtually ignored or at best treated briefly in an appendix (p. 18,12ff. etc.).

17. In the Vibhaṅga *dhyānāni* and *ārūpyāni* are treated as one.

18. The Vibhaṅga divides the list of the Kṣudravastuka into monads, dyads, triads etc., in the typical fashion of the Pāli Abhidharma, and in doing so extends them to excess. However, almost all of the rare and unusual concepts of the Kṣudravastuka reappear in the Vibhaṅga.

19. Note the repetition of concepts that have already been treated!

20. Cf. Dharmaskandha 7 (=8), 8 (=9), 9 (=7), 12 (=13). Sometimes extracts of varying lengths are given, as e.g. in 11 (=12), where the Vibhaṅga has incorporated the whole of the preparation for the *dhyānāni.*

21. These questions have been treated in my study *The Earliest Vinaya and the Beginnings of Buddhist Literature* (Serie Orientale Roma VIII), Rome, 1956.

3. *Dhātukāya*

22. The Sanskrit terms used here largely follow La Vallée Poussin.

23. DN No. 33, § 28; Tch'ang A-han Nr.9 T 1, p. 51c19ff.; Saṃgītiparyāya T 1536, p. 429a14ff.

24. VP, Introduction, p. XLI, calls this group *"une liste étrange"*.

25. Both appear separately in the Mahānidānasuttanta, DN, No. 15, § 20.

26. See below p. 33f.

27. Note the Kṣudravastuka in the Dharmaskandha mentioned above.

28. The reason for limiting the discussion to this small number of groups is not given.

29. See below p. 32ff.

30. See below p. 33f.

31. The distortions that it underwent are typical of the Pāli transmission.

32. That the *mātṛkā* of the Dharmaskandha was reworked in a similar fashion in the Sarvāstivāda school is demonstrated by the 7th and 8th chapters of the Prakaraṇa.

33. La Vallée Poussin gives an example, VP I, p. 153, notes.

34. VP, Introduction, p. XLI.

4. *Vijñānakāya*

35. "La controverse du Temps et du Pudgala dans le Vijñānakāya", (*Études Asiatiques*, publiées a l'occasion du vingt-cinquième anniversaire de l'École Française d'Extrême-Orient, 1925, I., p. 343-376). Cf. also VP, Introduction, p. XXXIII–XXXVI.

36. Mallavādin's Nayacakra, ed. Muni Jambūvijayajī, I, Bhavnagar, 1966, p. 61, gives further references.

37. These are the attributes enumerated in the five dyads. See above p. 5.

38. See above, p. 6f.

39. Cf. Abhidharmakośabhāṣya on II v. 61c (T 1558, p. 36b 11–13; VP p. 299f.).

40. See above, p. 5f.

5. Prakaraṇa

41. The reversed order of the 5 *dṛṣṭayaḥ* and the 5 *saṃsparśāḥ* can hardly be regarded as an intentional alteration.

42. It is characteristic that where clear, orderly explanations are given the correspondence is total, e.g. with the *dṛṣṭayaḥ*, *saṃsparśāḥ* and *indriyāṇi*. Where the explanation consists of more lengthy paraphrase, there are small divergences and omissions. Thus, these differences are apparently due to the transmission.

43. These explanations are not without interest. It is worth mentioning that the list of *caittāḥ* and *cittaviprayuktasaṃskārāḥ* incorporated into the *saṃskāraskandhaḥ* was taken from the Pañcavastuka. *Vedanā* and *saṃjñā*, which represent *skandhāḥ* in their own right, have naturally been omitted.

44. Both this and the following groups display points of correspondence with the *mātṛkā* of the Abhidharmasamuccaya, ed. P. Pradhan, Santiniketan, 1950, p. 16ff. [cf. p. 225, n. 12].

45. The isolated divergences that occur are so minimal that they can safely be attributed to the transmission.

46. The claim that it represents the "body" and the other works the "limbs" *(pādāḥ)* of the Abhidharma is in my view a later invention made in order to confer on the work (which did not originally belong to the Ṣaṭpādābhidharma) the status that a later age desired.

47. [After a lapse of seven years this article appeared in *WZKS* 15, 1971; s. p. 149ff.]

III. The Abhidharma of the Pāli School

1. A. Bareau, "Les origines du Śāriputrābhidharmaśāstra", *Muséon* 43, 1950, p. 69–95.

2. Cf. Harivarman's biography in Tchou-san-tsang-ki-tsi (T 2145), in particular T 55 p.78c9f.; also Seng-jouei's testimony in Ki-tsang's San-louen-hiuan-yi (T 1852) T 45 p. 3c11–14.

3. Cf. e.g. H. Oldenberg's introduction to his edition of the Dīpavaṃsa.

4. Cf. my remarks in *Earliest Vinaya.*

5. S. Lévi, "Ptolémée, le Niddesa et la Bṛhatkathā", *Études Asiatiques* II, Paris 1925, p. 1–55.

6. *Earliest Vinaya*, p. 186f.

7. There is still much exact philological work to be done here. Regretfully, I have only had limited access to the Pāli literature and the relevant secondary literature. I hope that I have not overseen anything of importance.

1. Vibhaṅga

8. Cf. the second chapter, "The Canonical [Abhidharma] Works [of the Sarvāstivāda School]", p. 15–27. I here repeat the most important points and add necessary corrections and supplementary material.

9. DN 16 Mahāparinibbānasutta, II p. 94, 12f. = DA T p. 16c10f. = Mahāparinirvāṇasūtra ed. E. Waldschmidt p. 224; DN 28 Sampasādanāyasuttanta, III p. 79,6-8 = DA T 1 p. 76c29f.; DN 29 Pāsādikasuttanta, III p. 99, 3-5 = DA T 1 p. 74a14f., and so forth.

10. Cf. VP, VI, p. 281.

11. The addition of *taṇhāvicaritāni* and *diṭṭhigatāni* at the end is odd.

12. This division has not, however, always been made in the same way in each case. Furthermore, in the case of the two sections 9 *(paṭiccasamuppādo)* and 17 *(khuddhakavatthuvibhaṅgo)*, a foreign text has been inserted into the first of these and in the second, the original *mātṛkā* had been changed to such a degree by immoderate expansion that the old commentary was no longer appropriate and had to be replaced.

13. Cf. above p. 16 and 19.

14. E.g. the formulations p. 249,13–18 and 20–25 etc., or p. 268, 24–269, 2; p. 269, 22–26 etc., which correspond to those in the 1st part of

the Dhammasaṅgaṇi. Cf. also the doctrine of the *kleśāḥ* and the *karma* in the former and the latter text.

15. We will encounter a similar list of numerous varieties of cognition in the discussion of the Śāriputrābhidharma. [Cf. p. 108ff.]

16. In particular SN XII, 63 Puttamaṃsasutta, II p. 83, 24–86, 15 = SA T 2 p. 102b18–c27 and SN XII, 11 Āhārasutta, II p. 12, 16–13, 20 = SA T 2 p. 101c25–102a11.

17. Cf. e.g. B. MN 10 Sammādiṭṭhisutta, I p. 72,4f. = EA T 2 p. 797b28; SN XII, 2 Vibhaṅgasutta, II p. 5,17f., = SA T 2 p. 85a28f.

18. The form *-vibhaṅgo* was evidently only added when the work was incorporated into the canonical Vibhaṅga.

19. In particular in the sections called "Koṭṭhāsavāra" and "Suññatavāra."

2. Dhātukathā

20. However, these also appear beside the first five in more extensive enumerations already in the canon. Cf. e.g. MN 111 Anupadasutta, III p. 90,1-3 and 13f.

3. Puggalapaññatti

21. p. 44,1–45,5, cf. AN III, 2, 3 Āsaṃsasutta, I p. 99,1–100,22.

22. p. 45,6–46,12, cf. AN III, 3, 2 Gilānasutta, I p. 111,1–112,10.

23. p. 23,13–25, 4; 108,1–11; 110, 1–111,22.

5. Yamaka

24. It is remarkable that the regular form of the presentation is almost always only adhered to in those sections which deal with the subjects belonging to the old list of the basic general concepts.

6. Dhammasaṅgaṇi

25. Cf. above p. 34.

a. Cittakaṇḍa

26. It is also frequently enumerated in what number of *kandhā*, *āyatanāni* etc., the elements cited are included.

27. Cf. above p. 21f.

28. Cf. e.g. Abhidharmakośa II v. 28–31.

29. This sentence concludes every enumeration.

α. *The Path of Meditation*

30. Cf. DN 33 Saṅgītisuttanta, III p. 172,14–16 = V. Stache-Rosen, *Dogmatische Begriffsreihen im älteren Buddhismus II*, Berlin, 1968, p. 88; DN 34 Dasuttarasuttanta, III p. 212,11–13 = Kusum Mittal, *Dogmatische Begriffsreihen im älteren Buddhismus I*, Berlin, 1957, p. 58; MN 128 Upakkilesasutta, III p. 232,4–16 = MA T 1 p. 538c2–539a2; SN XLIII, 3 Savitakkasavicārasutta, III p. 312,17–19 and XLIII, 12 Asaṅkhatasutta, III p. 315,1–6; AN III, 18 Rāgapeyyāla, I p. 280,1–4 and VIII 7, 3 Saṅkhittasutta, III p. 389,14–18. Here and elsewhere I give only those references which are of importance in the relevant case. For further references see the extensive collections in Ét. Lamotte, *Le traité de la Grande Vertu de Sagesse de Nāgārjuna*, tome III, Louvain 1970. In the present case cf. p. 1487ff.

31. Cf. Abhidharmakośa VIII v. 22d (see the translation by L. de La Vallée Poussin, VP, p. 180f.).

32. E.g. AN IV, 17, 2 Vitthārasutta, II p. 158,1–159,10 = EA T 2 p. 668a12–b13.

33. Only two variants appear in the case of the *abhibhāyatanāni* since *parittāni* and *appamāṇāni* have already been mentioned in the definition.

34. E.g. DN 33 Saṅgītisuttanta, III p. 170, 20f.

35. The variants are only presented with the *paṭhavīkasiṇaṃ*.

36. The variants are only presented with the first and third *abhibhāyatanaṃ*.

37. It is only here that variants three and four are introduced for the first time and applied to the previous cognitional complexes.

38. Missing.

39. This circumstantial categorization results from the fact that each of the two types, *suññataṃ* and *appaṇihitaṃ*, can produce all three types, i.e. *suññataṃ, animittaṃ* and *appaṇihitaṃ*, as *vipāko*.

40. Missing.

41. *chandādhipateyyaṃ* is also given where *suññataṃ* and *appaṇihitaṃ* occur on their own without any variants.

42. With the second to fourth *bhūmi*, the *vipāko* is not differentiated.

43. E.g. MN 25 Nivāpasutta, I p. 207,11–208,15; 26 Ariyapariyesanasutta (Pāsarāsisutta), I p. 224, 22–225, 30; 30 Cūḷasāropamasutta, I p. 253,24–254, 31 etc. The addition of the *saññāvedayitanirodho* in some cases results naturally from its character.

44. DN 16 Mahāparinibbānasuttanta, II p. 119, 23–120, 15 = DA T 1 p. 26b21—c8 = Mahāparinirvāṇasūtra ed. E. Waldschmidt, Berlin, 1950–51, p. 394–396.

45. DN 33 Saṅgītisuttanta, III p. 207, 8–14; 34 Dasuttarasuttanta, III p. 237, 13–20; MN 77 Mahāsakuludāyisutta, II p. 238, 10–18; AN I, 18 p. 41, 9–12; X, 3, 5 Kasiṇasutta, IV p. 135, 7–14; X, 3, 6 Kāḷīsutta, IV p. 136, 3–20; X, 3, 9 Paṭhamakosalasutta, IV p, 146, 7–20. Cf. Lamotte loc. cit. p. 1281ff., in particular p. 1286–1289.

46. DN 16 Mahāparinibbānasuttanta, II p. 86,21–88, 5; 33 Saṅgītisuttanta, III p. 200, 21–202, 2; 34 Dasuttarasuttanta, III, p 231, 3–232, 16; MN 77 Mahāsakuludāyisutta, II, p. 236, 17–238, 9; AN I, 18, I p. 40, 10–28; VIII, 7, 5 Abhibhāyatanasutta, III, p. 393, 14–394, 13; VIII, 11, III p. 429, 5–19; X, 3, 9 Paṭhamakosalasutta, IV p. 146, 21–148, 13. Cf. Lamotte loc. cit. p. 1281ff., in particular p. 1283–1286.

47. DN 16 Mahāparinibbānasuttanta, II p. 88, 6–18; 33 Saṅgītisuttanta, III p. 202, 3–18; 34 Dasuttarasuttanta, III p. 232, 17–233, 2; MN 77 Mahāsakuludāyisutta, II p. 236, 1–16; AN I, 18, I p. 40, 29–41, 8; VIII, 7, 6 Vimokkhasutta, III p. 394, 14–395, 3; VIII, 11, III p. 429, 20–430, 2. Cf. Lamotte loc. cit. p. 1281ff., in particular p. 1281–1283.

48. E.g. DN 13 Tevijjasutta, I p. 210,21–211, 9; 17 Mahāparinibbānasuttanta, II p. 142, 20–29; 19 Mahāgovindasuttanta, II p. 186,15–21; 25 Udumbarikasīhanādasuttanta, III, p. 38,27–39, 7; 26 Cakkavattisīhanādasuttanta, III p. 62, 8–17; 33 Saṅgītisuttanta, III p. 175, 2–10; MN 83 Makhādevasutta, II p. 301, 23–302, 9. Cf. Lamotte loc. cit. p. 1239 ff.

49. DN 22, II p. 220, 17–26. Cf. also Lamotte loc. cit. p. 1311ff.

50. Cf. Milindapañha p. 332,20–23 (Trenckner); p. 325,10–12 (Vadekar).

51. Saṅgītisūtra ed. V. Stache-Rosen, p. 151,7–10; cf. Yaśomitra, Sphutārthā p. 54, 33–55, 2; Vasubandhu, Abh. kos. VI, p. 337, 15–17.

52. DN Saṅgītisuttanta, III p. 172, 16f. = DA T 1 p. 50b1f.; SN XLIII, 4 Suññatasamādhisutta, III p. 313, 1–3; AN III, 18 Rāgapeyyāla, I p. 279, 25–27. Cf. Lamotte loc. cit. p. 1213ff.

53. Kathāvatthu XIX, 2 Suññatākathā, p. 497, 23ff.

54. It is incomprehensible why this is confined to the first *jhānaṃ*. This must surely be due to cursoriness, just as in the Abhidharma of the Pāli school excessive breadth at the beginning is often followed by carelessness at the end. I believe that the fact that only *dukkhapaṭipadaṃ dandhābhiññaṃ* is given out of all the variants is also due to carelessness.

55. E.g. when *sammādiṭṭhi* is given twice in the list of mental elements because the concept was taken twice from different contexts.

b. The Psychology in the Cittakaṇḍa

56. See p. 54 –57.

57. We shall only consider the *kāmāvacarā dhammā,* since everything else belongs to the path of meditation where the account of the mental processes is quite different and there is no corresponding description.

58. DN 33 Saṅgītisuttanta, III p. 170, 6–8 = DA T 1 p. 50a8–10; DN 34 Dasuttarasuttanta, III p. 212,18–23 = DA T 1 p. 53a26–28; MN 9 Sammādiṭṭhisutta, I p. 63, 6f and 13f.; MN 73 Mahāvacchagottasutta, II p. 184,12–15 = SA T 2 p. 246b26–28; AN III, 7, 9 Akusalamūlasutta, I p. 186–190.

59. Cf. e.g. Vibhaṅga, p. 460,11–13; Yamaka 7, II p. 81ff. It is remarkable that the *anusayā* are missing in the Dhammasaṅgaṇi (leaving aside the meaningless mass enumerations such as those on p. 240,22, and 255,3).

60. Cf. e.g. the Ñāṇavibhaṅga (Vibhaṅga 16, p. 366–408) and the relevant passages in the Kathāvatthu.

61. In the case of this word, too, this meaning would also seem to be more appropriate, since it is documented by the Sanskrit.

62. This cannot derive merely from the fact that most of the later members of the list are good or evil, i.e. do not come into consideration in

the case of the *avyākatā dhammā*. Why then are *samatho, paggāho,* and *avikkhepo* missing, quite apart from other discrepancies?

b. Rūpakaṇḍa

63. E.g. MN I p. 72, 6f.; p. 235, 16f.; p. 273, 21f.; III p. 57, 6f.; SN II p. 5, 18f.; p. 289, 1f.; p. 291, 18f. and so forth.

64. See p. 21,13–16 and p. 173,1–13. Cf. also Vibhaṅga p. 157, 19–158, 1 and Kathāvatthu 83, p. 346, 16ff.

c. The Commentaries

65. The commentaries are quoted with reference to the paragraphs in the Nālandā edition, since the passages which correspond in both commentaries can thus be located more easily.

66. They were similarly carried along in the Sarvāstivāda until the time of Vasubandhu and Saṅghabhadra (cf. Abhidharmakośa V v. 35ff.) and there as here had no significance for the system as such.

67. Cf. p. 233,7–13 and p. 277,17–19 and 24–27. In this case, the *saññojanāni* have nothing to do with the *akusalamūlāni*.

7. Kathāvatthu

68. "Notes Bouddhiques II. Le Vijñānakāya et le Kathāvatthu", *Académie Royale de Belgique. Bulletin de la Classe des Lettres,* 5e série, T. VIII/1922, no. 11, p. 516–520; "La controverse du temps et du Pudgala dans le Vijñānakāya", *Études Asiatiques* I, Paris 1925, p. 343–376.

69. I refer to L. de La Vallée Poussin's remark, loc. cit., p. 520: "Quant au Kathāvatthu, il n'est pas imprudent de penser que ce livre est fait de pièces et de morceaux. Certaines parties sont très vieilles, d'autres parties sont bien suspectes."

8. Paṭisambhidāmagga

70. AN IV, 17, 10, II p. 166, 8–167, 8 = SA T 2, p. 146c20–147a12.

71. SN XXXV, 85, III p. 50, 21–51, 8 = SA T 2, p. 56b21–c1.

72. This corresponds to the Saṅkhittasutta, AN V, 2, 3, II p. 281,11–13, cf. SA T 2 p. 185c20–24.

73. The text is even longer in this case.

74. Cf. the first part of this study, p. 45f.

9. Vimuttimagga and Visuddhimagga

75. For simplicity's sake I shall use only the Visuddhimagga here. P. V. Bapat gives a concordance of the two works in his book *Vimuttimagga and Visuddhimagga, a comparative study*, Poona, 1937. Concerning the relation of Buddhaghosa to his predecessors, I also remind the reader of the Samantapāsādikā and the Chan-kien liu p'i-p'o-cha (T 1462), of which P. Demiéville says: "Il n'est pas certain que le Chan-kien liu p'i-p'o-cha soit à proprement parler une traduction de la Samantapāsādikā; ce doit être plutôt la traduction d'un prototype de la Samantapāsādikā palie actuelle. L'ouvrage contient des éléments d'origine septentrionale et qui semblent parfois remarquablement anciens." ("A propos du concile de Vaiśālī", *T'oung Pao* XL, 1950–51, p. 289.)

76. I quote from the edition by H. C. Warren, Harvard Oriental Series, vol. 41.

77. Cf. above, p. 63f.

78. Cf. P. V. Bapat; *Vimuttimagga and Visudhimagga,* p. 38.

79. I believe that the *khaye ñāṇaṃ* found in the usual list is a later addition, even if it did find its way into the old sūtra texts.

80. In Upatissa's work, the first part is called "Pañca upāyā" and the second "Saccapariccheda".

81. Although the reformulations are not uninteresting, I cannot go into them any further here. Buddhaghosa's work is markedly more extensive than that of Upatissa. It is also striking that he quotes the Porāṇā more frequently than otherwise.

82. Cf. for example the advice given as to how the *asubhabhāvanā* should be practised (Ch. VI, 12ff.).

IV. The Śāriputrābhidharma

1. On this head, P. Demiéville says in his "A propos du concile de Vaiśālī", *T'oung Pao* XL, 1950-1951, p. 245, n. 1: "Dharmayaśas, cachemirien lui aussi, arrivé en Chine par mer entre 397 et 401 (il aurait été âgé alors de 85 ans), entreprit en 407, avec un moine indien nommé Dharmagupta qu'il rencontra à Tch'ang-ngan, une traduction de l'Abhidharma de Śāriputra. Ils commencèrent par coucher par écrit le

texte sanskrit, ce qui leur prit une année, après quoi il leur fallut encore dix ans pour apprendre le chinois et mener à bien la traduction. Ils la dictèrent eux-mêmes oralement jusqu'en 414; les rédacteurs chinois n'eurent plus qu'à réviser jusqu'en 415 (T 2145, X, p. 71a = T 1548, p. 525b; T 2059, I, p. 329b–c)."

2. For a detailed account and references to further literature, see A. Bareau, "Les origines du Śāriputrābhidharmaśāstra", *Muséon* LXIII, 1950, p. 69–95.

3. T 1428 (Vol. 22), p. 968b26f. The P'i ni mou king attests the same structure for the Abhidharma of the Haimavata (T 1463, p. 818a28f.).

4. I follow A. Bareau's reconstruction of the names.

5. a = enumeration and explanation of the concepts to be treated. b = discussion according to the *mātṛkā.*

6. Cf. my lecture "The Origin of the Buddhist Systems" [= chapter V, p. 99–111.]

7. In particular by T. Kimura, *Recherches sur l'Abhidharma,* Tôkyô, 1922. This work was unfortunately unavailable to me.

8. p. 15ff. and 43f.

9. It should nevertheless be pointed out that a work like the Pañcaskandhaka could also be based on the *āyatanāni*. Cf. p. 32f.

10. *pañcannaṃ khandhānaṃ kati kusalā, kati akusalā, kati avyākatā,* etc. (Vibhaṅga p. 70, 3f. etc.).

11. In addition to this, the list of mental elements from the Saṃprayoga is inserted between the *āyatanāni* and *dhātavaḥ*. However, it is clear that this is a later addition from the fact that this list is not considered in the discussion of includedness.

12. Cf. p. 21ff.

13. Cf. A. Bareau, op. cit. p. 69 and 84f.

14. Cf. p. 50f.

15. The rest of this section (p. 64–270) deals with different variants in characteristically self-important manner without adding anything to the basic ideas. It may thus be disregarded.

16. Cf. Puggalapaññatti p. 3f.

17. I shall return to the examination of the ideas of the Pudgalavāda in the discussion of the *kāyasmṛtyupasthānam* elsewhere. [Frauwallner never returned to this issue.]

18. Lesser developments would include the discussion of the *akuśala-* and *kuśalamūlāni* (I, 7–8), the *kāya-*, *vāk-* and *manaścaritam* (V, 5), the *akuśalāḥ* and *kuśalāḥ karmapathāḥ* (V, 8–9) and the *upāsakaḥ* (I, 10). The discussion of the *mahābhūtāni* (I, 9) and of *nāmarūpam* (V, 3) is unimportant.

19. The rendition of the Sanskrit terms here and in the following is merely tentative. Where there is a common expression in Sanskrit for the relevant term, I have used it, even if the Chinese translation seems to indicate that another form of the expression might be possible (cf. VP, Introduction, p. LXI, note 1).

20. In the repetitions in the commentary belonging to the *mātṛkā* of the first part (see below p. 113), the *kṣāntiḥ* has been dropped from the list of mental elements, but the *samādhiḥ* and *vicikitsā* added in fourth and penultimate place.

21. T 1544 (Vol. 26), p. 996b12–997a1 = T 1543, p. 873a21–c10. Cf. also Mahāvibhāṣāśāstra, T 1545, p. 760a20ff. and Abhidharmakośa III v. 30–31.

22. A clear survey of the doctrines of the various schools is given in A. Bareau, *Les sectes bouddhiques du Petit Véhicule,* Saigon, 1955, p. 266f.

23. AN I, 6 Accharāsaṅghātavagga, I p. 10,16–22: *pabhassaram idaṃ, bhikkhave, cittaṃ. taṃ ca kho āgantukehi upakkilesehi upakkiliṭṭhaṃ* and so forth.

24. The Rūpakaṇḍa naturally derives from the same tradition as the Vibhaṅga, but contains material that the redactors of the Abhidharma left out of the Vibhaṅga. The comparison of different versions of this kind is very instructive for evaluating the activity of the redactors. One can see how they organize the material, shortening it here and expanding it there. Sometimes mistakes occur, as, for example, in the Vibhaṅga (p. 85f.), where the *manāyatanaṃ* is suddenly discussed in a way that is normally limited to the *khandhā.* This should be compared with the discussion of the *manodhātu,* p. 110f.

25. In contrast to the Rūpakaṇḍa, the Śāriputrābhidharma, like the Vibhaṅga, only gives one variant here, that with *passati.*

26. SN III, 1, 48 Khandasutta, II p. 278,26–279,17 = SA T 2, p. 13b13–23.

27. Cf. chapter VI., p. 135ff.

28. In the case of the three *khandhā*, only the standard explanation of the Vibhaṅga is repeated. The kinds of *upādā rūpaṃ* given in the enumeration of the Rūpakaṇḍa, from *itthindriyaṃ* to *kabalīkāro āhāro*, are called *"anidassanaappaṭighaṃ rūpaṃ."* The *asaṅkhatā dhātu* is explained as *rāgakkhayo, dosakkhayo,* and *mohakkhayo,* which is justified by the old canon but for which other explanations normally serve. Here we have yet another of the many problems that the structure and composition of the Pāli Abhidharma confronts us with at every turn.

29. In order to preclude misunderstandings, I should like to emphasize that I have purposely avoided going into the question of borrowed heterogeneous material.

V. The Origin of the Buddhist Systems

1. Cf. p. 43ff.

2. It is further noteworthy that both inserted sections occur at the end of a part of the old tripartite *mātṛkā*, i.e., at an especially suitable point for an appendix.

3. Cf. chapter VI, "Pañcaskandhaka and Pañcavastukam", p. 135ff. A variation of the Pañcaskandhaka, where the *āyatanāni* form the focus of the work, is incorporated into the Prakaraṇa as Chapter 3.

4. Dhātukāya I and Prakaraṇa IV. Cf. p. 21–23.

5. Cf. chapter VII, "The Abhisamayavāda", p.149ff. In the Abhidharma we find only the doctrine of the *anuśayāḥ*, above all in Prakaraṇa V, but in a form which presupposes the path of liberation belonging to it.

6. See especially Vijñānakāya III.

7. Cf. p. 39–43.

8. The so-called five points which a part of the tradition attributes to a certain Mahādeva. Cf. my essay on the Buddhist councils, *ZDMG* 102, 1952, p. 243–249. Cf. also Lamotte, *Histoire*, p. 300–312.

9. Cf. chapter VI, "Pañcaskandhaka and Pañcavastuka", p. 135ff.

10. Dharmaśrī's achievements in general should not be underestimated. Above all, he demonstrates a fine understanding of the problems involved and he would merit a monograph, if for other reasons, as much as Vasubandhu.

11. The later, barren compendia, such as the Abhidhammatthasaṃgaha, do not count.

12. Quotations are from the edition by Pralhad Pradhan, which is adequate for our purposes [cf. p. 214, n. 44].

13. T 1646, p. 239–373.

VI. Pañcaskandhaka and Pañcavastuka

1. I quote from the Abhidharmakośa, since the Sanskrit text has unfortunately still not been published, according to the Bibliotheca Buddhica (BB) edition of the Tibetan text as far as this goes. However, I also refer to Hiuan-tsang's Chinese translation (T 1558) and give additionally the relevant page references of de La Vallée Poussin's translation (VP). [Since passages in the recent editions of the Sanskrit text are easily identified with the aid of the latter references, these have not been added.]

2. BB 7, 14ff.; T 1558, p. 1b28ff.; VP 6f.

3. BB 8, 18ff.; T 1558, p. 1c11ff.; VP 7ff.

4. BB 11, 12ff.; T 1558, p. 2a6ff.; VP 11ff.

5. BB 48, 8ff.; T 1558, p. 7a5ff.; VP 51ff.

6. BB 94, 3ff.; T 1558, p. 13a20ff.; VP 100ff.

7. BB 132, 4ff.; T 1558, p. 18b6ff., VP 143ff.: *vyākhāta indriyaṇāṃ dhātuprabhedaprasaṅgenāgatānāṃ vistareṇa prabhedaḥ. adhunā tu mimāṃsyate: kim ete saṃskṛtā dharmā yathā bhinnalakṣaṇā evaṃ bhinnotpādāḥ, utāho niyatasahotpādā api kecit santīti. santīty āha. sarva ime dharmāḥ pañca bhavanti rūpaṃ cittaṃ caitasikāś cittaviprayuktā asaṃskṛtaṃ ca* etc.

8. BB 135, 16ff.; T 1558, p. 18c27ff.; VP 149ff.

9. T 1558, p. 30a5ff.; VP 244ff.

10. T 1557. According to P. Demiéville, the attribution of this translation to Ngan Che-kao is probably correct (cf. *L'Inde classique,* Paris-Hanoi, 1953, Vol. II, § 2134).

11. More on this topic later [cf. p. 5ff.]. For the present I refer to the remarks in Bareau, *Dhammasaṅgaṇi,* p. 16ff.

12. T 1550, p. 809b24ff.

13. p. 809c15ff.

14. p. 810b17ff.

15. p. 810b29ff.

16. p. 811b4ff.

17. p. 811b14ff.

18. p. 830b27ff.

19. p. 830c20ff.

20. p. 831b6ff.

21. BB 132, 8ff.; T 1558, p. 18b14ff.; VP 144.

22. Information concerning Dharmaśrī's dates varies considerably. A useful date *ante quem* would seem to be provided by the information that the monk Dharmakāla, who came to China around the middle of the 3rd century A.D., became familiar with Dharmaśrī's Abhidharma at the age of 25 (Kao seng tchouan T 2059, p. 324c19f.; cf. Lin Li-kouang, *L'Aide mémoire de la vraie Loi,* Paris, 1949, p. 50f.).

23. T 1553. A retranslation of this work into Sanskrit was published by Shanti Bhikshu Sastri, Santiniketan, 1953 (Visvabharati Studies 17).

24. T 1553, p. 968c20ff.

25. p. 968c26ff.

26. p. 969a21ff.

27. p. 969b3ff.

28. p. 969b6ff.

29. T 1543–1544. The first two chapters have also been retranslated into Sanskrit by Shanti Bhikshu Sastri, Santiniketan, 1955.

30. T 1544, p. 929b10–c3. In Shanti Bhikshu Sastri's translation, p. 65–73.

31. T 1544, p. 943 b 7–16. In Shanti Bhikshu, p. 150–152.

32. I believe Ghoṣaka to be later than Dharmaśrī. However, this must be discussed elsewhere. [Frauwallner never returned to this issue.]

33. According to an incomplete manuscript edited by Pralhad Pradhan, Santiniketan, 1950 (Visvabharati Studies 12). Since the points that are of most interest to us are contained in this manuscript, I will restrict myself to quoting from this edition. For the rest, I limit myself purposedly to Asaṅga's Abhidharmasamuccaya. For the present, I am not going to refer to distant parallels such as e.g. Śāriputrābhidharma T 1548, p. 525c5ff., p. 534b9ff.; p. 543a5ff.; Prakaraṇapāda T 1542, p. 696b15ff.

34. T 1612 = No. 4059. Translated into Sanskrit by Shanti Bhikshu Sastri (*Laghugrantharatnaprabhāvaliḥ* 4) 1956.

35. This form of the name is attested by Yaśomitra.

36. *Die Philosophie des Buddhismus,* (Philosophische Studientexte. Texte der indischen Philosophie, Vol. 2) Berlin, 1956. p. 327.

37. For the present, I shall leave it open whether the work that has been preserved in Chinese translation (T 1556 and 1557) was the oldest work of this kind or not.

VII. The Abhisamayavāda

1. The theme is also treated in the Śāriputrābhidharma T 28 p. 584 c 11–589 c 3 and in the Abhidharmasamuccaya, p. 86, 1–92, 18.

2. Cf. VP, Introduction p. XXIX.

3. Cf. chapter VI, "Pañcaskandhaka and Pañcavastuka", p. 135ff.

4. The only surviving commentary by Dharmatrāta (T 1555) belongs, however, to a very much later period.

5. Abhidharmasāra IX v. 5–10.

6. T 28, p. 1b11f.

7. A description of the doctrine of the *anuśayāḥ* is also contained in the 5th chapter of the Prakaraṇa (T 26 p. 637a5–644a23 = p. 702a7–711b5). I shall be quoting texts of the Pāli canon from the Nālandā-Devanāgarī- Pāli series edition, Chinese texts from the Taishō edition of the Tripiṭaka, and, to facilitate reference, according to the volume and not the work numbers.

8. In the interests of brevity, I shall henceforth name the Sūtrapiṭaka "the old canon" or simply "canon" in contrast to the much younger works of the Abhidharma.

9. Cf. the author's *Geschichte der indischen Philosophie*, vol. I, Salzburg, 1953, p. 160ff.

10. An awareness of this was preserved right into the later period. Cf. Abhidharmakośa. V v. 1b–2a and v. 3.

11. Cf. the author's *Geschichte der indischen Philosophie*, vol. 1, p. 214f.

12. E.g. DN II, p. 187,20–27 = DA T I, p. 34a26–29; MN I, p. 45, 12–22 = MA T, 1 p. 596a10–17; MN I, p. 278, 18–279, 6 = SA T 2, p. 342b21–c3; MN II, p. 151,17–155, 9= MA T 1, p. 545c5–546c21; etc. Cf. also Abhidharmakośa. VI p. 370,16–18. Cf. also below p. 172f.

13. DN III, p. 35,18f.; p. 37,23f. = DA T 1, p. 48a28; b26; AN I, p. 142, 6f.; II, p. 255,6ff.; p. 386,2f.

14. E.g. DN III, p. 35, 19f.; p. 190,27; MN I, p. 132,24ff.; III, p. 39, 21f.

15. MN 2, I p. 10–17 = MA T 1, p. 431c13–432c29; cf. AN III, p. 96–99; EA T 2, p. 740a25–741b16; T 1, p. 813a3–814b5. The *dassanā pahābātabbā āsavā* are missing in AN.

16. The 4 Noble Truths are not named in EA.

17. Abhidharmasāra, T 28 p. 815c22–24; Upaśānta p. 844c11–14; Dharmatrāta p. 900b25–28; cf. Abhidharmakośa, p. 280, 12f.

18. Dharmaśrī's presentation of the doctrine consists of a systematic description of the path of liberation (v. 1–17) which is followed by a discussion of various individual questions (v. 18–26). We will here consider only the first part. Vasubandhu incorporated such a quantity of other material into the corresponding chapter of his Abhidharmakośa that it became the least structured and most unreadable section in the whole work.

19. Besides the mind, Dharmaśrī also mentions the mental factors (*caittāḥ*) and the conditioned factors which are not associated with mind (*cittaviprayuktasaṃskārāḥ*).

20. Cf. Abhidharmakośa VII v. 13; *yānataḥ* is perhaps merely a mistake for *nairyāṇikataḥ*.

21. Dharmaśrī has *lakṣaṇam* in stead of *kṣaṇam*; however, this would seem to be merely a mistake in the transmission, since Upaśānta and Dharmatrāta both have *kṣaṇam*.

22. I have not included here the statements from the 6th chapter of the Abhidharmasāra, since they belong to a later stage of development and are rooted in a different tradition.

23. See p. 154.

24. SN 12, 33, II, p. 48, 25–51, 13. SA T 2, p. 99c4–18 and c19–26 contains nothing relevant and appears to have been considerably shortened.

25. DN 33 Saṅgītisuttanta, III, p. 177,14f. = DA T 1, p. 51a18 (differs from Saṅgītisūtra ed. V. Stache-Rosen p. 100); DN 34 Dasuttarasuttanta, III, p. 214, 4f. = DA T 1, p. 53b21 (differs from Daśottarasūtra ed. Kusum Mittal p. 64 and T 1, p. 53a19). The later formation of groups of 8 or 10 *jñānāni* and the doctrines developed from them are not relevant to the current investigation.

26. Vibhaṅga p. 390, 21–391, 35.

27. E.g. DN 6, I, p. 133, 3–16; II, p. 187,18–27; 28, III, p. 83,14–84, 15 and so forth.

28. AN I, p. 216,1–217, 10; p. 217,11–218,11: cf. SA T 2, p. 210b 19–c12; p. 210c13–211a11; p. 211a12–b5; p. 211b6–29; AN IV, p. 25, 26–27, 9; SN IV, p. 177, 4–13 = SA T 2, p. 183b4–17.

29. Cf. SN Okkantasaṃyutta, II, p. 439,1–442,15 (missing in SA).

30. The distinction rests on the fact that of the two determinations, *kāyena phusitvā viharati* and *paññāya pajānāti*, either one or both are given. Cf. AN IV, p. 85,16–87,6. Besides this, a group occurs occasionally which consists of *kāyasākṣī*, *dṛṣṭiprāptaḥ* and *śraddhādhimuktaḥ*, which are distinguished by the fact that the *samādhīndriyam* is especially strong in the case of the *kāyasākṣī*, the *prajñendriyam* in the case of the *dṛṣṭiprāptaḥ* and the *śraddhendriyam* in the case of the *śraddhādhimuktaḥ*. Cf. AN I, p. 108,15–110,30. Concerning *prajñāvimuktaḥ* and *ubhayatobhāgavimuktaḥ* cf. also Abhidharmasāra. V v. 20.

31. MN 70 Kīṭāgirisutta, II, p. 168,24–170,18=MA T 1, p. 751c9–752a25 (with numerous variations in the wording).

32. Cf. SN 48 Indriyasaṃyutta, IV, p. 167ff., particularly p. 173,1–175,12 and 177, 4-13=SA T 2, p. 183a24-b17.

33. Cf. AN I, p. 110, 14–28; AN III, p. 383, 11–384, 4=EA T 2, p. 764c2–10; AN IV, p. 19, 25–20, 9=EA T 2, p. 767b27–c5. *phale ṭhito* only occurs in the verses AN III, p. 383, 17, and 384, 1.

34. AN Vajirūpamasutta, I, p. 113, 28–114, 24; taken over in Puggalapaññatti p. 48, 1–4. The terms *vijjūpamo* and *vajirūpamo* are also used in the *mātṛkā* of the Dhammasaṅgaṇi (p. 14, 17f.).

35. See above, p. 154.

36. DN 33 Saṅgītisuttanta, III, p. 169, 26 = DA T 1, p. 49c27; DN 34 Dasuttarasuttanta, III, p. 211, 28f. = DA T 1, p. 53a18, and so forth.

37. Cf. Nettipakaraṇa p. 15,6–8 *yaṃ pana evaṃ jānāti khīṇā me jātī ti idaṃ khaye ñāṇaṃ, nāparaṃ itthattāyā ti pajānāti idaṃ anuppāde ñāṇaṃ.*

38. See above, p. 168.

39. We have already encountered the *kāyasākṣī* among the 7 *pudgalāḥ,* see above p. 172. Particular attention should be paid to the Kosambisutta, SN II, p. 98, 20–101, 29 = SA T 2, p. 98c1–99a5, which L. de La Vallée Poussin takes as the starting point of his essay "Musīla et Nārada", *MCB* 5, 1936–1937, p. 189ff.

40. Cf. e.g. the Satipaṭṭhānasaṃyutta, SN IV, p. 122–166.

41. DN 22 Mahāsatipaṭṭhānasutta, II, p. 217–235, MN 10 Satipaṭṭhānasutta, I, p. 76–89 = MA T 1, p. 582b7–584b29; EA T 2, p. 568a1–569b12.

42. Cf. for example MN I, p. 177, 4f. *api nāyaṃ Ariṭṭho bhikkhu gaddhabādhipubbo usmīkato pi imasmiṃ dhammavinaye*; see also p. 317, 22f.; see also the use of the word *khanti.*

43. AN IV, p. 61, 3–65, 5.

44. SN IV, p. 355,1–9 and 10–19 have *pajānāti*; p. 355,20–356,13 and 356,14–357,2 have *abhisamayo* and *abhisameti*; p. 357,3–16 and 357,17–358,5 have *abhisambujjhati*, and so forth.

45. I am thinking here of Maitreyanātha's Abhisamayālaṃkāra and the works in its tradition.

VIII. The Sarvāstivāda

1. "The Origin of the Buddhist Systems", see chapter V, p. 119ff.

2. *Abhidharmakośabhāṣya of Vasubandhu*, ed. P. Pradhan, Patna, 1967, p. 295,2–301,16.

3. A-p'i-ta-mo chouen tscheng li louen, T 1562, p. 621c5–636b16. Cf. also the A-p'i-ta-mo tsang hien tsong louen (Samayapradīpikā) by the same author, T 1563, p. 900c1–902a25.

4. *Abhidharmadīpa with Vibhāshāprabhāvṛitti*, ed. Padmanabh S. Jaini, Patna, 1959, p. 256,8–282,8.

5. I shall refer to them as A, B, and C respectively.

6. A-p'i-ta-mo ta p'i-p'o-cha louen, (Mahāvibhāṣā) T 1545, p. 393a9–396b23.

7. A-p'i-t'an p'i-p'o-cha louen, T 1546, p. 293c19–296a2.

8. Pi-p'o-cha louen, T 1547, p. 464b22–466b28.

9. *Tattvasaṅgraha of Śāntarakṣita with the commentary of Kamalaśīla*, ed. Embar Krishnamacharya, Baroda, 1926, p. 503–519 = *Tattvasaṃgraha of Shāntarakṣita with the commentary of Kamalashīla*, ed. Dwarikadas Shastri, Varanasi, 1968, p. 613–633.

10. *avasthāntarato dravyāntarataḥ* in the manuscript. Missing in the Chinese and Tibetan translations. Cf., however, Vibhaṅga B p. 295c25f., C p. 466b25; also Mahāvibhāṣā p. 396b10f., Saṃghabhadra p. 631b2f., and Abhidharmadīpa. 260, 8.

11. A poor copy of this text also ultimately found its way into the Yogabhāṣya. Cf. L. de La Vallée Poussin, "Le Bouddhisme et le Yoga de Patañjali", *MCB* vol. 5, 1936–37, p. 237–239.

12. Cf. Abhidharmakośa. V, p. 297,13f. *yady atītam api dravyato 'sty anāgatam api, kasmāt tad atītam ity ucyate 'nāgatam iti vā.*

13. Missing in versions B and C.

14. Also missing in versions B and C. The rejection of the first two doctrines is added to the end of the Mahāvibhāṣā, prompting the impression that it is a later addition.

15. The differentiation between the characteristics on the different levels of time according to their *vṛttiḥ*, as can be found in Yaśomitra's work, for example, seems to have arisen at a later date and subsequent to the doctrine of *kāritram*.

16. Already present in all three versions of the Vibhāṣā.

17. Only Kamalaśīla includes it in an abbreviated version (p. 504, 20f. = p. 614, 22f.).

18. Abhidharmakośa V, p. 297,8–13; Nyāyānusāra V, p. 631b11f.; Abhidharmadīpa V, p. 261, 1–9.

19. The whole text is a colorful patchwork and deserves to be analyzed in its own right. For present purposes the first few passages are sufficient.

20. A p. 393a9–17; B p. 293c20–26, C is missing.

21. A p. 393a18–b29, B p. 293c26–294b5, C p. 464b22–465a25.

22. A p. 393c1–6, B p. 294b5f. and 293c18–20, C p. 465a25–29.

23. A p. 393c6–11, B p. 294b6–11, C p. 465a29–b2.

24. A p. 393c11–16, B p. 294b11–17, C p. 465b2–7.

25. A p. 393c16–23, B p. 294b22–25, C is missing.

26. A p. 393c23–394a2, B p. 294b17–22, C p. 465b7–9.

27. A p. 394a2–4, B p. 294c5–7, C is missing.

28. A p. 394a4–8, B p. 294c7–8, C is missing.

29. A p. 394a8–15, B p. 294b25–29, C is missing.

30. A p. 394a15–21, B p. 294b29–c2, C is missing.

31. A p. 700a26–b2, Jñānaprasthāna T 1544 (vol. 26), p. 987b5f., cf. T 1543 (vol. 26), p. 862c4.

32. A. Bareau reckoned there were five Vasumitras, for example.

33. Chos-mṅon-pa'i mdsod-kyi bśad-pa'i rgya-cher 'grel-pa don-gyi de-kho-na-ñid ces-bya-ba. No. 5875, p. 273a7–274b4; cf. also Pūrṇavardhana, Chos-mṅon-pa'i mdsod-kyi 'grel-bśad mtshan-ñid-kyi rjes-su-'braṅ-ba śes-bya-ba, No. 5594, p. 143b5–144a5.

34. *adhipatiphalam* is missing in Sthiramati.

35. A p. 394b19–395a1; B p. 295a6–28; C p. 465c11–466a6.

36. I think it probable that this paragraph was taken over from a later reworking of the Vibhāṣā, where the first paragraph was reformulated in this manner. The phrase *asti paryāyaḥ* is also missing here.

37. Vasubandhu cites two of these alternatives at the end of his presentation (p. 301,13-16) as evidence that the nature of things cannot be

logically established in every case (*dharmatā nāvaśyaṃ tarkasādhyā bhavati*).

38. *tseu fen* in B = *svabhāgaḥ* must be a mistaken reading for *svabhāvaḥ*.

39. *i cheu kou* B, *in cheu kou* C; I believe Hiuan-tsang's translation *iou in iuen kou* to be a modernization.

40. The translations vary; I presume *yathāsvaḥ* after *jou k'i fa* in B.

41. T 1562 (vol. 29), p.409a7ff.

42. p. 449c27ff.

43. p. 409b4–6.

44. p. 409c23ff.

45. p. 631b20 = p. 902a16; p. 631c12. The varying mode of expression frequently gives rise to confusion. That the definitions of cause and condition are thrown together on p. 631b20 and p. 902a16 is obviously a mistake, possibly only in the translation.

46. p. 409a23–28.

47. p. 409c25f.

48. p. 410a1–3.

49. p. 631c5ff., cf. also p. 900c14f.

50. Probably. I believe that the text is corrupt here.

51. Cf. Nyāyānusāra p. 635a4ff.

52. p. 301, 10–13. The text should read like this in my opinion. Re *ātmakāmena* cf. Paramārtha's translation p. 259c10 and that of Hiuan-tsang, p. 106b2f.

53. Nyāyānusāra p. 632a16–19; but cf. also p. 632c16f.

54. p. 631c25–28; p. 625a19–b2 = p. 900c18–29; cf. Tattvasaṃgrahapañjikā p. 509,3–5 = p. 620,12–15.

55. p. 632c12–14.

56. I hold *kien* to be the correct reading in p. 632a24.

57. Cf. p. 632a20–b13.

58. p. 632c25–633a8.

59. E.g. p. 632c14. Cf. also the account of the doctrine of the Sautrāntika in the Abhidharmakośa, p. 278, 20ff.

60. *tuṭiḥ* = *truṭiḥ* = *trasareṇuḥ*.

61. E.g. Abhidharmadīpa., p. 278,6f.

62. Cf. Foreword, p. xf.

Name Index

Indian

Arhats of Kaśmir, 36
Asaṅga, 39, 115, 119, 131–134, 144–145
Aśoka, 124; A.'s missions, 40, 42; inscriptions, 42
Ābhidharmika, 60, 151
Āḷāra Kālāma, 63
Uddaka Rāmaputta, 63
Upatissa, 89, 91, 130, 221
Kamalaśīla, 187, 194, 196, 231, 232
Kātyāyana, 150
Kātyāyanīputra, 13, 36, 141, 152
Kumārajīva, 36
Kumāralāta, 39, 207–208
Girnār, 42
Ghoṣaka, 140, 143, 145, 189, 202, 227
Ceylon, 41–42
Dārṣṭāntika, 190–192, 206–208
Devakṣema, 13
Devaśarman, 13, 28
Dharmakāla, 226
Dharmagupta, 97
Dharmaguptaka, 97
Dharmatrāta, 188, 192–193, 203, 205, 227
Dharmayaśas, 97
Dharmaśrī, 128, 132–133, 137–143, 145, 150, 152–153, 161–162, 165, 167, 176–179, 181, 225–229
Nāgārjuna, 197
Paramārtha, 233
Pūrṇa, 13, 27
Buddhadeva, 189
Buddhaghosa, 73, 89–90, 92, 130–131, 221
Buddhavarman, 152
bhadanta-Kumāralāta, 207
bhadanta-Vasumitra, 193
Mallavādin, 213
Mahākātyāyana, 13
Mahākauṣṭhila, 13
Mahādeva, 224
Mahāmaudgalyāyana, 13
Mahāyāna schools, 131
Mahāsaṅghika, 211
Mahīśāsaka, 133
Maitreyanātha, 131, 230
Maudgalyāyana, 13, 28
Milindapañha, 218
Yaśomitra, 13, 27, 211, 219, 227, 231
Yogācāra, 131, 144; Y. school, 11
Vardhamāna, 121
Vasubandhu, 3, 8, 24, 32, 39, 119, 128, 129, 135–140, 142–145, 150, 152, 174, 185–188, 190, 193, 195–197, 199, 202, 219–220, 225, 228, 231, 232
Vasumitra, 13, 27, 32–33, 36, 150, 152, 189–193, 206–207; five V., 232
Vātsīputra 92
Vātsīputrīya, 28, 126
Vidiśā, 42

Vibhajyavādin, 190, 191–192, 207
Vaibhāṣika, 207; V. school, 195, 206
Vaiśeṣika, 146, 192, 193
Śāntarakṣita, 186, 193, 205, 231
Śāriputra, 13, 14, 121
Śrīlāta, 202
Saṃghabhadra, 3, 130, 150, 174, 185–187, 190, 196–197, 199, 201–6, 220, 231
Sarvāstivāda, 21, 100, 108, 115, 130–132, 135, 137, 151–152, 184–186, 190, 193, 196–199, 203, 205–208, 220
Sarvāstivādin, 28, 31, 36–37, 39, 43, 48, 83, 86, 103–104, 109, 111, 143–144, 150, 186, 191, 202
Sāṃkhya, 146, 188, 193; epic text of the Sāmkhya, 146
Sautrāntika, 186, 234
sthavira-Vasumitra, 193
Sthiramati, 194, 232
Haimavata, 222
Harivarman, 39, 132, 133–134, 215
Hīnayāna school/s, 131, 144

Chinese

Che-t'o-p'an-ni, 142
Hiuan-tsang, 13, 225, 233
Mou-lien, 28
P'ou-kouang, 13, 17, 27–28
Seng-jouei, 215
Tao-yen, 152
Tsing-mai, 20

Subject Index

Abhidharma, early: catechesis, 7, 10, 150; degeneration, 9, 11, 122; dogmatics of, 147; method of explanation, 4–11, 17, 40, 51, 53–54, 58, 88, 90, 105, 142; scholastic formalism, scholasticism, 7–8, 11, 19, 31, 45, 142, 210
Abhidharma, Pāli: 17–19, 41, 100, 212; Sarvāstivāda, 41; seven works of, 48
Abhidharma, six-membered: its chronology, 152
Abhisamayavāda, 37, 45, 69–70, 129, 149, 153–184
activity, 195, 202, 206; two kinds of, 195. *See vyāpāraḥ*
acts, doctrine of, 47, 79, 82, 127, 129; retribution of, 47
arhan, 125
atoms, 136, 138, 140; theory of, 128

being, state of: 205. *See bhāvaḥ*
beholding, 183. *See abhisamayaḥ*
Brahminical sūtra, 40, 150; sūtras of the Brahmanic philosophical systems, 5

canon, old: 154–156, 161, 169, 172, 174, 177–178, 181, 183–184, 228
capacity: twofold, 201. *See* power
categories, 146; five, 135–136, 139, 145
causal: activity, 199; processes, 195, 199
causality, doctrine of: 9, 30, 50, 124, 127–129, 136, 138, 139, 199, 201, 205–206
causes, 107, 198–200; four kinds of, 28, 30; 24 kinds of, 50; distinction between c. and condition, 200–201; doctrine of, 108; six c., 127–129
chain, 200. *See* moments
characteristic, own. *See svalakṣaṇam*
characteristics, of conditioned elements: 189
cognition, 28–30, 173; causality of, 28; complexes of, 55; doctrine of, 29; intuitive, 182–183; liberating, 63, 92, 157–159, 164, 166–167, 178, 183; process of, 74–76, 175; single, 154; 16 moments of, 154, 164, 167; supranatural, 182
commentaries, 112, 115, 121, 142, 151; on the Dhammasaṅgaṇi, 79–80, 82–96, 123, 127; written c., 150
commentators, later: 73, 80
compilation, 129; systematic, 114
compilers, 53
concentration, 129
concepts, doctrinal: collections, lists of, 15, 121, 141; commentary, oral, 15, 40; explanation, 15, 45; systematic description, 128. *See* lists of
conditions, 106, 198–200, 203–204; 4c., 127–129; 10 c., 105, 107; 24 c., 105

connectedness, 48–49. *See saṃprayogaḥ*
contemplating, 158, 175. *See bhāvanā*
contemplation, 173, 181; two paths of, 165
contradictions, 153
council, 125
cycle of existence, entanglement in: 17, 23, 129
dependent co-arising, 16, 125, 200; doctrine of, 121
development, 115, 124, 127; doctrinal, 109, 112, 116, 187; of psychological ideas, 109; of systems, 94, 126, 131; tendencies of, 104; two stages of, 147
diamond, 178
doubt, 161

effect: giving of, 195, 199; grasping of, 195, 199
efficacy, 190, 192, 193–201, 204–206; as state of being, 196; concept, development of, 195; definition of, 201; doctrine of, 190, 192, 196, 231. *See kāritram*
elements: enumeration of, 146; 18 e., 131; of being, 145–147; origin of, 138, 140; systematic compilation of all, 114, 136; theory of, 123
embryo, human: 200
enlightenment, 181–182
errors, 157, 159–160
Erschauen, 183. *See abhisamayaḥ*
essence. *See* things, *svabhāvaḥ*
evolution: doctrine of, 146
experiences: meditational, 179, 183; supranatural, 182–183
examples, 95, 131

faith, 173; five capacities of, 173
fate of beings, 129
fluxes: cognition of, 159, 167; disappearance of, 157; elimination of, 157, 181. *See āsravāḥ*
future. *See* past and future

groups, five: 126, 128, 131, 136

human beings: types of, 49

ignorance, 161
impurities, external: 112
includedness, 48–49, 222. *See saṃgrahaḥ*
insight, 164
intuition, 183. *See* cognition, intuitive

justification, 188

karma. *See* acts
knowledge, 122, 129; of destruction, 154; of not arising again, 154; 10; kinds of, 32
liberation, 65, 69, 121, 153, 170, 175, 181; doctrine of, 37, 111, 124, 126, 129, 134, 153, 155–156; path of, 16, 69, 79, 90, 92, 100, 123, 125–126, 130, 133, 147, 153–154, 157, 162, 168, 174, 181, 183, 224, 228; of Dharmaśrī, 162–184; old path of, 154, 157, 166, 175, 178, 180; ultimate moments of, 176; process of, 177
lightning, bolt of: 178
lists, of doctrinal concepts: *See mātṛkāḥ*

material elements, 80, 81, 86
mātṛkā, 3–11, 16, 21, 25–27, 34, 40, 43–46, 48–49, 51, 79–80, 82–84, 88, 99–100, 102–103, 109, 115, 121–122, 137, 141, 150, 211, 213, 216, 224; *m.* of the Abhidharmasamuccaya, 214; *m.* of the Dhammasaṅgaṇi, 45, 49–50, 53, 54, 79–80, 82–86, 107, 123, 209, 211, 230; *m.* of the Dhammahadayavibhaṅga, 57; *m.* of the Dharmaskandha, 40, 43–44; *m.* of the Śāriputrābhidharma, 103, 109, 113, 115; *m.* of the Vibhaṅga, 40, 43–44, 48, 100–101, 103, 108, 122, 123, 215; *m.* in early Yogācāra works, 11; "attribute-*m.*", 5, 9, 31, 34–35,

Index of Terms

Terms in numerical groups:

Index of Texts

Indian

Chinese

12264504R00154

Made in the USA
Lexington, KY
03 December 2011